NewsTalk II

**Wadsworth Media Interview Series**   Shirley Biagi, Editor

*NewsTalk I: State-of-the-Art Conversations with Today's Print Journalists* by Shirley Biagi
*NewsTalk II: State-of-the-Art Conversations with Today's Broadcast Journalists* by Shirley Biagi

From the Wadsworth Series in Mass Communication

*Media Writing: News for the Mass Media* by Doug Newsom and James A. Wollert
*Uncovering the News: A Journalist's Search for Information* by Lauren Kessler and
    Duncan McDonald
*When Words Collide: A Journalist's Guide to Grammar and Style* by Lauren Kessler and
    Duncan McDonald
*Interviews That Work: A Practical Guide for Journalists* by Shirley Biagi
*Communication Research: Strategies and Sources* by Rebecca B. Rubin, Alan M. Rubin and
    Linda J. Piele
*Reporting Public Affairs: Problems and Solutions* by Ronald P. Lovell
*Free-Lancer and Staff Writer: Newspaper Features and Magazine Articles*, 4th, by
    William L. Rivers and Alison R. Work
*Newswriting for the Electronic Media: Principles, Examples, Applications* by Daniel E. Garvey
    and William L. Rivers
*Writing for Television and Radio*, 4th, by Robert L. Hilliard
*Creative Strategy in Advertising*, 2nd, by A. Jerome Jewler
*Copywriting for the Electronic Media: A Practical Guide* by Milan D. Meeske and R. C. Norris
*Advertising in the Broadcast and Cable Media*, 2nd, by Elizabeth J. Heighton and
    Don R. Cunningham
*Public Relations Writing: Form and Style*, 2nd, by Doug Newsom and Bob Carrell
*Announcing: Broadcast Communicating Today* by Lewis B. O'Donnell, Carl Hausman and
    Philip Benoit
*Modern Radio Production* by Lewis B. O'Donnell, Philip Benoit and Carl Hausman
*Audio in Media*, 2nd, by Stanley R. Alten
*Television Production Handbook*, 4th, by Herbert Zettl
*Directing Television and Film* by Alan A. Armer
*Sight-Sound-Motion: Applied Media Aesthetics* by Herbert Zettl
*Electronic Cinematography: Achieving Photographic Control over the Video Image* by Harry
    Mathias and Richard Patterson
*Broadcast/Cable Programming: Strategies and Practices*, 2nd, by Susan Tyler Eastman,
    Sydney W. Head and Lewis Klein
*World Broadcasting Systems: A Comparative Analysis* by Sydney W. Head

# NewsTalk II

State-of-the-Art Conversations with Today's Broadcast Journalists

SHIRLEY BIAGI

California State University, Sacramento

Wadsworth Publishing Company
Belmont, California
A Division of Wadsworth, Inc.

*Senior Editor:* Rebecca Hayden
*Editorial Associate:* Naomi Brown
*Production Editor:* Gary Mcdonald
*Print Buyer:* Karen Hunt
*Designer:* Paula Shuhert
*Copy Editor:* Toni Haskell
*Compositor:* Omegatype Typography, Inc.

\# 13525731

Printed in the United States of America      19
1 2 3 4 5 6 7 8 9 10—90 89 88 87

ISBN 0-534-06858-8

**Library of Congress Cataloging-in-Publication Data**

Biagi, Shirley.
  Newstalk II.

  (Wadsworth media interview series)
  Includes index.
  1. Journalists—United States—Interviews.
2. Television broadcasting of news—United States.
I. Title. II. Series.
PN4871.B53  1986      070'.92'2      86-9254
ISBN 0-534-06858-8

105273

F<small>OR VIC</small>

# FOREWORD

*NewsTalk II* is the second in a series of interviews with American journalists about what they do. In *NewsTalk I,* 12 recognized American print journalists discuss their jobs. *NewsTalk II* focuses on 12 broadcast journalists.

The Perspectives section at the beginning of each interview suggests three topics of special knowledge or experience from each interviewee. At the end of each interview is a sample script or a transcript from a story by the interviewee. In the Overview Index on page 227 are some suggestions to help compare and contrast the interviewees with one another on topics common to many of the interviews.

Because they are published in a series, *NewsTalk* interviews offer a consistent format. What they also promise is a more comprehensive overview than one lonely book. *NewsTalk* offers insight, variety, depth, breadth and practical advice. The goal of this series is to produce a dialogue with professional journalists that is provocative, substantial, timely and important.

# PREFACE

"A sense of history," David Brinkley was saying, "is what journalists need today." Here, sitting across from me in his office in Washington, D.C., was journalism history—40 years of it. I was working on another project, for which I was interviewing Brinkley, and it had nothing to do with what he was talking about. But what he was saying, I felt, was important for journalists to hear. How could I share his knowledge, and the knowledge of other broadcast journalists, with people who would never have a chance to talk with David Brinkley and his colleagues? *NewsTalk*.

Print journalism has chronicled its past fairly well, but every day broadcasting literally erases much of its history, as scripts are filed and tapes are erased to make room for the crowded record of each new day's events. Because of their schedules, broadcast journalists rarely have time to talk about their profession, except with other journalists. Here, for the first time in manageable format, 12 of the country's best professional broadcast journalists with varying levels of responsibility for presenting information to the American public share ideas about how they work every day.

The people in *NewsTalk II* represent a diversity of backgrounds, geography, opinions, ideas and experience. David Brinkley began broadcasting network television news in 1947. Bill Whitaker started in 1984. Judy Woodruff began in Atlanta, Don Oliver began in Montana, Sam Donaldson began in Texas, Susan Wornick began in New Hampshire. Seven of them studied journalism. Three of them have master's degrees. One has two master's degrees. Two of them didn't graduate from college.

On the same topics, many of them disagree. However, most of them seem to agree that the way broadcast news is presented to the public is changing. Some are more outspoken and critical about the changes than others.

These people talked about their profession for as long as six hours, sometimes over two days, or even in two conversations six months apart.

Together they shared more than two centuries of professional experience. Here for people interested in television news is the benefit of all that knowledge without all the work.

This is the second book in a series of interviews with working journalists. The first book, *NewsTalk I,* contains 12 interviews with print journalists throughout the country.

**Acknowledgments** The 12 people who were interviewed for this book deserve the most credit. Despite frenetic schedules and mind-wearying commitments, they managed to fit me in, often for several hours. I'm very grateful.

Becky Hayden also has been centrally important to me because she believed in the idea for the Wadsworth Media Interview Series before anyone else did. The other people at Wadsworth who have helped me beyond what any author should expect are: Gary Mcdonald, Robert Kauser, Paula Shuhert, and Naomi Brown.

For special help with this book I would like to thank Norm Hartman, Mari Hope, John Martin, Barbara Sherwood, Harry Silberman, Jerry Sugarman, Mike Sugarman and Linda Zecchino. I could not have met my deadlines without transcription help from Jan Haag.

I am also grateful to the reviewers who offered their suggestions and enthusiasm: Charles Burke, University of Florida; Charles Coates, University of New Mexico; and Sarah Toppins, University of Illinois.

*Shirley Biagi*

# CONTENTS

# 5

## Sam Donaldson, White House Correspondent, ABC News 85

# 6

## Byron Harris, Investigative Reporter, WFAA-TV News 103

# 7

## Marlene Sanders, Correspondent, CBS News 121

# 8

## David Brinkley, Host, "This Week with David Brinkley," ABC News 137

# 9

## Bill Whitaker, Correspondent, CBS News 153

# 10

## Susan Wornick, General Assignment Reporter, WCVB-TV 171

# 11

## Don Oliver, Correspondent, NBC News 189

# 12

## Charles Osgood, Correspondent, CBS Radio and Television 211

# News Talk II

CBS News

*We have an immense audience, and to think that we can inform them about something they didn't know is enormously worthwhile. People say to me all the time, "I didn't know that." And that, to me, is the best compliment.*

# SUSAN SPENCER

A yellow lamp in the corner is the major decorative accessory in Susan Spencer's office at CBS in Washington, D.C. She does not have a window—"I was on assignment when they gave out the offices," she says. On the floor in a large leather bag is a pair of tennis shoes. On the wall is a poster of Richard Nixon, his arms upraised in the familiar "V" sign. The poster says "Political Art—83." The artist is Spencer's cartoonist husband, Pat Oliphant.

Spencer received her B.S. degree in 1968 from Michigan State University and she majored in journalism at Columbia University, where she received the Sevellon Brown Writing Award. She spent a year in a film production house in New York until she was hired by public television station WKPC-TV in Louisville, Kentucky. From there she went to WCBS-TV in New York as a researcher, and was hired a year later by WCCO-TV in Minneapolis. She covered general assignment and eventually became co-anchor of the station's hour-long 10 p.m. "Scene Tonight" newscast.

When she decided to leave WCCO after five years, she applied to all three networks. CBS hired her and brought her to Washington, D.C., as a correspondent in 1978. She covered the Kennedy campaign in 1980 and the Mondale campaign in 1984. In between, she covered Congress and did some general assignment reporting. Now Spencer, 39, specializes in science and health issues for the "CBS Evening News." Like many CBS reporters who work in television, she also does commentary for CBS radio.

As a reporter on the science beat, she has covered the effects of anti-psychotic drugs, alcohol abuse, overeating and dyslexia. But her beat is science in the widest sense, so sometimes she gets a different challenge, such as a story she did about the replacement of library card catalogs by computers. The story was challenging, she says, because she was forced to make an inherently static, non-visual story work for television.

3

Sitting behind a metal desk in her windowless but cheerful office at 5 o'clock on a weekday, she is comfortable in a casual, but appropriate, loose-fitting dress. At about 5′10″ tall, she is graceful and willowy. She eases herself into the desk chair, ready to talk. ❖

*from Susan Spencer*

- Campaign reporting
- Convincing people to talk
- How to avoid bad questions for television

# Beginnings

When I was a junior in college, I took an aptitude test to find out what I was suited for. I didn't have any idea. And the first thing that came up was nightclub singer, so that didn't help very much.

I knew a woman who was in TV and radio and I just thought it was sort of a kick. I didn't think of it, at that point, as a particularly serious journalistic subject. I started taking electives in journalism and I just got more and more interested in it.

My major at that time was German literature, so my parents thought I wanted to be on the public television station giving German lessons. I graduated with a double major in television/radio production and German literature.

I applied to a whole bunch of places including Columbia. When I got accepted at Columbia, everybody said, "Nobody gets accepted at Columbia, you have to go to Columbia." And so, to be candid, Columbia was more of a job mechanism, and I think it helped, particularly at CBS. There are a lot of Columbia women here.

At Columbia, I got a master's degree in journalism. Another reason I picked Columbia for graduate school was because the program was nine months, not a year. All very sound, terrible reasons.

The school helped focus me, and I really do think that a name like that on a resume doesn't hurt. At that time it was at least as competitive a market as it is now. When I graduated in '69, there was a notice on the bulletin board saying that there were no jobs available in any Associated Press office in the world, that we should not apply. That's how tight the job market was.

I didn't get a journalism job. I went to work at a film production house in Louisville, Kentucky, and I wrote ads. Then I went to the public television station in Louisville and worked on a public affairs program, "Metroscope," where I shot my own film. I did everything—some hard news, some features, sort of a magazine.

## MOVES TO WCBS AND THEN WCCO

I don't remember my first story. I can't imagine it was watchable. It was done with silent film and narrated. We shot it, wrote it, read it. I'm sure it was terrible. Then the money for that show ran out. I ended up going to New York and getting a job as a political researcher at WCBS. It was an election year. It took me four months to get a job, and I had been to film production houses, all the affiliates and all the local stations.

I worked there for a year and then moved to Minneapolis [WCCO]. I was in Minneapolis for five years, and then came here. For a while, I had the environment as sort of a specialty. The last two years I was there, I was anchoring the evening broadcast. I'd come in and do a story for the six o'clock news, get dinner, come back and write the late news. I never went home.

Then I wanted to come to Washington. I'd been at WCCO for five years and I felt that was long enough. I applied everywhere. I applied at the other two networks, I applied at local stations. I don't know why they [CBS] hired me. I don't have any idea.

I thrust myself on them. I said, "I'm going to be in town and I want to talk to you." I had to send a tape. I talked to the bureau chief and then talked to someone in New York. It was a fairly lengthy process, waiting around a lot.

## COVERING MONDALE FOR CBS

I've been here now [at CBS] for eight years in July. The first couple years were pretty much general assignment. In 1980, I covered the Kennedy campaign. In '81 and '82, I covered the House. In '83, I covered environmental stuff and the agencies. I spent all of 1984 with Mondale.

The Mondale beat was depressing because the outcome was never in question. Every now and then there was a little blip. But it didn't lessen the workload, despite the fact that this was irrelevant. You were out there in your own little world and the broadcast didn't care, the country didn't care, nobody cared. The people who were on the [campaign] bus were the only people who really cared.

In a way, all campaigns are the same. It's all long days and weeks away from home. Covering Kennedy [in 1980] had the added edge to it that everybody wanted to know about everything, from almost a gossipy point of view. And you always had to worry about him getting shot.

I don't think I ever thought to myself one time, "Walter Mondale may get shot." There just wasn't that same drama about it. Ever. Mondale was sort of like pathos, but not the same sort of, "Oh, my God, don't ever take your eyes off this man." That's the way we were with Kennedy. Eight months—where is he, why hasn't he come out yet?

## CAMPAIGN REPORTING

We [reporters] change politics because we're there. There might not be any if we weren't there. We change schedules. Everybody does things according to our deadlines.

On a campaign, you can never let up, ever. Even, as in Mondale's case, when there isn't much interest in him, it doesn't change the dynamic of what's going on. I always had to know why something happened, even if nobody in America would care why something happened. If we were going to Columbus and instead we went to Cleveland, I wanted to know why. On the campaign, a couple of hours would be the average amount of time I had to write a story, sometimes an hour, but not very often. And sometimes half the day.

So much of your activity is spent ferreting out completely irrelevant information. But it's the only way to do it. It's just physically, emotionally and intellectually an incredible strain. Unbelievable. I think it took me a good two months to decompress from that.

We started out on January 3rd and we finished on November 4th, and during that time I was home maybe 10 days or two weeks, but not consecutively. So when the campaign is over, you have this total readjustment. Suddenly, you've got your own little nest and a bathroom and it's sitting still. All your things are there. And you think, "This is funny. Someone in the hotel has unpacked my furniture."

The interminable process of picking a vice president also wore us out. But there again, as dull as it was, you had to pay attention to it. I found the convention fascinating. I really thought the convention was great.

It was my second convention. I went in '80 with Kennedy, but the only drama at the '80 convention, apart from the speech itself—"The hope lives on, the dream shall never die"—was whether Kennedy would tell his delegates to go to Carter or whether he would tell his delegates to take a hike.

The 1984 convention was so much fun to watch. On the road you would hear that [Jesse] Jackson had called Mondale on Tuesday and you wouldn't find out about it till Thursday, whereas in the hotel at the convention, it was all happening right there.

## COVERING CONGRESS

What makes the House so much fun to cover is that it's like a little village and you know all the people who live in this little village and they're all different. You know many of them very well, and some of them you don't know very well at all, but they all mesh. The House is a very gossipy sort of place that feels it's the only place there is in the world, very self-important.

That makes it hard to cover because usually you can't say "The Democrats think . . ." or "The conservative Democrats think . . ." or "The ultraconservative Republicans think. . . ." There's not often that much consensus. We tend to want to categorize politics, but people have so many competing interests and they're so tied to back home—as they're supposed to be.

It's probably not my place to say, but I sometimes think that both print and broadcast reporters too often go with stories that start out, "The president says . . ." without some analysis about whether or not what is coming out of the White House is right or justified.

It seems to me that the information is not put in much of a context unless the White House or the president, whoever it is, is flat out wrong. If he's flat out wrong, there's "But, contrary to what the president said, it was actually 42, not six." Sometimes it's as if reporting "The White House says . . ." is enough.

## WHY I LIKE TELEVISION AS A MEDIUM

I just enjoy the way you can make things work visually and how that can add so much to what you're saying. I think it's an acquired skill—pacing and how to make the pictures work best and how to grab people at the beginning.

There are two things that people who come from print to broadcasting underestimate—one is to make the pictures work for them and the second is the complete inaccessibility that they discover in sources that they've known forever.

You say the magic three letters, CBS, and most people won't talk to you, but there's a definite disadvantage to always having to have a camera. I'm doing a piece on dyslexia. We want to go to the NIH [National Institutes of Health] and shoot people being tested. They said, "You can't do that. You bring a camera in here and you'll screw up the tests. Nobody will act the same." They're right. But the dyslexia people will figure out something so we can come in. Because everybody wants to be on television.

Those are things that print people who make the change to broadcasting have to get used to. The 5,000-pound pencil is very cumbersome.

## CONVINCING PEOPLE TO TALK

Half of this job is convincing people that they should reveal their most private moments to a strange television crew. It's not convincing them to talk, it's convincing them to give you access with all this equipment. It doesn't have anything to do with journalism, but it's always something you have to think about.

For instance, we did a story on a fertility research foundation. And you say to someone, "All right, look. You're going to go in and have this exam. We'll be discrete, but I'm sure you won't mind if we tape the exam." And I say to myself, "My God, if anybody came to me and said that, I'd say, 'Get out of here.' "

I just did a story, it was on last night, on obesity. This woman we ended up interviewing and I had three very long conversations. One was at least half an hour on the phone. I tried to explain to her that a story like that needs a person who knows and can talk about the problem firsthand.

We weren't going to ridicule her. But we would really appreciate it, and maybe she could help other people understand what she'd gone though. You can't do a story like that without somebody saying, "This is what this is like." That's one of the powers of television, to have the person look at you and say, "This is what I'm going through. Think about me." All of this is true, but you still feel like a snake oil salesman. She finally said, "OK."

I don't want to overplay this. It's not the biggest part of the challenge. Obviously, getting the story, getting it right, getting all of it and writing it in a way that people can understand is the main part of the job.

## WHAT MAKES A GOOD TELEVISION REPORTER

The ideal situation is to have gone to a liberal arts college and majored in politics and history, to have a natural gift for writing, to go to a local station for x years and then give the network a shot.

Someone must be really interested in the business and really care about it because if you aren't interested, it's too hard. And you have to be able to distill things quickly, and not spend a lot of time gnashing your teeth over all the stuff you can't include.

You have to adjust to the fact that television pieces are not documentaries. You may know an awful lot, and everything that you know probably helps what you end up being able to put on the air, makes it more clear. But you can't say everything you know or you'll consume the whole broadcast: "Good evening. This is Dan Rather and here's Susan Spencer. Let's hope she's finished by the time our time is up." It's true.

Half the time, when I get ready to write a piece, I think, "This is the one I can't do. This is hopeless. No way can I cram all this stuff into two minutes." But it's always gratifying when I do it.

## WHERE TO FIND STORIES

I'm working on three things right now, actually. One is the story on dyslexia. One is a cute feature story on the 25th anniversary of the Xerox machine. And one is a story that we're still trying to sell. The Japanese are heavily into industrial ceramics. This is yet another area where we're being overtaken by the Japanese. You think of ceramics, you think of a porcelain dish. But this is the stuff that you make engines from.

The dyslexia idea came from the producer, as did ceramics. The Xerox idea was mine. The way our system works we have one person here who is in charge of getting all the potential stories together. He can reject any stories he thinks are not going to fly. The ones that he likes he presents to people in New York. There's one person who channels the daily stories and another person who takes care of the longer-term stories. So he will then talk to the people in New York to get their reaction. When they say, "Go ahead," a producer is usually assigned and a correspondent.

## ETHICAL DILEMMAS

There are ethical questions I ask myself about the way television covers the news. Because of the beat I'm in now, I don't run into many issues involving classified documents or leaked documents or anonymous sources or whispered phone contacts.

I have much more problem with, "OK, your son died. How do you feel?" We get very sensitized to that and yet, after any kind of real disaster, people want to talk about it. People are grateful that you're interested. You can say, "Well, that's fine, but they're also under a lot of stress and, even though they think they're grateful, is this really right?" I have questions about that. But there's no way in a situation like that, as a reporter, you're going to think somebody's telling you too much.

## WHAT MAKES A GOOD TELEVISION STORY

I think one of our biggest challenges is to take a story that isn't good for television and make it interesting. Television is naturally drawn to picture stories and those are easy. It's the subcommittee that met today and said such and such that gets hard.

We did a piece about three months ago on card catalogs. There's just nothing more boring than an old card catalog sitting there. And this was about the replacement of card catalogs by computers.

Computers—you think that's going to be neat TV, but when you see it, computers get really boring after a while. It is not interesting. We shot some of it at the New York Public Library in sort of low light and from weird angles and with the drawers hanging out and tried to make it sort of artsy. We used a segment from "Ghostbusters" with all the cards flying around. Those are just some little tricks that you do to keep the thing going.

We're often criticized for that kind of stuff, but my feeling is that if it's the way to keep the person watching interested, then it's justifiable. If the story doesn't have good pictures, and the pictures are so boring that people don't care what you're talking about, it defeats the purpose of doing the story.

The approach we took on that story was that this was the end of fountain pens. It is just one more sign that everything's changing, that there will be adults in 20 years who have never seen a card catalog. This is now ready for the Smithsonian. So it was a nostalgic approach.

Then we found out that half the librarians were delighted. They got so sick of the goddamn card catalog, they couldn't stand it. They couldn't wait for everything to be computerized.

---

## HOW TO ASK GOOD QUESTIONS FOR TELEVISION

Let me say what a bad question is. A bad question is a question that states the answer and then continues to talk. If you say, "Mr. So-and-So, I understand the reason that we're having a drought is because the westerly winds are a thousand miles farther north than they were six months ago. Is that correct?" That's a bad question. You need to ask questions in such a way that the answer stands by itself, that it doesn't depend on the question being heard to be usable. With the drought question, you would say, "Why is there a drought?" Let him tell you.

Also, sometimes you need to ask and re-ask and re-ask questions because it takes people in interviews time to get their thoughts together. Sometimes if you ask the second question again at the end of the interview, they will have condensed the answer and made it more usable.

It's silly in interviews not to remember while you're doing them that they're going to have to be short. It doesn't do any good to interview someone for an hour and then end up with sound cuts that are all a minute and a-half long, which you can't use.

And there are some people who are terribly hard to interview, who just don't ever stop sentences. Everything will be dependent upon the previous dependent clause. And everything will be qualified and the subject and the verb will be so far apart that you can't put them together.

So you have to listen as you interview to be sure that this person is not only comprehensible while you listen to them there in person, but that it can be used, that the point is made quickly enough so that you can use it on television.

## MISTAKES REPORTERS MAKE

Those are the two biggest ones—stating the question and then saying, "Isn't that right?"

I can think of somebody else's gaff which, of course, is easier. There was an unnamed reporter at WCCO who went out to cover a story involving a small town that had banned dogs—no dogs in the town. And the mayor had a dog. And the mayor's wife loved her dog and, in fact, may have had several dogs. She liked dogs a lot.

The piece was all about the town and outlawing dogs and how complicated this was going to be and how much it was going to cost. And the punch in the stand-up was going to be that the mayor has a dog. But the words that came out of the reporter's mouth were, "To top it all off, the mayor's wife has a fetish for dogs." It wasn't me. I swear it wasn't me. I always liked that. It's just a malaprop.

## HOW PEOPLE PERCEIVE MY JOB

I don't think people think we're particularly left-wing politically. I think that's a myth propagated by people who aren't. I think surveys show that.

I don't think people understand how hard we work. I don't think they appreciate how much real agonizing goes on to try to make a story fair. I just don't think they understand that. I don't think my parents understand that.

Politics is probably the easiest kind of balancing act. But there are all kinds of other stories that we do where opinions aren't black and white, and where there are a lot of different points of view. In a short time, to try to make that clear and still make it a story, is very hard. I don't think people have any sense of reporters making those sorts of considerations.

I don't think people understand my job at all. They think the reporter only reads what other people write, which is completely wrong. I think they think that most of the things they see on television are arranged.

I'm just reminded of these people at NIH [the National Institutes of Health]. They've dealt with television a lot and yet they say, "We can't let you come in with your cameras and show one of our patients, but we'd be happy to have one of the technicians here pretend that he's a patient." And you say, "No, we can't do that."

We go to absolutely elaborate lengths to make sure that doesn't happen. We cut ourselves out of great pictures by refusing to stage events. I think it's done much more at the local level, and it's just assumed that the network does those things.

On a local newscast, whenever you see a shot from the camera's point of view—a door opening and then suddenly you're inside and the door is closing—they didn't just happen to be there. They can't do that. They have to have the door open and close twice to get that shot. And if they did it twice, they staged it.

If you look at how reporters are portrayed in movies, it's not far from what it used to be, with the press card in your hat. The cumulative image in people's minds is really inaccurate.

I don't know if people think this is glamorous or not. I mean, I think they think being on television is sort of glamorous because it's also the entertainment medium.

But you've got to really care about it because it's very, very hard work. There are times when you do things and you think, "I did that the very best I could, didn't I?" There's a lot of second guessing that you do with yourself. Maybe there's even more in print because it's there and you can keep looking at it. Our stories are gone.

## HOW TO PREPARE TO BE A REPORTER

If ever I talk to college kids, I tell them to experience the business while they're in school. That's the only thing that gives you a leg up on the next guy and really helps you figure out if this is what you want to do. This isn't all fun, and I think a lot of people think it is.

This business allows you to go out and ask people anything you want, and you get to go to a lot of neat places and they pay you a lot of money. That's a lot of fun. But there's a serious side to it.

What's not fun is the pressure, this constant need to capsulize things—the feeling that sometimes you're not able to give a subject as much time as you'd like. You'd really like to say more—the realization that there are 22 minutes in that broadcast and every piece can't get on.

"Well, that's the way it is." That's why Walter Cronkite said that all those years. He was talking to all the reporters whose pieces didn't get on. It wasn't for the public. It was for us.

## THE IMPORTANCE OF WRITING

It's certainly true that a lot of people can't write in television, but if you can write, you've got an enormous advantage. There are people out there who can both write and master the equipment and if someone can't write, their deficiency will be quickly spotted. It's a very competitive business.

To believe that you don't have to learn to write is nonsense. For one thing, when you get to this level, you have very little to do with the equipment. Somebody else is doing the equipment. You can't touch it. It's all unionized. I can't run an editing machine or a camera.

But when someone asks, "Why am I learning about the equipment?" the answer is, "You're learning about it because when you get to the network and you're writing and putting together those pieces, you have to know what the equipment is capable of doing. You may not be doing it, but you have to know what it can do so you can use it effectively. Now write."

Some people go through a lot of drafts, but I do the changing as I go. I block it out and then write the first sentence until I like the sentence and then go on to the next. Some people will do something rough and then go back. I don't do that.

I think writing is absolutely critical. It's true that if you listen to local news, a lot of those people can't write. It's just awful. I used to have a bulletin board of local news-isms. It started with the night that Billy Kilmer retired from the Redskins. The local anchor here came on and looked in the camera and said very, very soulfully, "Good evening. The end of an era is over." It was great. You could just feel that people all over the city were howling. That started my wall.

## WHAT HELPED ME SUCCEED IN TELEVISION

I can write. I don't know why I can, but I can. At least, that's what other people say. I think that's been an enormous advantage. And there are people here [at CBS] who can't, and everybody knows who they are.

The end product is nine times out of 10 the correspondent's. And if you can't write and somebody else is writing for you or fixing everything you do, then you're also not going to read it too well because it's not going to be the way you'd express it.

## MY GOALS IN TELEVISION

Is what I'm doing worthwhile? I hope so. I don't know what else to say. I spend all these hours. Of course it has to be worth it. In a general sense, my goal is to present interesting, informative pieces that are clear and that tell people something they didn't know. I think that's a worthwhile goal. It's not particularly lofty. I'm not trying to change the country.

We have an immense audience, and to think that we can inform them about something they didn't know is enormously worthwhile. People say to me all the time, "I didn't know that." And that, to me, is the best compliment.

## WHAT COMES IN THE MAIL

Most of the mail you get is complaints. People who like what you do, don't usually write. I'll tell you what I got the most mail on—this radio commentary I did called "News Notes." I think people listen in their cars on their way to work and if they hear something that infuriates them, they get to work and they write at work. That's my theory. They don't have to pay the postage, they don't have to go to the post office. It just makes them so mad, they write and off it goes.

I got an enormous amount—I got seven letters, that's an enormous amount—when I did a commentary saying that the biggest problem about Ronald Reagan going to Bitburg, Germany [to a commemorative ceremony at a cemetery where German soldiers were buried] was that he didn't understand why he shouldn't. And I got a lot of "You crazy liberals, why are you beating up on our president?" sort of mail.

I also get a lot of mail that says things like, "Dear Susan, Did you used to live in a trailer park in Portland, Oregon, in 1953? We knew a Spencer family." I also get a lot of mail from people who say, "Dear Susan, We're doing a history of the Spencer family tree. Did you ever . . . ?" You know what else you get is a lot of mail from prisons— inmates: "Dear Miss Spencer, I think you're beautiful. Write me a letter. Love . . . " Diane Sawyer says that when she was on the "Morning News" she always got a lot of these sad and lonely letters. That's the "Morning News" audience.

## THE IMPORTANCE OF APPEARANCE

Unfortunately, appearance is still important. If you look at the women who are currently in television, they're not all gorgeous, but for the most part, they're at least average looking. No, they're better than average looking. I don't know how many average-looking women there are out there who would be perfectly wonderful television reporters, but they aren't considered qualified.

Nobody asks, for example, how a male reporter looks. People don't say things like that. In one piece this week one of the female reporters at CBS had a stand-up, and the comment here afterward was, "Boy, so-and-so just looked terrific in that piece." Well, I have never heard anybody say, "David Martin looked terrific" or "Bob Schiefer looked terrific." That's still sort of an unspoken expectation.

That's still going to be tested. We just hired a woman in Chicago who's 42, which is a good sign. A very good sign. I don't think that what women are going to be allowed to do in their 50s and 60s has been tested yet. I suspect it'll be a battle as long as there's sexism everywhere else. Marlene [Sanders] is in her 50s.

This is a fairly open-minded business, probably with less of a protective kind of mentality. Not that there's not the old boys' network, but women are getting closer to it.

That's what's going to help us old biddies—there are a lot more of us and there are a lot more of us with experience and we have become valuable to them in spite of themselves. They need us.

# The Learning Disability Called Dyslexia

DAN RATHER: With back to school in mind, last night we reported the latest research into the learning disability called dyslexia. That condition, which may affect as many as 25 million Americans, makes it difficult, if not impossible, for an otherwise bright person to learn to read and write. In tonight's report, Susan Spencer looks at how dyslexics cope in a world of words.

SUSAN SPENCER: Todd Hanley had great success as a carpenter's assistant this summer. Here he didn't have to read. He could forget about being dyslexic.

TODD HANLEY: It's almost like being blind, but you're blind to words. You know, there's nothing wrong with the rest of the parts of your body, it's just that you're blind to words.

SPENCER: Dr. Richard Jed Wyatt, also dyslexic. He has no trouble analyzing tissue samples under a microscope, but just ask him to read the paper.

DR. RICHARD JED WYATT [reading newspaper]: "His discomfort with racial stereotypes stems from an ever-present fear that it could happen again seems an especially important statement."

SPENCER: Then ask him to summarize it.

*Susan Spencer mentions this story on p. 10. © CBS Inc. 1985. All rights reserved. Originally broadcast September 4, 1985, on the "CBS Evening News."*

DR. WYATT: I have no idea what I just read. I have absolutely no idea what I read. I was concentrating on getting the words, and I have no idea of the meaning of them.

SPENCER: Wyatt and Hanley are among the 25 million or so Americans who have dyslexia, a learning disorder which makes it difficult, sometimes impossible to learn to read and write. It's thought that roughly one in 10 schoolchildren is affected. These are language problems that have nothing to do with how smart you are or how hard you work, though schools sometimes make that mistake.

EDWARD FLETCHER: You know, you read outloud and someone in your own classroom tears it apart, and you just—you begin to have a nervous breakdown right there.

AMY MacDONOUGH: Well, the—the school where I went to mainly I felt like I was dumb, you know, and like I couldn't do anything, you know. I mean they knew I wasn't retarded or anything, and—but at times I thought I was.

ROBERT WEAVER (Psychologist, Carroll School): They're all very different, but if there's one thing in common, it's that they have failed and they failed consistently as a result of their efforts. They have—they begin to predict failure.

TEACHER: Slick.

SCHOOLCHILDREN: Slick. Slick.

SPENCER: That can be a self-fulfilling prophecy. So at Boston's Carroll School, which specializes in teaching dyslexics, educators go to elaborate lengths to erase that sense of failure, to build confidence.

BOY: Even if you have to grab on with two hands, you're not going to fall.

SPENCER: Outside the classroom, they encourage hair-raising activities like this, part of a program called Bounders. The premise is— well, if you can do this, maybe you can even learn to read.

TEACHER: Objectable.

BOY: Objectable—objectionable.

TEACHER: Good.

BOY: Object—objectionable.

TEACHER: OK.

BOY: Whatever.

SPENCER: Inside the classroom instruction is intense. Classrooms are limited to six students and many are even smaller. The emphasis is on what seems to work best, very basic instruction, repetition and drills.

GIRL: R—I—N—G.

SPENCER: Some day this may be done on a computer, with a program Carroll is developing to help dyslexics retain the fundamentals.

VOICE OF COMPUTER: Fetch the dog and see what happens. (Student presses diagram of dog and computer makes barking sound.)

SPENCER: But no matter how sophisticated, how concentrated the instruction, no one has found a magic cure for dyslexia.

OCTO BARNETT (parent): I doubt our kid will ever be a great writer, because expression is a very difficult thing, but that doesn't say there's many other areas of endeavor that he couldn't be amazingly successful in.

SPENCER: Ten-year-old Megan already has her own ideas of success.

MEGAN SOLO: It's going to be hard to get there 'cause I'm going to have to memorize a lot, but I want to—I basically want to be either an actor or a rock star.

SPENCER: For Todd Hanley, being successful means finishing his struggle, with the help of audio tapes for the blind. Neuropsychiatrist Richard Jed Wyatt already is successful thanks in part to a med school that let him take oral exams, an obsession with science and a refusal to be beaten.

DR. WYATT: 'Cause I think we fail all through life and I think failing early is a good experience rather than a bad one, if one doesn't fail too hard and—and one has some resilience.

SPENCER: Wyatt even thinks finding clever ways to cope can turn dyslexia into an advantage, a challenge. The trick, he says, is to remember that as important as it is, reading is a recently acquired and highly specialized skill. And that just as some people can't learn to sing, and some people can't learn to draw, some people can't learn to read.

Susan Spencer, CBS News, Washington.

---

KNBC-TV

*When I said to my father, "I want to be a reporter," he said, "You've got to be kidding. A reporter is nothing more than a professional wiseguy."*

# DOUG KRIEGEL

Doug Kriegel is wearing a charcoal three-piece pinstripe suit, exactly what you would expect the business editor at KNBC, Los Angeles, to wear. But after 15 minutes of work, Kriegel tosses his coat carelessly over the back of a chair, running across the newsroom to chase a phone call. After half an hour, he loosens his tie and unbuttons his vest. Soon the right rear tail of his laundered pink shirt is hanging out below the vest.

A stocky 5-foot-6, Kriegel looks more like a baseball catcher than a television reporter. As a teen-ager in Brooklyn, a baseball catcher is what he hoped to be. Instead, he has two master's degrees—one in economics from the University of Stockholm and the second in journalism from Columbia University. He has been called a "stand-out" by one Los Angeles newspaper for his clear approach to reporting about money issues.

Stand-out is one way to describe Doug Kriegel, but unconventional is probably more appropriate. Kriegel has been known to wear wooden clogs to work with his suits, and his approach to reporting is a cross between a kid playing baseball in the streets of Brooklyn and an experienced journalist with an eye for the ironic.

"During college I had a summer job at Morgan Guaranty Trust as an accounting clerk, and I was riding the elevator with one of my buddies," Kriegel says. "Two economists were in the elevator talking—[deep voice] 'Well, you know, if the demand is all right, we'll get interest rates down and then Treasury bills will go up.' [regular voice] And they walked out, and my buddy turned to me and said, 'Who are those guys trying to scare?' About 10 years later, I was one of those guys, saying 'If interest rates go down . . .'"

Kriegel, 46, spent a year as a stock analyst before deciding to attend Columbia in 1968, where he was a classmate of Susan Spencer. He has worked in local television news since 1969. He began as a courier for KPIX in San Francisco and worked in Seattle and Sacramento as a television reporter before joining KNBC News in 1978. KNBC made Kriegel the Money Editor in 1983.

He picks up a tattered file folder from his desk at one end of the newsroom and carries it to a desk at the other end, where he will do a quick promo on camera for the day's story. Juggling the folder under one arm, then the other, he tucks in his shirttails, tightens his tie, buttons his vest, and lifts on his coat.

His grooming consists of a pat to the top of his hair and a question to the nearest person—"Is my hair sticking up?" Satisfied about his appearance, he hops on the desk with the newsroom as a backdrop, opens the folder, promotes the night's story on camera, jumps down and unravels his clothing until he looks as he did before he began his journey across the newsroom. "It's very weird how almost every element of my background comes into play in this job," he says. "I'm enjoying it." ❖

*from Doug Kriegel*

- ■ Personal involvement in the stories you cover
- ■ How to find good business stories
- ■ Conflicts of interest for business reporters

# Beginnings

When I was a kid growing up in Brooklyn, I used to work at the Dodger games selling hot dogs, and I used to have to sneak into Ebbets Field. The cops would chase me. There were 16 different ways you could sneak into Ebbets Field. But I noticed, as a kid standing out there every day with my friends, that the reporters at the press gate were getting in free.

I was 12, 13, 14. Right away I thought there seemed to be something to this job. Any job that could enable a guy to get into a ballgame free and get paid to see a baseball game sounded like my kind of work.

I used to read the papers all the time. When I said to my father, "I want to be a reporter," he said, "You've got to be kidding. A reporter is nothing more than a professional wiseguy." I thought that was a great definition.

That's a pretty concise, efficient definition—he was a businessman—of how businesspeople see reporters. And of course, he grew up in the '20s, '30s and '40s, when reporters were simply professional wiseguys. They chewed gum and cracked wise with each other. He didn't feel that it was a very substantial kind of career.

I went to my high school newspaper to work there and they told me, "How can you want to work here? You're the worst kid in school.

We don't want you on the school newspaper." I was at the top of the bad list at Wingate High School in Brooklyn. There were a lot of gangs. But for some reason, with all the loonies in that school, I don't know why, I was at the top of the bad list that year. I was always in trouble in high school. I had a 66 average. I majored in fun. I worked at the ballpark a lot.

I graduated from high school in 1958. I was 18. I wanted to be a professional baseball player, but I wasn't good enough. In high school, I was captain of the baseball team, although I was suspended from a number of games. I used to play catcher and third base. I went to Florida to try out for the Baltimore Orioles but I didn't make it.

I came home and went to work for my father. He was in plastics manufacturing. He used to make looseleaf binders, tote bags, travel bags. That was when New York had a lot of manufacturing going on right in the city. My father was part of that industry. I was a shipping clerk.

I was unsuccessful in my career as a shipping clerk. I used to sit on the sidewalk at lunch hour, drinking beer with a guy who worked for my dad. My father felt that it was undignified for the boss's son. And I wasn't really a good shipping clerk. The trucks used to complain— they'd back into the loading dock, and I'd say, "Back, back, back"— zzech! I was directing the drivers into the wall. "Some kid you got here. He just backed me into the loading bay."

My dad said he thought I needed some discipline. So he suggested I join the Marine Corps. I had one older brother who had been in the Marines. I joined the Marines in 1960. It was a reserve six-month program, and then I went to five years of reserve meetings after that. It did help.

I was in a platoon on Parris Island where, for the first five weeks of the three-month training, the drill instructors were violating the rules by beating us up. They said it was a shortcut and real Marines could take it. It was really quite an experience to have these grown men working you over. But they got caught about six weeks into the training and there was a court martial.

---

## COLLEGE AT NYU AND IN SWEDEN

In some ways, it really did teach me discipline. I learned how to sit still for the first time in my life. I think I had what they realize now is a hyperactive problem. So when I left the Marines and went to NYU, I was able, much to my surprise, to sit in the library as I never could before for three or four hours and read a book. I became a good student, actually. I got a C average and went on to get even better grades as I learned how to study. Really, it's kind of a craft, studying.

I majored in economics. I really liked economics, and I had a lot of friends who were studying economics. We used to argue in the cafés around Greenwich Village. I loved it. I did take one journalism course in print journalism. My minor was English.

I graduated in 1963, in about three and a-half years. I didn't know what I wanted to do, but I knew I didn't want to work. I had worked all through college in my dad's business, driving a delivery truck. I had many jobs. I was a waiter in a Quaker boarding house. I worked on Wall Street at Morgan Guaranty Trust.

Having observed work in a lot of different spots, when I graduated college, I knew I didn't want to go to work. I wanted to see the world more than anything. So I applied to study in Sweden, at the University of Stockholm, and I was accepted. They had a special graduate program for foreign students in economics—the American Scandinavian Foundation. You didn't have to be Scandinavian, anyone could go. I went to Sweden in the fall of 1963.

That was a one-year program. We learned Swedish, in addition to studying economics, and the Swedish economy is a very interesting economy. In my senior year in college, the rage was a book called *Sweden, the Middle Way* by Marquis Childs. I thought it was fascinating to read about the [Swedish] economy—low rates of unemployment, low rates of inflation, high tax rates, yes, but they're running an economy with very few people out of work. It's an alternative to the American system and an alternative to the Russian system. I felt that was interesting and that's why I wanted to go over there and study economics. My master's thesis was on labor economics. It was an econometric investigation of certain things that happen in Sweden called wage drift.

I'd been there about three years and I wanted to see more of the world. England at that time was having a money crisis. There was the first major run on the pound, the first softening of Western currencies in the mid-'60s. It was getting real interesting. They were having big strikes and I wanted to see England anyway.

I was married, with a son, so we went to England and I worked in Southampton as a researcher. I think my salary was 1,000 pounds a year, which wasn't very much money. Then Barbara and I went back to Sweden and we lived there for a while trying to figure out what to do. One year I worked as a window washer.

---

## RETURNS TO THE U.S.

I thought about living the rest of my life in Sweden or in England. I came to think I could live anywhere. But my home was America. Finally I came to America in 1968 and with my economics background I got a job on Wall Street in the first week. It's easy to get a job on Wall Street.

I got a real good job at one of the best investment houses, Lord Abbott. They manage mutual funds and pension funds. I worked there for a year as a stockmarket analyst. Every analyst in these firms has certain industries. My industries were international gold, the South African gold mines.

Every Wednesday morning they had a meeting: "Hey, this fund has several million dollars. Where should we put our money?" These guys argue. I found myself sitting in those meetings—I was the youngest analyst in the firm—and I don't think I ever said one word. I learned so much just listening for 12 months at those meetings. Sometimes when I look at other financial reporters, I think, how many reporters are lucky enough to work inside a fund for 12 months and listen to the senior guys argue the merits of the economy, stocks, industries, the economic policy of the government?

About six months into the job, I said, "I like this job, but the physics of this job don't appeal to me." What an analyst does most of the time, especially a young one, is to come in in the morning and sit down at a desk and read numbers. You call people at companies, but basically you read until noon. You go to lunch on Wall Street or sometimes you eat lunch standing up at Chock Full O'Nuts. Then you come back to your desk at 1 and you read until 5.

So it's interesting and all that, but I used to read the papers because I was following the gold industry in South Africa. I used to read the London *Financial Times,* which is really a well-written newspaper. I found that I was daydreaming, wishing that I were writing these stories rather than just reading them. So I decided, after about six to eight months, that I wanted to become a journalist.

---

## ACCEPTED AT COLUMBIA

I heard that Columbia University had a graduate school in journalism, and they had a special scholarship for students with a background in economics. I like to write. I like to meet people. I like to be at interesting situations. So I applied for the scholarship while I was on Wall Street and in the spring of '68 I learned that I was accepted.

I graduated from Columbia in 1969 when I was 29. Some professor told me, "Why don't you go to a section of the country where you want to live and start looking for a job there?" So I went to San Francisco.

The second day I was in San Francisco, I put on this suit that I had folded up in my suitcase and I called information for the numbers of the four TV stations in San Francisco. I called up the news director at KPIX. He said, "Well, why don't you come over? Somebody left last night."

## WORKING AT KPIX

It was the lowest job, as a courier. I said, "How much does the job pay?"
He said, "$125 a week." I said, "Actually, I have two master's degrees—
one from Columbia. I couldn't possibly work for $125." He said, "Well,
I have this stack of resumes here. I want you to make up your mind in
about a minute. Half of these people will work for free. I'm offering
you $125 a week." I said, "I think I'll take it." Having studied supply
and demand, I could see if there was that much demand for the job, I
should accept.

I said, "When do I start?" He said, "Right now." And I rented a
house and my wife Barbara and my son David moved out here. But it
was only a summer job. So in October the news director said, "Well,
maybe we'll try you as a film editor." I'd never edited film, but they
taught me how to edit. Then I put the political reporter in what I
thought was an "artistic" shot. The guy complained to the news director.
He said, "This guy can't edit." So I was laid off.

## HIRED AT KXTV

Then a guy I knew at Channel 10 in Sacramento got another job and he
called me to come up and apply. So I was hired as the 6 o'clock
producer. You'd write the show and you'd carry the script to the anchorman. I'll never forget one day I was carrying the script to the anchorman and I tripped and dropped all the pages. He had to read the show
out of order.

We had a crowd of guys at Channel 10 who were the funniest, most
amusing guys. One of my buddies was the only TV reporter in the
country who refused to wear a tie. "What will my wearing a tie add to
this story?" He used to ask questions like that. So they said, "Look, we
want you to buy clothing." He said, "I don't have the money. Loan me
$1,000." The manager loaned him $1,000, and the two of us went to
Reno and blew $700. He then took the $300 and bought Mexican style
clothing. Still no tie. He bought a ruffled shirt, tight pants, and he went
into the station with these ruffled shirts. He was the most incredible
guy I ever met.

I was completely intrigued as a local reporter. Covering crime,
covering cops—doing everything I'd wanted to do as a reporter. No
economics, of course. Just being a general assignment reporter in the
'70s was the most fascinating experience a guy could have. I really
consider myself tremendously fortunate.

Plus, I was in a place where there wasn't a lot of pressure. Now
there's a lot of pressure in these news departments. There wasn't a lot
of pressure then, so we could experiment. You could do anything you

wanted at Channel 10 and it went on the air. You could make a million mistakes and come back tomorrow and try again.

## AN UNUSUAL APPROACH TO ANCHORING THE NEWS

They did let me anchor once. It was on a Friday. And I knew I had to be on as little as possible. So the half-hour show was about seven pages long. It was all, "Today in Washington . . ." and they'd go to Roger Mudd—that was when Roger worked for CBS. Then they'd come back to me and I'd say, "Today in Los Angeles, a murder happened. Terry Drinkwater reports."

So all I would have to say was, "And today in Yuba City . . ." It was only introductions. But wouldn't ya know it, we had technical problems. I read the first story, came out of that, and I started to read the second story introduction and they didn't have the tape. I said, "Well, we'll be back in a minute," and they rolled a commercial. I read another intro, and we didn't have the tape again. So we went to another commercial.

By about 15 minutes into the show, they had run all the commercials. The director told me in the last commercial, "We have no more commercials to go to. You still have 15 minutes and you'll have to fill it all." So I panicked. But I knew there was a large Channel 10 sign on the wall behind me, so when I went back on the air and read the next story and the tape didn't work, I said, "We don't have that tape. We'll be back in a minute."

And I pointed to the 10 on the wall and I put my head down on the desk. The camera was pointed over my head behind me on the wall. It was like a test pattern. So I would wait a while and then I would lift my head up and say, "Now, from Los Angeles . . ." And when they didn't have the tape again, I put my head down on the desk again. And that's how I got through the program. The next Monday when I came to the station, the general manager said to me, "I hope you don't hope to become an anchorman." I said, "No. I just like being a reporter."

I was lucky enough to arrive in Sacramento when so many fascinating things were happening there. It seemed to me like the center of the earth. One time I lived in a commune for two weeks in Mendocino, and they accepted me at the commune. They were all naked, they were all dropping LSD, but I did a five-part series on Morning Star Ranch. What a beat—the communes, Lake Tahoe, Ronald Reagan, Jerry Brown, the Zodiac killer, Patty Hearst.

## THE MURDER OF GEORGE MOSCONE

The assassination of [San Francisco Supervisor] Harvey Milk and [San Francisco Mayor] George Moscone was the biggest story I ever covered. I knew Moscone fairly well when I was a capitol reporter. One day I was standing on the street in San Francisco and a man said, "The mayor's been shot."

I went to city hall and I was one of the first reporters on that scene. I'd done so many murder stories. But here was the body of a friend of mine. I'd played cards with him. I liked him. I thought he was an important man. I thought he might change society in some way. Watching his body being carried out of city hall was a very emotional experience for me.

I remember my boss said, "You did a great job on that story, better than any of the network correspondents." I think sometimes if you're genuinely moved, you do a better job. If it strikes a chord in your soul, you really do a better job.

That used to be one argument at Columbia—should a reporter care about a story? Or should you be totally neutral? Of course you've got to care. If you don't care about the story, I don't think you do a good job, you don't understand its importance. You're really just a storyteller. You've got to understand why people should care.

## QUALITIES OF A GOOD TV REPORTER

You need a lot of energy. You need the ability to see stories in pictures and to link pictures together. A visual sense is important.

You also need to know how to write with economy. That's very important. You must tell things briefly because you don't have a lot of time. It's not like a newspaper where wordiness is an asset. You have to tell things with brevity.

I think it helps if you're interested in the subject. That's tremendously important and often taken for granted. It's never taken into account when people are hired—what is this person interested in? Is he interested in himself, is he interested in being on television, or is he interested in the world out there?

Someone who is genuinely interested in the world will be a better reporter, given all the same attributes, than someone who is interested in himself. Because a good reporter is reading magazines, he's reading books, he's talking to people. When he goes out on a story, he'll be more curious.

When they hire people in television, they look at the tape—how he looks, how the voice sounds, how he writes, maybe. But they don't ask, what are this person's interests? Through what sort of lens does this person see the world? That's very hard to find out about a person you're hiring, but that's very important, his vision of the world.

## LEAVES FOR KNBC

Then in 1977, I got a job in Seattle at a station where the general manager would do outrageous editorials: "Personally, I think all gays should be put in jail." You'd come to work at that station through a picket line. The gays would be picketing. I was there for six months. Then I was hired by KNBC.

Before I was hired at KNBC, they said, "We hear you're a little offbeat. You think you can work for a conservative company like NBC?" I said, "Yeah, I think I can, boys. Underneath this veneer, I'm a serious, sober kind of guy."

I think it helps me relate to bums on the street. I have no trouble relating to virtually anybody because I've had a lot of experience, from window washers to presidential candidates. I have an egalitarian approach to people. All people are basically the same. It doesn't matter whether you're a head waiter or the head manager.

## ASSIGNED TO THE BUSINESS BEAT

I came to this beat about two years ago. The business editor was fired. And the news director said, "You know, Kriegel's got a master's degree in economics. Why don't we make him the business editor?" So they called me in and I said, "No. General assignment is the most fun." So they said, "We'll give you a raise." I said, "OK. I'll consider it."

This used to be the throwaway job. When they didn't know what to do with somebody, they made him the business editor. He'd come on at the end of the show and give the stock market report and read some wire copy.

I've been saying for a long time that the number one story is the economy. But whenever they did a story about business, they used to interview somebody in a suit and tie who worked in an office. They didn't consider the guys who sell hot dogs, the people who wash windows as part of the business report. So I changed the way it was done. I started covering actual money stories. I said, "I want to be called the Money Editor." So they said, "All right."

Most local stations still ignore the local economy. They don't know how to cover it. Economic news involves people, money and work—three of the most vital things in everybody's lives. What's more important than that? Everybody works—conditions of work, that's a story. Money— who's got it, who doesn't have it? And people themselves—who gets breaks in business, who doesn't? I do one two-minute report every day. I find the story and then I assign it to myself and I go out and do it.

## HOW TO FIND BUSINESS STORIES FOR TELEVISION

Drive around the city, keep your eyes open and look for stories that way. You won't find all your stories in *The Wall Street Journal*. There are a lot of stories involving people trying to make money, struggling for existence. That's the center of economic stories.

We did a story on a guy who came to Los Angeles from Egypt five years ago with one oven. Now he owns four pita bread factories across the country. That's fascinating. Of course, the immigrants here are an interesting part of the economic stories, immigrants who are tremendously motivated, and their view of work and money is totally different from the Americans' view of work, money and prices. Asian immigrants, Mexican immigrants are some of the hardest working people who ever came to America.

I like to bring in stories about small businesses. That's one thing that America offers that a lot of other countries don't. I love stories of immigrants who own nine restaurants, who do what our grandparents did. I like that story. It's a great story.

So I look for stories that involve people, not necessarily the Dow Jones average. If you do the Dow Jones average, you've got to tell people why they should be interested in the Dow Jones average. Virtually everybody with pension plans, health plans—that money has got to be parked somewhere and is usually parked in securities that move up and down. You don't know about it, we don't hear about it, your retirement plan doesn't tell you about it.

The banking system—is your money safe in a bank? The fraud that gets committed in banks. I've done a lot of stories on banks and savings and loans and how tenuous they are. There are a lot of investment scams. People are confused by all the investment alternatives—money market accounts, T-bills.

Everybody wants to get rich quick. I did one story on how to get rich slowly—drive an old car, don't spend a lot of money. I did kind of a parody on financial advice. I said, "Imitate the immigrants. Imitate your grandfather because the biggest increase in wealth in the history of the world probably came between 1900 and 1950. The people who lived in America during those years may have quadrupled the national wealth, just on the sweat of their backs and their willingness to work hard."

All these other people try T-bills, then switch in three days to a money market account, then swing into a couple of stock options. That's not the way. The old-fashioned values in finance and economics still obtain—the importance of just saving money. If you can control your spending, you don't have to worry about finding T-bills or the best stock investment.

You can find stories anywhere—driving to work, phone calls. Basically you tell people stuff they didn't know was interesting, whether it has to do with the safety of a bank, an investment fraud, why the GNP growth rate is important. Just telling people things they don't know, I think, is the most interesting kind of story. In economics and finance, there's a lot of stuff people don't know.

Why should we care if the GNP is growing at 3 percent versus 1 percent? Well, if it only grows at 1 percent, unemployment's gonna rise. Economies never stand still. Jobs are threatened, incomes are threatened and that could spiral.

## HOW TO TELL A BUSINESS STORY WELL

Economics is called the dismal science. But there's nothing dismal about money and nothing dismal about work, in terms of people's interest in it. There's nothing dismal about home prices and interest rates, and whether someone should get an adjustable or a fixed-rate mortgage. That stuff's not dismal, but you have to sell the story.

To tell the story, you have to add a little flavor. I remember doing a GNP story by saying, "How do you find out if the economy's getting better or worse? Do you look out your window? Do you call up your mother? Do you ask your girlfriend? No. The government tells us. Once a quarter, it comes out with this number, and here's what it means." With economic stories, unlike stories which are inherently interesting to people, sometimes you have to set the story up, tell them why they should be interested.

I hate to use the word, but it does require a little showmanship, whether you do it with tape or with writing. With these economic stories, you can just hear someone say, "That business news is coming on. Turn it off."

I actually worked on a real interesting story today that I'll have to save for tomorrow. Because of the interpretation of the law, there's a savings and loan here in Southern California that has $800 million in deposits. They've invested a lot of the depositors' money in fast food, in Love's and Wendy's, both of which are losing money.

So, in a sense, if you put your money in a savings and loan, you're not aware that they're investing your money in Wendy's and Love's. These guys are gambling venture capital with people's deposits. That's serious stuff. Savings and loans in California were created to invest in real estate, safe investments. But there was a window period when they were allowed to invest in some riskier stuff, and this savings and loan went overboard.

I used to go to this Love's over on Hollywood Boulevard, and this guy called me. He said, "Did you know we're owned by a savings and loan?" So I called up the S & L and asked them about it. They didn't talk to me. They were typical. I told them that it's a story that involves their business. There are a lot of depositors out there who'd like to understand. But they saw it as just a lot of bad publicity.

## WHY BUSINESS PEOPLE WON'T TALK

Covering business is a little different from covering politicians. Politicians can't avoid you—they ran for office, they made a million promises. They gotta talk to ya, sooner or later.

With a businessman, it's a little different. The guy says, "Hey, this is a private business. I don't want to talk to you. Goodbye." In a hostile situation, they just duck you. Often, they're not used to dealing with reporters, especially television reporters. So I think we have an obligation to be extra fair to these people.

## ETHICAL CONFLICTS OF INTEREST

NBC does have a conflict of interest policy which says you have to declare any interest, especially financial interest, in any story that you report. In practice, I don't have any investments. I'm really not fascinated by investing money in the stock market or T-bills, My theory is, if you're going to try to get rich, do it slowly. Don't try to get rich quick.

But there are potential conflicts of interest. You don't want reporters doing a story on XYZ company the day after they bought stock in that company. That's obvious. In economics, if a reporter has transactions in the stock market and the money market, I think his boss is entitled to know what those transactions are, just so everything's above board.

People say, "Well, you hear stuff before anybody. Can't you make money?" Actually, that sometimes reflects a lack of understanding of how money is made. In financial markets, there's a saying—buy on the rumor, sell on the news. By the time the news people hear about it, by the time you see it in the paper, it's too late to make any money out of it. The insiders have already made money. In practice, I don't hear stuff that could make me rich.

I don't think the ethical conflicts in business reporting are terribly different from anyplace else. You basically just try to be fair to people. The only element you sometimes have to add with business stories is that people's livelihood is at stake. You can hurt a person's business dramatically. You have to be a good reporter. You have to get your facts right. If you do the series "Is Your Money Safe?" you don't want to start a run on the banks. You have to be responsible.

## THE ROLE OF MANAGEMENT

An advertiser called me here once and asked me not to show a picture. They were told very directly by management never to call a reporter in

*Doug Kriegel*

the newsroom. If they have a problem, call the station manager. There's been no interference at all.

I was the only person who ever put on the ratings of California banks. There's a service in New York that charges $5,000 and they rate the banks and savings and loans. Well, that was leaked to me and I put that on the air and they wanted to sue me. But the station backed me up, so we went on the air with a story that said, "Gibralter Savings is D. American Savings is E. Bank of America is C, just average. Home Federal is a B, that's good." The service that does that, they threatened lawsuits and they were furious. But we did it. And we got a lot of response to that—"Thank you. We now know which banks are good, which ones are a little shaky."

## WHETHER I MAKE A DIFFERENCE

Maybe I do help some people understand money and the economy and banks and investments a little better. I think I do that. It's a unique position. If I were doing general assignment reporting, I don't think I would really add much to people's lives except a little amusement and a little information.

But I think this position at this particular time has opened up financial alternatives to everyone, especially older people. In that series "Is Your Money Safe?" I think in my own little way, I did help people understand how the banks and savings and loans work and how risky certain kinds of investments are. I think I was doing a service there. I think I do help some people.

## WHAT MY ROLE IS

I'm the Money Editor. That's my title. My job is trying to explain the sort of complicated world of money and economics and finance to the people out there who would like to know its significance. Should I buy a house now? Should I not? What's happening to home prices? I think that's a legitimate role.

Sometimes the boss here will say, "We need you back on general assignment," and I say, "I think this is an important role we have here." Not a lot of stations have a guy who covers the money scene, and I think I have a unique background in that. I've studied theoretical economics, I've worked on Wall Street, I've been a general assignment reporter, I've worked in small businesses. It's very weird how almost every element of my background comes into play in this job. I'm enjoying it.

When my father said a reporter was a professional wiseguy, I felt it was just the opposite of that. But I still think it's a great definition of the job. If you had said to me at 17, "You're going to be a reporter," I would have felt, "Well, it sounds like something I'd like to do." I don't think it's a real sharp left turn.

I had a friend who used to claim, "You know, Kriegel, you're always interviewing. We walk to the subway and you're always talking to people, conducting an interview right here on Kingston Avenue." He claimed I was always interviewing people, talking to old ladies. He'd say, "Kriegel, you can spend 10 minutes talking to an old lady."

I wasn't interviewing them. I always enjoyed conversation, talking to people, listening to people, hearing what they have to say. That's partly why I went abroad. I wanted to see the world and see what people were like. I didn't just want to see a country. I wanted to live in it and get the experience of learning the language fluently, and learning something different. I was tremendously curious always.

I don't know if it's a logical progression of where I was as a kid, but it's not illogical. I was really a bad student as a kid but it was because I was a discipline problem. I still am.

---

# Is Your Money Safe?

DOUG KRIEGEL: There are more than a thousand banks and savings and loans with serious financial problems according to government regulators. But the government refuses to make public the list of troubled savings institutions. Now this is especially crucial now that so many savings and loans are losing money.

(FILM CLIP)

KRIEGEL: Remember this classic savings and loan commercial? (OVER CLIP OF COMMERCIAL) John Wayne endorsing Great Western? The image of John Wayne, solid as a rock, was good for the savings and loan industry.

These commercials also helped attract billions of dollars in new deposits to Great Western Savings, which is one of America's most profitable S and L's. Actually, most California savings and loans are making a profit; most are in good shape.

But 25 percent of California's savings and loans are losing money. That's one in four, a big chunk of the industry operating in the red. And it's worrying lots of people.

---

*Doug Kriegel talks about this story on p. 32. This is a transcript of the second story in a four-part series by Doug Kriegel, "Is Your Money Safe?" Courtesy of KNBC-TV News.*

American Savings, the nation's biggest S and L lost five hundred ninety million dollars last year. Beverly Hills Savings lost a hundred million before it was shut down last month. Central Savings' loss was forty-three million dollars.

Southern California Savings lost seventeen million dollars. Santa Barbara Savings reported a five million dollar loss. Valley Federal's loss was four hundred thousand dollars.

What went wrong? Deregulation. Freedom to enter new areas of lending confused many savings and loans.

SAL SERRANTINO, BANK ANALYST: The industry was not prepared to handle partial deregulation. The management was not capable enough to make these changes and do it successfully.

KRIEGEL: California savings and loans were created to serve savers; their money would be loaned out to people who wanted to buy or build homes. But deregulation has changed the rules.

It means that Butterfield Savings of Santa Ana, which lost six million dollars last year, could invest depositors' money in a chain of Love's Barbecue Restaurants, which are also losing money. Eight Wendy's Hamburgers are also owned by Butterfield Savings.

GERRY FINDLEY, BANK ANALYST: They're using people's money for venture capital bases. I think it's a misuse of the savings and loan charter and a misuse of the purpose of savings and loans.

KRIEGEL: But how does a person find out if their savings and loan or bank is healthy? Well, it can be difficult and expensive. The Keefe Bank Watch Service rates financial institutions, but it costs five thousand dollars a year. And last time we broadcasted Keefe's bank ratings, they threatened to sue us.

In Orange County, Gerry Findley, bank analyst, charges two to four hundred dollars a year for ratings on all California banks and savings and loans. Generally, you can bet your bank knows more about you than you know about them.

SERRANTINO: Frankly, I think it's a one-way street, that they have so much information on their customers—loan applications, forms filled out that you won't believe. But try to get some basic data on financial institutions on a current basis and that's very hard to come by.

KRIEGEL: Government accountants who are regularly monitoring banks say more than a thousand financial institutions are having serious problems. But government regulators will not make public the list of troubled banks and savings and loans. Herbert Chin, FDIC, West Coast:

HERBERT CHIN, FDIC: Actually, I don't think we should make it public. That kind of thing could cause a run on a bank and that could cause a bank to fail.

KRIEGEL: Now that more banks and savings and loans are failing, more people are beginning to wonder if their money is safe. Federal insurance funds don't have enough money to reimburse all insured depositors.

Ultimately, the United States Treasury stands behind the banks. In a sense, the people of America are the lenders of last resort.

(END FILM CLIP)

KRIEGEL: Incidentally, Butterfield Savings defends its investments in Love's and Wendy's, saying the failure rate in fast foods is lower than the default rate on home mortgages. But this week, savings and loan regulators are asking Congress to crack down on S and L's and force them to invest depositors' money in things like home mortgages not hamburgers, chicken and ribs.

NICK CLOONEY: Just to re-emphasize again, when you say these banks and S and L's lose money—the depositors, what's their position? What happens to them?

KRIEGEL: Well, their deposits are safe up to a hundred thousand dollars. That's how much the federal government insures.

---

The MacNeil/Lehrer NewsHour

*People turn to television for that extra visual dimension that they don't get in the print media. The question is, how do we provide that visual dimension and not be controlled by it?*

# JUDY WOODRUFF

Tacked haphazardly to the wall beyond Judy Woodruff's desk are drawings from her 3-year-old-son, Jeffrey. On September 14, 1981, Woodruff had worked all day at her job as NBC White House correspondent. Jeffrey was born at 3 the next morning, and his birth was announced on the NBC evening news.

Woodruff, 38, now works for "The MacNeil/Lehrer NewsHour" during the week, produced by PBS in Washington, D.C., where she is chief Washington correspondent. On weekends, she travels to Boston to anchor the PBS weekly documentary series "Frontline."

She graduated with a degree in political science from Duke University and went to work at WQXI-TV in Atlanta in the newsroom, answering phones and filing scripts. Her first on-air assignment was as a Sunday evening weather reporter at WQXI before she convinced someone at WAGA-TV in Atlanta to hire her for general assignment reporting. She covered Jimmy Carter when he was governor of Georgia, covered his presidential campaign, then covered Carter and Ronald Reagan after she joined NBC as White House correspondent in 1977.

After Jeffrey was born, Woodruff stayed home to write a book about her White House experiences, *Judy Woodruff at the White House*. "Even in the best of times, the television news business is crazy," she wrote. "The competition is fierce, the money at stake is huge, and the potential impact is heady and sobering. And even in the best of times, covering the White House is crazy. The constraints are rigid, the demands are relentless, and the stories are complex.

"But combine the business of television news with the business of covering the president of the United States and the result can be chaotic. Toss in what has been called the fine madness of Washington, a town filled with people driven by ambition and a lust for power, and you have summarized my job."

In 1983, she left NBC to join MacNeil/Lehrer as their Washington correspondent. She says MacNeil/Lehrer gives her a chance that she didn't have at NBC to do stories about Washington that last longer than NBC's customary two minutes.

Upstairs from the lobby on the second floor of WETA, the Washington, D.C., PBS station where MacNeil/Lehrer is produced, Judy Woodruff sits at her desk in front of Jeffrey's five drawings in red, green, pink, blue and yellow blots. On the desk sit several empty used paper coffee cups from the Weanie Beanie Drive-In across the street. Woodruff's IN box is piled with reference materials—*Washington Dossier, The New York Times, The Atlantic* and *Ms.* magazine. Traces of her Tulsa, Oklahoma, background creep into her speech, in spite of her efforts to overcome her Southern accent.

At 11 a.m., 15 D.C. schoolchildren and their teacher pass by the open office door on a tour of the station. Then the conversation is interrupted by a phone call from her husband, Albert Hunt, Washington Bureau Chief of *The Wall Street Journal.* At 12:30, Woodruff races in a taxi to a meeting at the downtown Marriott hotel. By 2:30, she is back at her desk, working on a 12-minute story about Pentagon spending.

Woodruff is a thoughtful, constructive critic of television's coverage of politics. She also has been a consistent advocate for women in broadcasting. In 1983, in a speech to the national conference of Women in Communications, she said, "Women who seek to be equal with men simply lack ambition." ❖

*from Judy Woodruff*

- The dangers of pack journalism
- The president as a celebrity
- Pictures in politics

# BEGINNINGS

I was studying political science at Duke [University] and got a job as a summer intern for my congressman for two summers in Washington between my junior and senior years.

Almost as a whim, I thought about television journalism. It just intrigued me for some reason more than anything else. I'd never really done much writing and didn't really think about the print media, but I did think about television.

I went back to school my senior year and took a course in politics and mass communications—that was my one bridge to journalism—and wrote the three TV stations in Atlanta to see if anybody wanted to hire somebody with no journalism and no training, no nothing. Fortunately for me, one of them was foolish enough to want somebody with a bachelor's degree in political science, but no training in television.

One station said come in for an interview. I came down on my spring break and interviewed with the news director at the ABC affiliate in Atlanta. We had our interview sitting in the lobby of the TV station. And I thought we'd had a nice chat about my background in political science. We finished the interview and I stood up to leave and he said, "Well, I think we can work something out. Besides, how could I turn down somebody with legs like yours?" This was 1968. I just gulped and looked at him and said, "Thank you. I'll look for your letter in the mail." I was absolutely stunned.

I got the job as a secretary. I cleaned the film and researched, answered the telephone and made coffee and all those things that secretaries do. This was from June of '68 to January of '70. The last year I was there I was chomping at the bit to get some reporting experience, but we already had a woman reporter, as I was repeatedly reminded—not by the news director who had hired me, but by his successor. They already had a woman and I should be patient. My turn would come.

What did happen was the Sunday night weather person, who happened to be a woman, was fired. They asked me to audition and I said, no, I wasn't interested in doing the weather. I wanted to do news.

The news director pulled me aside and said, "If you're serious, you better get some experience. This is the way the real world works." I reluctantly agreed. So my first on-air job was doing the weather on Sunday nights at 11 o'clock at the ABC affiliate in Atlanta. I did the weather for six months. Sunday night, once a week. Absolutely hated it.

They wouldn't let me touch the news. Occasionally, I would finagle my way out with a crew and a reporter to observe. I would ask a lot of questions—"How are you putting the story together? Who did you talk to? Why did you write it this way?" I was 21 in 1968 when I started as a secretary and I was 23 when I was hired to be a reporter at the CBS affiliate and went to cover the legislature.

## MOVES TO CBS AFFILIATE IN ATLANTA

For five years, I covered politics at the statehouse. I also anchored the noon news. Then for one year of my five-year tenure, I anchored the evening news. I was anchoring noons and evenings and reporting, too. But I still wanted to go into network.

I applied to NBC and was told at first that my voice was too Southern, but mainly it was too little-girl-like, that I needed to take voice lessons and get back to them in six months. This was in 1974. I immediately rushed off and signed up for voice lessons and had barely taken one lesson when NBC called me back and said they needed a reporter in their Atlanta bureau. Could I send them another audition tape? I did, and they hired me right away. I never did have time for the voice lessons.

They hired me with my little-girl voice. I did try to make my voice sound more mature or more sophisticated, to get rid of the Southern accent. I didn't entirely succeed. I still lapse back into it—walkin', talkin'.

Literally the third day I was at the CBS affiliate in Atlanta, the news director said, "Go cover the legislature." I learned from my cameraman, who had covered the legislature for several years. He knew who to talk to and how to hold a microphone—stand here and when you do a stand-up, look this way.

## FIRST-YEAR MISTAKES

Everything was an error the first year. The first several years. But there was nobody who really ever came along and said, "You ought to do it this way." I was never sent to any kind of school—this is the way to cover a story, this is the way to write a story, this is how you speak on camera. I was constantly asking questions, but at the same time you're so busy covering stories, you don't have time to take a lesson.

It's really a sink-or-swim philosophy, television news. I've found at the network level, you get in and you either make it or you don't. They kind of throw you in and see how you do. If you make it, great. If you don't, there's somebody else waiting in line.

## WHAT MAKES A GOOD REPORTER

Well, certainly [you need] some amount of intelligence, an awareness of what's going on in the world around you and just a basic awareness of and familiarity with the subject matter you are covering.

I include common sense in that, a feeling about the right way to turn when things don't come out exactly as you expected. You've got to have a great deal of curiosity to know why, to ask how, and to keep asking questions because frequently in our business, especially when you're covering politics, people don't want to tell you everything you want to know.

Another thing that doesn't get much attention is an ability to bring people out so that when you walk into a room to get information, you don't turn people off. You should be able to get them to relax around you to open up.

## QUALITIES THAT I HAVE

I can't say how smart I am, that's for somebody else to say. I like to think I have enough intelligence to put my shoes on in the morning and to get to the office. Some days, that's about it.

I've always had what I think is a great curiosity about how things work and why things happen. Of course, I'm much more interested in some things than others. My great fascination is with politics, with the way government works and how it ultimately serves or doesn't serve the people.

I was raised as an Army brat—we did a lot of moving. I was uprooted year after year when I was growing up until I was about 13 years old. I think this contributed to my ability to sort of roll with the punches. And I'm convinced that it helped me to meet people I didn't know before, to survive in a new situation.

That's what you've got to do as a reporter because you're constantly having to deal with people you don't already know. If you're a general assignment reporter, it's even more true, because you're asked to go cover something you have no familiarity with whatsoever. You've got to be able to pick up information very quickly, absorb it and get people to talk to you about it.

## HOW TO BECOME AN EXPERT—QUICKLY

I remember when I had just been hired by NBC, I'd been working for them about six months and I was based in Atlanta. I was covering the Southeast—10 states in the Southeast and the Caribbean. I had been in New Orleans covering one story, I think there was an oil drilling rig accident, then I was in Texas doing something on migrant workers. Overnight they just decided they wanted me to go cover a story about a problem with school desegregation in Alabama. We had some names the researcher in New York had given me. But I was getting all of this information on the road. I wasn't even near a newspaper file.

We got off an airplane in Montgomery, or wherever it was, and drove to this place and had to figure out, in 12 hours or less, what was going on—had to get to know the key people on the school board, talk to some of the parents, talk to some of the influential people in the black community.

The entire time I was thinking, "This isn't the way it ought to be done. If you're going to cover something like this, you need a reporter who knows the local situation." Yet I was the closest thing the network had to an expert because I was in the Atlanta bureau, which was supposed to know about everything that was going on in the entire Southeast.

If you're a network reporter and you arrive someplace where you are a complete stranger, you're very smart to turn to the local reporters. If I'm working out of an affiliate, I will talk to their reporter, if it's a city big enough to have a TV station. I'll also try to talk to some of the newspaper reporters. I'll just look at a byline, call up a reporter and say, "I'm with MacNeil/Lehrer, and we just arrived. Can you give me some help?" Frequently, these people are more than willing to help.

## REPORTING IN THE SOUTHEAST

Those two years that I was doing general assignment in the Southeast, I loved it and I hated it at the same time because I was living out of a suitcase.

I loved the stories I did about the Vietnamese refugee camps. I also did some stories near Miami on the Cuban refugees. But it all comes back to politics. I covered Jimmy Carter when he ran for governor in 1970, when nobody thought he was going to win even the governor's race. I covered his four years in the governor's office and state legislature.

You had a whole collection of colorful characters. I covered Lester Maddox as governor and as lieutenant governor. You remember he had the restaurant in Atlanta and chased blacks out with ax handles. He was crazy, irrational. Everything that his reputation was, he lived up to. He loved the limelight, he loved publicity, he loved getting attention at whatever cost. And he truly milked his reputation as a segregationist.

He continued, even to the day after he left the legislature and was a small businessman again, to look for ways to get the press to cover him. When Carter, of course, was governor, Lester Maddox was lieutenant governor, and there were weekly brouhahas between the two of them. They hated each other, bitterly.

## HOW THE PRESS CAN BE MANIPULATED

Maddox was on the news every night with some colorful saying. It was there that I think I learned a lot—in watching Maddox and some of the others who were so good at getting press attention—about how people manipulate the press. They learned how to get their names in the news and get their point across on television, to at least get their faces on the air or their names mentioned.

Maddox knew that he could do something outrageous and get on the news. Then there was a city councilman, a member of the state legislature for a while, black, who had been active in the civil rights movement who was equally adept at getting his face on television and getting his name mentioned in the newspaper. He would call a small demonstration or he would call a news conference and all the press would come, even though there was very little to be announced. It was just his daily salvo. And Maddox would do the same thing. Both sides were good at figuring out how to keep us nipping at their heels.

## THE HAZARDS OF PACK JOURNALISM

We are too often guilty of waiting until something is a headline, a big story, until there's been a disaster of some sort, until a mine explodes or a political problem becomes a political crisis. We wait until it's big news before we pay any attention to it. Then sometimes we overcover it.

We don't do the background kind of reporting because we're afraid people won't be interested enough and they won't read it or they won't watch it. Then we cover it and we all cover it—pack journalism takes over. Everybody's trying to outdo everybody else in the number of sidebars we can do. That's not to say we shouldn't cover it. We should. But do we need to devote all our energy to competing with our competitor down the street and saying, "We've got more sidebars than he does"?

Pack journalism truly takes over when there's a political convention—no better example. We all send a hundred reporters and we all do the same thing when there's virtually no news. We all put it on the air and interview each other. The press was interviewing itself in 1984 in Dallas [at the Republican National Convention] and in San Francisco [at the Democratic National Convention].

There was not much of a story in San Francisco. We tried to pretend there was still a contest between Jesse Jackson and Gary Hart giving Fritz Mondale a run for the money. In Dallas, you had a coronation for four and a-half days.

There were trailers lined up behind the convention hall, representing every major television station and local station in the country. All of them had to have their local reporters and anchors there in Dallas covering the convention. I'm not saying they don't have a right to do that. They do. I just think it's remarkable that our resources and our energy are so misplaced. We oversaturate. The Dallas newspapers interviewed every moving object in Dallas. It was extraordinary.

It's a misplaced sort of information we're giving people. We do a great job of showering the president with cameras when he goes to the helicopter. How many people go to the White House briefings now? I covered the White House for six years and by the time I left, that briefing room was a mob scene. We're better about ferreting out news, but we still don't do a good job, I think, of covering how government as a whole serves the people.

## THE PRESIDENT AS A CELEBRITY

Everybody goes out and reports the same thing, which is very little. The president's on the network news almost every night with this or that quick comment. There are four reporters for each network covering the White House. Do you know how many reporters cover the Congress for each network? Two. One or two. And they get on the air less often. How many people cover the agencies for the networks? Very few. One person may cover three agencies.

That's because the president is a celebrity. It's easy to put this person on whom we've turned into sort of a hero/celebrity—personality journalism. It's much easier to do a story about a person and infighting in a place like the White House where you can identify personalities and show pictures of them.

It's much easier to do that kind of reporting, especially the president and Nancy and the kids, than it is to do the long, hard, slogging kind of reporting about how well HHS [Health and Human Services] grants are doing the job they were intended to do. Are they reaching the people they were supposed to reach? Or is this Education Department program that started five years ago to help a school system still doing what it is supposed to be doing? Somebody needs to start thinking about that kind of journalism.

Television lends itself to pictures and faces and fast-moving stories and quick quips. The president's great at it. We now are creating a generation—forevermore probably—of politicians who can't succeed unless they're good on television. As Fritz Mondale said, "You can't be successful unless you come across well on the tube." That's the way it is.

If you're a good interviewee, if you can give us quick answers and look sparkly, we'll put you on a lot. We don't want to interview somebody on television who's thoughtful but who can't get it out very quickly, who talks in long sentences. You've got to be [snaps finger] like this. I don't want to be all negative because I also think we are doing some good things.

---

## CAPTIVES OF TECHNOLOGY

We are captives of our wonderful technology and we are so good now at being able to respond when there's a crisis. When the "Today" show wants to go to Vietnam or New Orleans, or "Good Morning America" wants to go to Rome and meet with the pope, they can do that. We can do that very, very well.

The question then becomes, is that driving what we're doing? Are we doing what we're doing because we now have the capability to do it? When there's been a terrible disaster in Beirut and 256 Marines have been killed because a barracks was blown up in a truck bomb accident, we can get the pictures out in a matter of hours by satellite.

But are we as good at analyzing the problem and helping people understand what's going on over there and why? Yes, the pictures are necessary and yes, we need them. But should that drive what we're covering? I don't think so.

We're still too much a slave of the picture. We think that if we've got a picture, that governs what news is and that's not always the case. It's good to have the picture but it's not enough. There are lots and lots of things that happen around the world that we don't have pictures of or that don't lend themselves to pictures very well. Washington is a perfect example of that.

## COVERING PRESIDENTIAL CAMPAIGNS

During the [1984] campaign, the president would give the stump speech he'd been giving day after day, and we would all put it on that night because the balloons had gone up and the crowd was cheering and it was a beautiful scene.

Even if the White House correspondent said something skeptical about the president, the people who work at the White House figured out that didn't matter. The public was only keying in on what they were seeing on television, and whatever the correspondent said went in one ear and out the other. As long as they have pictures of the president and the crowd smiling, that was what was going to come across.

The Mondale people didn't quite figure that out as skillfully. I was with Mondale when he showed up at a factory gate and the shift changed and nobody came out. We did lots of stories about how Fritz Mondale didn't know how to run a campaign. What we were saying was, he didn't know how to run a campaign for television—that was a legitimate thing to say. Because it's true—he was having trouble putting together a campaign for television and television is terribly important.

I also still raise questions about whether we ask the tough, in-depth questions of our candidates. Are we doing stories about the candidate's character, about the issues? Are we approaching the issues in a way that makes a candidate responsible for what he said? Do we hold him to account for his proposals?

Reagan would be very vague. He'd say, "Everything's going to be fine. The economy's going to work out great." Mondale would say, "We're going to be able to get the budget in shape. I can't tell you exactly what we're going to cut out, but we're going to cut something." Hold their feet to the fire when they're vague.

We all assume the public has such a short attention span, but you can't keep on doing stories day in and day out that say the same thing: "Once again today, Walter Mondale didn't explain how his budget was going to be cut. And once again today, the president didn't address the deficit."

We would mention it, but we would still show the pictures of the balloons. They've got us like little puppets on a string. They can manipulate us, if they're good at it. The Reagan people were good at it and the Mondale people got better as the campaign went on.

I did a story during the campaign, a 12-minute piece, on how skillful the Reagan people were at orchestrating the campaign and having an event turn out just so. We showed the advance work, but you can't do that day in and day out. You show it once, but people still see the smiling Ronald Reagan and the good news White House.

## WORKING AT THE WHITE HOUSE

You come to the White House in the morning for the press secretary's early morning briefing. Then you do what other reporters do in Washington. You talk to your producers, you figure out what the story of the day is and you start calling sources. If nothing is going on, you may just do background reading.

On the road, it's long hours, especially during the campaign, not much sleep. On the road, you're all thrown together. If you're in Europe with the president, you're all on the same plane and you're bouncing ideas off each other—pack journalism takes hold.

Some of that to me is fine. You're with your colleagues. There's nothing wrong with sharing ideas and talking to each other. I do think it's a problem when we get on a story and we all want to outdo each other.

## PICTURES IN POLITICS

You try to point out in your story the weaknesses, the inconsistencies, the fact that you're not getting all the details, but it's very difficult. The print media, to an extent, make the same sort of mistake, but it's different with them because they can go on for pages about an issue or an inconsistency, if they want. But television has a special problem. How do we suddenly become independent of the picture? We can't.

We do have a special function to perform that newspapers don't. People turn to television for that extra visual dimension that they don't get in the print media. The question is, how do we provide that visual dimension and not be controlled by it?

The Reagan White House has an awareness and an ability to take advantage of what TV needs. They think like TV producers. They give you a picture that works on television. They give you a speech with little sound bites that they know you will want to use—the sound bite that makes the point is one where the president pounds his fist on the podium or whatever. Or they never make him available to answer questions, so you have to use that excerpt.

How often has this man been available for questions? News conferences are a joke—they're staged. I don't mean truly staged. Everybody goes in and works on questions—and I did that, I worked very hard on my questions—but it's so easily controlled by the president. It's only 30 minutes long. He can deflect a question he doesn't want to answer.

If he doesn't want to answer a follow-up, he can kiss it off with some cute line and go on to some other reporter and say, "Oh gee, I hate not to be able to answer all your questions." He's very good. He's very engaging, and I give him enormous credit. You've got to give those people credit. They've figured out what the media want and they give it to them.

Or he's on the way to the helicopter, he cups his hand to his ear and yells out a few words, and they keep the motor running so you can't hear him. The White House is good at that. Or you'll only hear a word or two—a two-word quip, and that's what makes the news that night. Or somebody will say, "What did you think about Mr. Gorbachev's statement about so-and-so?" And he'll say, "What'd you expect from the Russians?" And that's all we know about how policy is made in this administration.

## HOW PRESIDENTIAL COVERAGE SHOULD BE CHANGED

I don't think we should put him [the president] on as often. I think one network should have the guts—and we are able to do it here [at MacNeil/Lehrer] because we have a more accordian-style newscast—if he doesn't make any news, we don't run it. On the other hand, because we don't have the resources, we are not able to send teams of investigative reporters out to every agency to do the kind of in-depth background reporting that I think ought to be done.

I did a 12-minute piece a few weeks ago. The basic question of the piece was, are we getting our money's worth for the trillion dollars we spent on defense in the last four years? We did a lot of interviews and used graphics and so forth. Basically, it was interviews with people, asking them, "Why is it this way?"

I'm working on another piece now on the whole defense procurement problem. You start out with this little, modest special set of specifications—we need a missile that destroys radar to protect these pilots. And 10, 15 or 20 years later you end up with something that's much more sophisticated and 50 times as expensive.

If you've got the time, you can do it. You can do it on the morning news shows, when you're willing to take the time. But it takes money to pay for human power for weeks to go out and ask questions, time to work on the piece and time to put it on the air.

## WHITE HOUSE AGENDAS

If you could cover the White House and do the kind of in-depth, analysis type of reporting that ought to be done—the presidency, the executive branch of government—that's one thing. But that's just not possible. The way the White House [beat] is structured you're called on to be there every day—day in, day out, rain, sleet, sun—and to go on all the trips and to be herded around like a bunch of cows, and be told what the story of the day is.

For all the twists you put on it and for all the skepticism you express, they're still setting the agenda, and you're pretty much regurgitating to the public what the president said today. You can do some enterprise reporting, but not enough, not nearly enough.

## WHAT YOU LEARN ABOUT COVERING GOVERNMENT

You learn, number one, that so much more depends on the personalities involved than the way a law is written or what it says on a flowchart about the way decisions are supposed to be made. I learned this from covering the state legislature and the county commission and, ultimately, at the White House.

So much depends on how clever the White House people are, how they deal with other people and how good they are at getting their way. That's probably the paramount lesson. Somebody may tell you that in political science class, but you don't really see that until you cover it.

What else? You learn the critical role that the news media play in government policy-making, government communications with the public, the way politicians use the press to get their points across to the public and also to communicate with one another, the way the press is used to send messages from one politician to another, to an agency, from one member of Congress to another, to threaten somebody.

I'm not covering it day to day, but what you're seeing now with the tax reform story is an attempt by the people in the administration and the Congress to float ideas. They will use the press to float an idea and see how it's received, to see whether people are going to knock it down or build it up. That's done all the time, what they call trial balloons.

Those who are good at doing that are really a marvel to watch. Their fingerprints are very seldom on their work. They put the word out without letting the reporters use their name for attribution, so the reporters have a quote from a high administration official or a senior administration official or a White House aide. The White House people are very good at that. They don't want to go on television, but they love to give you not-for-attribution quotes.

## WHAT I LIKE ABOUT TELEVISION AS A MEDIUM

I like the ability to use pictures to tell a story. It does reach more people than any other single news medium. I like the ability to work with videotape and film. I've learned that I have some skill at being able to make pictures and stories work together. To me, that's a real challenge.

The beauty of being able to work with the camera and the pictures comes with the drawbacks. You can't get some people to do interviews when they know their picture's going to be on television. That's a frustration you never get used to. You know your colleagues in the print media go in and take pages and pages of notes and may or may not use a quote or may or may not attribute it to someone. In television, somebody has to agree to be on camera, unless it's going to be a chase-em-down-the-hall interview. I envy my print colleagues sometimes because they can blend into the woodwork and stand there and take notes. When we're there, the camera's there. We're very obvious.

Some people in government find publicity a hindrance because it prevents them from doing their jobs. There are a lot of people in the White House, for example, who don't want their names used because they figure they're more effective. A lot of lobbyists in this town won't grant you interviews because they find it a hindrance to be publicized.

## TELEVISION AS ENTERTAINMENT

We are in the entertainment business to the extent that we've got to survive—public television aside for the moment. We've got to have enough viewers so the people who make the program decisions decide it's worth keeping MacNeil/Lehrer on the air.

To what extent do you abandon the principles of journalism to satisfy the public's desire to be entertained? Hopefully, not at all. Occasionally, certainly in the case of television, I think we've gotten to be captives of this notion that the public has a short attention span and if you don't get it on and off in 30 to 60 seconds, they're not going to watch it. That's terribly unfortunate.

I think we underestimate the public. I also think we've spoiled the public. We've given them news in short bursts to the point that many of them think that's all they can stand—hence, *USA Today* with the three-paragraph news story.

I'd like to see us start moving back in the other direction. That's probably a pipe dream. I'd at least like to see ventures like MacNeil/Lehrer succeed because we can show there's an alternative, that there are some people out there who want more than a minute-15, and are willing to sit still for 10 or 15 minutes and hear the hows and the whys of a story and not just the who, what, when and where.

## WHAT YOU SHOULD KNOW TO COVER NEWS

If you're going to be a reporter, it seems to me you're better off getting as much of what I call a liberal arts background as you possibly can. Take as many English and history and philosophy and psychology courses—whatever courses you're most interested in. You need that basic, academic foundation. Yes, you can pick it up by reading, if you're self-disciplined enough, but most of us need some kind of guidance.

If someone says, "Should I major in journalism?" I generally say, it depends on what you want to do. If you want to be a reporter, if you think you want to cover politics, if you think you want to cover foreign affairs, study what it is you're interested in, and learn the how-to later.

You ought to find time to learn the writing skills, but there are a lot of different ways to learn it. There's no question that I would have benefited if somebody had told me how to write a story. I didn't know. I had to sit down with the news director and we had to go over my copy.

As much as you learn in school, you learn much more on the job. Being there, covering the Assembly [in Atlanta], I learned much more about politics than I did reading about it in a book, but that's the way everything is. The book is there to whet your appetite and give you the foundation.

## GLAMOUR AND EXCITEMENT

Before I came to Washington, I thought it was all glamour and excitement, that it was the crème de la crème of the television news business, that nothing could be more interesting and exciting. And it is. I still find it extraordinarily fascinating. I wouldn't want to work anywhere else.

But on the other hand, there's a lot of slogging around and standing outside at the White House and waiting for people to come out of meetings and making sure you have cameras at all the gates so you don't miss anybody leaving, and waiting for people to return your phone calls, and browbeating secretaries to put their bosses on the phone so you can get through to them to ask a question. It's fun, but it's not glamorous.

Sure, it's glamorous to be on television and be recognized, but only to a point. I don't get a great deal of joy out of standing outside the west wing of the White House for an hour in the snow or the hot sun, waiting for a group of businesspeople to come out and tell me what the president said in a meeting. I don't feel like I'm committing great journalism when I'm doing that. I know somebody's got to do it, and to me, that's the problem with the White House beat. It's great for a few years, but six years for me was more than enough. It gets to be too much like a police beat, in the sense that they set the agenda, for the most part, and you cover it.

## ETHICAL DILEMMAS

To me, one of the most difficult questions is, to what extent can you be acquaintances or good friends with the people you're covering? How can you maintain objectivity about a story if you get to be good friends? And yet that's how Washington works.

You get to be good friends with people and then they talk to you and they know they can trust you and they give you information. The more dependent you are on them as sources, then it seems to me the greater the conflict if the time came to be tough and scrutinizing in your reporting.

I don't know of a single reporter who claims not to be able to do that with perfect objectivity. They say, "Oh yes, I can be friends. I can stand back. But when the time comes, I'll be just as tough and objective as anybody else." I don't know. That bothers me.

Some reporters are pretty scrupulous about it. They just don't believe in socializing and inviting somebody over to dinner or getting to know somebody well if they're covering them. Others thrive on it. They think that unless you take somebody to lunch and get to know them and their wives and husbands and families and see them on the weekend, you can't really be a good reporter, that you've got to get to know every aspect of the person.

I think there are some clear things that you should avoid. I certainly don't think you can get personally involved and have any sort of romantic relationship. If you're a single reporter, that's absolutely out of the question. Just like I think, how can you be married to somebody you cover? And there are examples of that, too.

Beyond that, can you be good friends? How do you then cover them? My husband [Albert Hunt, Washington Bureau Chief of *The Wall Street Journal*] has said there were a couple of people he got to know extremely well that, if the situation ever arose where that person was the subject of a story involving some controversy, he would have to excuse himself from that. I would like to think that all of us would have that capacity—that if someone we considered ourselves close to as a friend were involved in a story we were covering, we would somehow step back. But that's much easier said than done.

If you cover the White House, you obviously take these people to lunch, you get to know them, you know their wives and husbands, their children. How do you then totally turn around and skewer them? It may never arise. But if it did, what do you do?

Bert Lance was someone I had known very well in Atlanta. He and his wife were nice people. I had covered him when he was director of the transportation department under Governor Carter. He got along very well with the press. He knew a lot of reporters.

And here he was, a few months after he arrived in Washington, in the middle of this terrible scandal over his overdrawn bank account and the way he'd run his bank in Georgia. My first reaction was, how can Bert Lance, this person I've known all these years, be involved in something like this? Well, you learn somehow by osmosis when you come to Washington, to stand back and be more objective. But it's not always the easiest thing in the world.

I knew his wife. I'm not saying we were close friends, but I had seen them at a few social dinners and they knew who I was, and I would run across them in Washington. And they were having a very, very difficult time, and I felt very awkward because I was reporting on what was happening to them. It was tough. They are very warm, likable people. They came away, understandably, from that whole experience very bitter toward the Washington press. But there were some pretty serious charges involved that Lance never did totally respond to. It wasn't all cooked up. It wasn't a creation of the press.

## WOMEN IN NETWORK NEWS

They really didn't start hiring women until the early '70s, about the time I was hired to work in television, so we don't really have a big generation of women who are in their 50s yet. Barbara Walters is in her 50s and she has been an extraordinary success, but she's an exception.

There is a group that is my age, a group in our late 30s and early 40s who are sort of the vanguard. It remains to be seen what will happen to us. You don't see any of us anchoring the evening news, which I think is a telling point. You see one woman on each of the morning network news shows, except that those are not all news shows. They're mostly entertainment with a little bit of news. You see a woman anchoring a weekend show here and there on NBC. Beyond that, the vast majority of network correspondents are still men. The people who are making the decisions—most importantly—behind the scenes, deciding what stories get on the air and what stories don't, are mostly men. That's slowly being changed, but very slowly.

NBC has just made a woman number two producer on the evening news, which is a big deal. CBS has a woman who was in charge of their convention coverage last year. But it's rare. We really have a long, long way to go in terms of being in a decision-making role, and in being in the most powerful on-air jobs. I find that the jury's still out.

In the '70s, a lot of pressure was being put on television stations and networks by the FCC [Federal Communications Commission] to hire more women. But the pressure's not really there anymore and you're not seeing as many women hired. It's about 20 percent at each network and the figure has held steady for many years. I mean, we are 50 percent of the population. But I don't like television to be singled out because I don't think newspapers are any better. The number of women in editorial positions or columnists at newspapers is depressingly low.

At the network, in television, they originally would say, "A woman doesn't have credibility with an audience," or "An audience isn't ready to hear news from a woman." Network management tells you that the audience isn't prepared to accept women. I think that's baloney. I really believe that the audience is prepared. That doesn't mean that any woman could be put on the air, nor could any man be put on the air.

*Judy Woodruff*

But there are enough of us around who qualify, so that the time has passed when they can use that as an excuse. But that's what they argue.

---

## FAMILY LIFE

I'm very fortunate in that I'm married to another journalist who understands the crazy life that we lead, who understands the pressures, the highs and the lows. I'm married to somebody who is, number one, a journalist, but equally important, somebody who's very supportive and who wants to play a big role in raising our son. Al is completely devoted to Jeffrey, as I am, and we both just try to make time.

We're fortunate enough to be able to afford full-time help, which we need, given our schedules. We couldn't do it alone. We really do it no differently than any other working couple does, who are both trying to have full-time careers.

When I have an opportunity to go somewhere and make a speech, I do take Jeffrey with me. It may be the only chance I have to be with him. Whenever we can combine work with family, we try to do that.

---

## HOW WHAT I DO MAKES A DIFFERENCE

I don't have illusions that journalists change the course of history. We can influence the public's perception of the issues, personalities, the great subjects of our day. Then I think we do have some kind of effect on what happens, on people. We help them in a small way as they make up their minds when they're going to vote, or about whether our president is doing his job, or what American policy ought to be.

Obviously, some stories like Watergate are much more influential than others. But most stories aren't that dramatic. Most stories are much smaller, stories about tax policy, about what our attitude should be toward Nicaragua, how much we should spend on defense.

---

## WHAT THE JOB DOES FOR ME

Just great joy. That's part of it. I like to feel that I'm making some contribution toward the public getting a better understanding of what's going on around them so they can better make decisions about their daily lives. That, to me, is the most important thing. If I didn't think anybody was watching or heard what we were doing, I wouldn't do it. I'd do something else that I thought would make a difference. Plus, I just get great joy out of the work. I just love the whole game of politics.

| | |
|---|---|
| VTR SOT (Reagan) | SOT "spending for defense is investing in thgs priceless-peace & freedom." |
| SOT (weinberger) | SOT ..."size of the defense budget." (outcue) |
| SOT (reagan) | SOT "we must not relax efforts to restore mil. strength just as we near goal of fully equip, trained and ready professional corps." |

*nois?*

| | |
|---|---|
| NATSOT INTER-SPERSED, AND CONTINUES | NATSOT (missiles, airplanes, carriers, etc.) |
| VO ⟶ | |

*military pictures —*

To reach all those goals—the Reagan administration has spent almost one trillion dollars for defense over the past four years—~~the president~~ *the president* wants another 313 billion this coming year. The new request is meeting with resistance from republicans as well as democrats—And before congress approves it, it's asking how well the administration spent the first trillion— —a question being heard from even the pentagon's strongest supporters.

*Sen. John*

SOT STENNIS

SOT "now tell me what we've gotten for that money. that's what the people want to know... what we've gotten for that money..."

VO ⟶ The ~~most~~ *basic* question people have is how do we stand compared to the Soviet Union. In terms of strategic nuclear weapons, most experts agree the balance between the two superpowers is

*Graphics:*
*U.S. vs. Soviet*

# What Price Defense?

JUDY WOODRUFF: Pick up any consumer's guide and you'll find buying tips to help you decide which product gives you the most for your money. Unfortunately, we cannot normally do that with the items the federal government buys with our tax dollars. But because defense takes up such a large part of that budget and the President is asking for even larger sums for the Pentagon in the future, we decided to ask some experts to try to answer the question anyway: have we been getting our dollar's worth out of defense?

Pres. REAGAN [February 6, 1985]: Spending for defense is investing in things that are priceless: peace and freedom.

CASPAR WEINBERGER, Secretary of Defense [at hearings]: Certainly no one who's looked at the behavior of the Soviet Union could possibly say that there's been any diminution in the threat. Actually there's been a substantial increase, and that has to be the thing that determines the size of the defense budget.

Pres. REAGAN: We must not relax our efforts to restore military strength just as we near our goal of a fully equipped, trained and ready professional corps.

WOODRUFF [voice-over]: To reach all those goals, the Reagan administration has spent almost $1 trillion for defense over the past four years. The President wants another $313 billion this coming year. The new request is meeting with resistance, from Republicans as well as Democrats. And before Congress approves it, it's asking how well the administration spent the first trillion, a question being heard from even the Pentagon's strongest supporters.

Sen. JOHN STENNIS, (D) Mississippi [at hearings]: Now, tell us what we've gotten for that money? That's what the people want to know. What have you gotten for that money?

WOODRUFF [voice-over]: The basic question people have is how do we stand compared to the Soviet Union? In terms of strategic nuclear weapons, most experts agree the balance between the two superpowers is essentially unchanged after four years of the Reagan presidency. That's because the Soviets have matched or more than matched any gains by the U.S.

LAWRENCE KORB, Assistant Secretary of Defense: Just think of how bad it would be if we didn't spend the money. And remember, we're not in this game by ourself; the balance implies two people. And the Soviets, and there's no doubt about it, have continued to modernize their force, which is basically the reason that we had to modernize ours.

*Judy Woodruff talks about this story on p. 50. Courtesy of "The MacNeil/Lehrer NewsHour."*

*Three*

WOODRUFF [voice-over]: A look at the American strategic nuclear arsenal shows there is considerable modernization under way or planned. But as of now, the number of land-based intercontinental ballistic missiles is fewer than when Mr. Reagan came into office. The number of such submarine-based missiles has increased slightly. But the number of strategic bombers, which carry nuclear weapons, has stayed the same.

JAMES SCHLESINGER, former Secretary of Defense: The deterioration of our force posture relative to the Soviet Union, which was going on in the '70s, has been arrested. We have not improved our relative position. Whatever the deficiencies of our force posture in 1981 that the President then talked about and Cap Weinberger still talks about are still there.

WOODRUFF [voice-over]: The improvement in conventional military forces in terms of units designed for combat is slightly more visible. The Army has added one fighting division to make 25 in all, and the Navy has added 44 combatant ships, bringing the total to 523. Among them, the forces have poured billions into new hardware: planes, tanks and missiles. But in some instances, like fighter planes, these were smaller improvements than those made by the Carter administration, which President Reagan has criticized for neglecting the forces.

JAMES FALLOWS, author, "National Defense": The improvement in the actual hardware of the military has been very slight. If you look sort of category by category, wings of fighter planes or how many ships are steaming, there has not been a very substantial increase in those categories, especially in light of how much money has been put into them.

WOODRUFF [voice-over]: Behind the hardware, changes are measured by other standards as well. The quality and the morale of the people in uniform is unanimously agreed to be vastly improved over what it was four years ago, thanks both to pay raises and the recession, which drove job seekers into the all-volunteer military. The readiness of these forces to fight is also said to have improved, but by how much is a matter of considerable debate. Finally, their ability to sustain themselves in combat is also said to be better.

EDWARD LUTTWAK, military analyst: The number of U.S. Army battalions that could really fight has greatly increased. So you can look at the Army and say, "Gee, we spent all this money, but the Army hasn't got any bigger"—it hasn't. But so much more of the Army is real and has real combat capability.

WOODRUFF [voice-over]: Indeed, Reagan administration officials claim that after four years they have a lot to show for the almost trillion dollars they've spent.

Sec. WEINBERGER [at hearings]: In summary terms, we have acquired a substantial amount of additional readiness, and additional sustainability, and an additional credibility to both our deterrence to war and to our foreign policy.

WOODRUFF [voice-over]: But several studies, including one by the nonpartisan Congressional Research Service, concluded that improvements have come only at the margins. And even administration supporters like President Ford's national security adviser Brent Scowcroft say there doesn't seem to have been a plan behind all the spending.

Lt. Gen. BRENT SCOWCROFT, former National Security Adviser: We have not applied the money quite as much in a priority order as I would have done it. It has been more the sense that everything has been underfunded in the past, and that we have to build up everything, so we in fact have tried to put money everywhere.

WOODRUFF [voice-over]: Democratic critics are even harsher.

Rep. THOMAS DOWNEY, (D) New York: Well, I think you put your finger on it when you said, "What's wrong with his priorities?" There aren't any. It's "Buy everything." It's "Everything is okay." I mean, I believe what happens in the Department of Defense is that the service secretaries—the Army, the Navy and the Air Force—come up with their wish lists, and Caspar Weinberger basically puts it together, binds it and sends it off to Congress and says it can't be touched.

WOODRUFF [voice-over]: One of the items on the so-called wish list that critics most often mention is the 600-ship Navy, a goal adopted by the Pentagon under President Reagan.

HAROLD BROWN, former Secretary of Defense: So far as I can tell, the 600-ship Navy was picked out of a hat. It doesn't follow very clearly from any believable plan and scenario. It includes 15 carrier battle-groups, whose exact purpose has still not been made very clear to me.

Mr. LUTTWAK: We essentially have been perpetuating the force structure of the Second World War. A big Navy, as if we were fighting the Japanese, instead of a big Army. Now, we're dealing with the Soviet Union; we don't have nuclear superiority; we ought to have strong continental forces and we don't have them.

Rep. DOWNEY: What do you need a 600-ship Navy for? I mean, what is the purpose? Because we once had it, does that mean you need it again?

Sec. KORB: We're liable to need a very large Navy to keep open the sea lines of communication. If oil should be cut off either to ourselves or to Western Europe or Japan, we could use just about the whole Navy to deal with that, let alone to fight, you know, in a war in the NATO or the North Atlantic area.

WOODRUFF [voice-over]: However, even conservative Republicans like Georgia Congressman Newt Gingrich complain that the administration could have gotten more from its big buildup by making dramatic changes in the way the Pentagon spreads its money around.

*Three*

Rep. NEWT GINGRICH, (R) Georgia: They inherited a system which they did not think they could reform, and they made the decision to avoid spending any of their political capital reforming the system, and instead spent all their time and energy building it bigger. I sympathize with them; I just think in the long run they're wrong, that in the long run we have to rethink—the Congress and Office of Management and Budget and the Pentagon—or we're not going to survive as a country; that we have real structural crises in defense.

WOODRUFF [voice-over]: But some critics of the way the Pentagon operates still defend the big expenditures. Analyst Edward Luttwak, who's just written a book on reforming the military, points out that some of the money that's been spent has gone for weapons not yet built.

Mr. LUTTWAK: A lot of the trillion dollars is not with us because it is being built. Two aircraft carriers, lots of other costly ships, a lot of tanks, advanced procurement of a lot of aircraft. So a lot of the trillion dollars is invisible right now because the weapons haven't arrived yet, or the construction hasn't been finished.

WOODRUFF [voice-over]: The plus most often mentioned is the psychological advantage the President has restored to the United States, cited even by those who disagree with Mr. Reagan's premise that the U.S. was behind the Russians when he was first elected.

Mr. FALLOWS: And so you have a situation very much like that that was recommended often during Vietnam of declaring victory and leaving, where the President can now say our forces are improved. Even though there's not that much difference in what the forces are, but he can say that we're proud again, the balance has been restored, we can deal now with the Soviet Union from a position of strength. And to the extent that psychology matters in domestic politics and international relations they've accomplished their end.

WOODRUFF [voice-over]: But getting back to the basic question at hand . . .

Sen. SAM NUNN, (D) Georgia: When people say that the defenses have not improved over the last four years, I don't agree. But when someone says to me, "Senator Nunn, have we gotten our money's worth for the amount of money we've spent in the last four years?" I have to say I frankly do not think we have.

WOODRUFF [voice-over]: Surprisingly, many thoughtful critics say the major problem is not waste, the $600 toilet seats or even much more outrageous examples of overcharging—all very well publicized.

Mr. LUTTWAK: If we take all the waste and all the fraud and all the mismanagement and put it all together, it may amount to 1% of the defense budget, perhaps 2%—I'll give you 3%. That's a lot of money, billions. Right to be angry about it. But let's not kid ourselves that it's important. What's far more important than that is a question of the money that is not being wasted, defrauded or mismanaged—is that being spent well?

WOODRUFF [voice-over]: And that raises a point brought up by every defense expert we spoke with, both pro- and anti-Reagan administration, that under this President there has been no coherent and credible military strategy upon which to base the Pentagon budget, much less the huge increases in spending we've had the past four years.

Sen. NUNN: They have a strategy—the strategy is to be able to fight the Soviets on three fronts as long as necessary. That strategy is as broad as universal salvation. And when you ask whether we will ever have enough money to implement that strategy, the answer is no.

Sec. BROWN: It's an increase in requirements that's much greater than the increase in U.S. military capability that has occurred in the last five years or will occur over the next few years as this additional money finds its way into equipment and force structure.

Lt. Gen. SCOWCROFT: This administration has been quite innovative in developing ideas. But I don't think any of them have really been adopted as our national military policy, notwithstanding that they've gotten substantial amounts of the budget. And I think we need to decide clearly and publicly in the sense of getting the Congress involved, what it is we're planning to do. My impression is that we're sort of going in several directions at once without any clear priority among them.

WOODRUFF [voice-over]: The administration obviously disagrees.

Sec. WEINBERGER [at hearings]: As the secretary of defense I'm often asked what is our strategy, and not infrequently it turns out that what I'm really being asked is for an explicit account of just where and when and how we would use our military power under any and all conceivable circumstances. And if the questioner doesn't hear precisely what he wants to hear, why then he says we have no coherent strategy.

Sec. KORB: It's very easy when you're not like Secretary Weinberger and you're outside to, you know, pontificate about what will happen. But he's the person who's sitting here, and if something does happen he has to be able to deal with it. And so I think he's acting like all of his predecessors have in this particular job, trying to present—to cover his bets, if you will, so that no matter what the circumstance he can assure that the security interests of the United States are protected.

WOODRUFF [voice-over]: In any event, the alleged lack of strategy has led, critics say, to serious weaknesses in those very spots around the world where the U.S. might one day have to confront the Soviets.

Sec. SCHLESINGER: The greatest weaknesses of the Western defense posture I think still are in the Persian Gulf. The emphasis has not been placed upon the Persian Gulf to the extent that it should have been.

Sen. NUNN: No one can tell you how we're going to take on Soviet tank armies if they try to take over the oilfields in Iran. But that is what we're building for. We're not going to be able to prevent them from coming across their own border with huge divisions right on that border stationed there. We simply cannot realistically do that, but that is the kind of goal we're aspiring to.

WOODRUFF [voice-over]: Just as troublesome, these experts say, is the advantage they contend the Soviets have in conventional weapons in Europe. The Reagan administration's stress on building up strategic nuclear forces, they say, has taken its toll.

Sec. BROWN: There's always a shortage of procurement money at the margin, and if you put a lot more into strategic procurements, say $10 billion in a given year, the things that you'd really like to have to beef up the conventional forces may just not be purchasable.

WOODRUFF [voice-over]: But Assistant Defense Secretary Lawrence Korb says the strategic side of the military budget had to have the extra attention this Pentagon has given it.

Sec. KORB: The strategic had been underfunded for about a decade. If you take a look at the decade of the '70s you'll see that the strategic budget was getting 7% of the overall defense budget. It has come up to about 15%, but that's the peak—it will not go any higher. And the reason it had to is we had to modernize all three legs of the triad simultaneously, because all three were wearing out together 'cause they had all come in together some 20 years ago.

WOODRUFF [voice-over]: For all the criticism, the bottom line, the administration insists, is that we are better off than we used to be.

Gen. JOHN VESSEY, chairman, Joint Chiefs of Staff [at hearings]: If I were the Soviet chief of the general staff ⌐ would be far less inclined to agree to an attack on NATO and the United States today than I would have been four or five or six years ago.

WOODRUFF [voice-over]: Critics agree, but with a warning.

Sec. SCHLESINGER: I think it was Bismarck who said that God takes care of fools, drunks and the United States. That's been true to this point, but we should not assume that that will always be true. It'd be better for us to have a sounder defense position.

WOODRUFF We did a little calculating and found that over his first four years in office, President Reagan got from Congress an average of 95 cents for every dollar of defense spending he asked for. For all the griping from Capitol Hill that we're hearing this year, and all the dark warnings that his Pentagon request will be severely slashed, the cut made by the Senate Budget Committee last night actually amounts to giving him 94 cents on the dollar—a penny less than he received when the mood was supposedly more pro-defense than it is now.

CBS News

*Some people read about events in the newspapers. We go out and witness life in all its variety. I think there's a little boy or little girl in all of us who likes to be where the excitement is, where the action is.*

# DAVID DOW

To get to David Dow's office at CBS in Los Angeles, you walk past the line of people outside the CBS studios at the corner of Beverly and Fairfax, where today a woman is dressed as a purple tomato and a man buzzes around the parking lot in a green and black bumble bee suit. These are not news subjects. They are waiting to get into one of the soundstages where CBS produces game shows.

Behind the soundstages and down a hallway is the CBS bureau, a series of small offices full of metal desks and brilliant ceiling lights, but no windows. A front page from *USA Today* with the headline "Red Letter Day for Dow" is hanging on the wall opposite David Dow's desk. A Dodger pennant hangs near two shelves full of videocassettes. More tapes are stacked on the floor.

"Do you know about any news stories?" David Dow asks. He has been in the bureau for two days without a story for the network and he is agitated. He wants something to do.

When Dow graduated from Stanford in 1959 with a degree in journalism, he went to work for *The San Diego Union.* "I liked the excitement of the moment," he says. "I had always been active in sports. In fact, I went to college on a partial baseball scholarship, and there were teamwork elements of journalism that reminded me of a sporting contest. In essence, several reporters working on a story were like a backfield, the quarterback handing off to a halfback or passing to the wide receiver. Like so many other things in news, you can't assign a definition to it. There was a feeling of rightness about it all—this is where I belong, this is what I should be doing."

Dow felt that television was not an especially promising career in 1959, so he stayed with newspapers. He left the *Union* when he was drafted for four years in the Navy. In the fall of 1964, he was hired by *The Sacramento Bee.* Then the newspaper's owner bought a television station and recruited Dow. He learned on the job.

In 1972, he returned to Stanford for a year on a journalism fellowship and then was hired by CBS in New York to work as an assignment editor and reporter. In 1975, he became a correspondent. He opened a bureau for CBS in Buenos Aires, where he lived with his family and worked for three years. He has reported from virtually every country in Latin America. In 1978, he came to work in Los Angeles.

Dow, 48, has covered the eruption of Mount St. Helens, the Voyager and Pioneer space missions and the 1984 presidential campaigns, but his specialty is Latin America. He covered the negotiations leading to the Panama Canal Treaty, Pope John Paul II's visit to Central America, the fall of Isabel Perón and the civil war in El Salvador. ❖

*from David Dow*

- ■ The cosmetics of television news
- ■ The unpredictable life of a correspondent
- ■ Reporting in a foreign culture

# B EGINNINGS

Television was, in my mind and in the mind of virtually all of my classmates, certainly not a serious device for the spreading of news when I got out of college in 1959. Broadcasting was just not a big part of the journalism curriculum at Stanford. There were courses. I took none of them.

I happen to disagree with those who say journalism curricula are of no use. I think good journalism courses can contribute to the ability to perform. They were a help for me. The most valuable course of all, my senior year at Stanford, was what we referred to as "city practice," an internship program where, for one academic quarter, we worked a couple of days a week with the old *San Francisco News* and one day in the Sunday section of the *San Francisco Examiner.*

I was thinking I might want to be a sportswriter. I had a couple of short stories published in *Sequoia,* the Stanford literary magazine, one of which was later anthologized in *Ten Years of Stanford Short Stories.*

My game plan was to get out and see the world via the exciting vehicle of daily journalism and maybe somewhere down the line, to pull back with all those experiences neatly banked, and write the Great American Novel. I would ease myself into a successful career of writing important novels and short stories. You've heard this story before? Sure. I've never written the Great American Novel.

## LOOKING FOR A JOB

I got a job for one year through the Copley Training Program at *The San Diego Union*. My first paycheck, take home, was $71.14 a week. Since I had all of about $50 in the bank, that was a terrific haul.

After my year at the *Union* was over, my draft number was up and I joined the Navy and served four years as a junior officer from 1960 to 1964.

## FIRST TV AUDITION

In the fall of 1964, I got a job at *The Sacramento Bee,* which had just purchased KOVR-TV. Eleanor McClatchy's [the owner's] idea was that all the good journalists were on newspapers. So her notion in building up the news department at KOVR was to recruit from the paper. The first audition I took, evidently I didn't impress anybody because I didn't get the job.

For my audition we just took some wire copy and rewrote it—just as many people audition today—right in front of a camera and read it. Fortunately, I'm sure the tape has long since disappeared. But I got a second chance about a year after that. They were still enlarging the [television] news operation, and this time I moved over to television in the late summer of '66.

I was very, very naive about broadcasting. I had never really taken a critical eye at a television newscast. The hardest thing to learn, and it's still something that I fight to this day, is the ability to write very tight, to say a lot very quickly.

When you grow up learning your first journalism for newspapers, every lead has five Ws and an H in it. It took me a while to realize that there are different forms of communication and different rules that apply to them.

My first script was probably pretty bad. But I was beginning to think that television really had a future. In 1971 and 1972, I returned to Stanford on a fellowship program for journalists, and then I joined CBS.

I guess one of the things that made me think I could do television was that I fancied myself as a pretty good newspaper writer and it occurred to me early on that television rewarded writing as well. I fancied myself as—quote—a creative person, whatever that was. Television struck me as a field that could be even more creative than newspapers simply because you were dealing with not only words but with sounds and with pictures that could be woven together in communicating a story. It struck a couple of my fancies. It played to them quite nicely.

# QUALITY OF TELEVISION REPORTING

Number one, you've got to split the question up into networks and local television. There's a lot more local television news than there was when I started, but I don't think the reporting is much better. The technology has come along to help make some improvements. Even local stations can now create graphics to help illustrate an economics story. It's certainly more pleasant to watch an anchorman, even in a little, tiny market, who is working with a TelePrompTer instead of constantly trying to establish eye contact—up and down, up and down.

But there is a transiency in local television, the race to the big markets, the big bucks. And some people's ideas of television news have not helped us. We wasted a lot of time and talent on happy talk and all its derivatives and all these cosmetic things that entertain people. At the same time this established a norm for many viewers, not of news, but of entertainment, an expectation that television news would be entertaining. That's not served us well at all.

It's amusing to go out in some markets and interview people who get interviewed a lot by local reporters. Their expectations of how you're going to do the story are interesting. Sometimes they will suggest ways to get me involved in the interview because involvement reporting is a big deal in a lot of markets.

I have a friend who worked at a station where involvement reporting was a big thing, and he once showed me an audition tape in which he had managed to weave himself into a story involving a senior citizen marriage. Suddenly the camera widened out and there he was, standing next to the groom's party at the altar, narrating this thing. To those of us who still think news is a serious business, involvement reporting really undermines the credibility of television news.

Also, live television can bring you the immediacy of an event and that's terrific—we all know that. But it's like any other new toy—it got played with too much. Sometimes it was played with in the wrong events in the wrong instances at the wrong time. It dictated news judgment.

You still see stations that are leading with a story simply because they can get a live unit there. The story has some visual excitement to it and they can get a reporter in front of the visual excitement, whereas the more important story may be down at number three or four in the show's lineup.

Live television has created a whole new dimension of the television personality. When we gather in tape from affiliates, an event has happened when we were not present and we want their tape to put the event on the air. If we want it, you know it was a big story in the local community. So we get their tape and it's a fire or a disaster of some kind that wasn't really very well covered. And it wasn't well covered because they spent most of their time shooting the reporter talking about the event. They didn't get the pictures.

## THE ECONOMICS OF LOCAL TELEVISION NEWS

Local stations have discovered that news makes money. And if news makes money, what follows is a ratings race involving news. The ratings races involving news have gotten far more intense over the years than they ever were when I started out.

[Ratings] sweeps week in a big market like this one [Los Angeles] is really something else. It brings out the best and the worst in local television. Locally, sweeps week always seems to bring out at least one titillation series—"New Fashions in Lingerie," "Sex Therapy—Where Is It Headed?" or something like that.

Another phenomenon is that local stations are sending reporters to places once reserved for the networks. The last time I was in El Salvador, I bumped into a reporter from our Dallas affiliate who was down there doing a sweeps week series. To his credit, he was looking for angles that we weren't covering. He did a feature on a U.S. military adviser who happened to be from Dallas. So this competition has brought out terrific excesses and some benefits.

Where the money has gotten bigger, it has meant a turnover in personalities. I haven't got the figures to prove it, but you smell it, you see it. Agencies are doing audience surveys about how the audience likes various on-air people—not just the anchor people, but field reporters.

When it's a big bucks race, if there are cosmetic reasons why you are losing some of the bucks, the guy or the woman goes. There's always been an element of that in television, but as the stakes have gotten higher, it's gotten much more prominent. And when you're making judgments on news that aren't based on news judgments, there's always a danger of demeaning or undermining the product.

## WHAT TO EXPECT IF YOU WORK IN TODAY'S TELEVISION

Someone who wants to be an on-air television reporter is going to face the reality of being scrutinized cosmetically much more heavily than when I got in. I would have gotten to be on the number 200 market if that had been the case when I got in. That's the reality.

But I want to put in something parenthetically here. I don't want to sound like one of those holier-than-thou people who says cosmetics, cosmetics, how terrible it is. I certainly believe, and it's fairly obvious to everybody, that you've got to have some ability to communicate. If that means keeping yourself well groomed and taking care of your body so it doesn't look hung over and wizened, obviously you do that. Communication is the business here and you keep your attributes in good shape.

I'm not saying that you go out and hire the three ugliest people you can and put them on the air. I'm not saying that at all. It's the excesses that bother a lot of us—where cosmetics is so clearly the motive for keeping some people on the air and washing out others. That's the thing that bothers me.

Someone who wants to be in this business should practice the basic communication tools of speaking well into a camera and making sure they keep their appearance as good as they can with what God's given them. Beyond that, the people who go far, if they ever have a notion of working for a network, inevitably they're going to sink or swim on those same old journalism basics—the ability to interview well, the ability to think and organize information, to edit, to decide what's important and what's not important. And last, but perhaps most important, to write. I certainly know that people applying for jobs at CBS sink or swim on their ability to write. If they can't write, they don't get the job. It's as simple as that.

## THE IMPORTANCE OF BEING A GOOD WRITER

Often, people will say, "Who writes your stuff for you?" And I say, "I write my stuff for me. What do you think I am?" "Oh, you do? You write your material?" What do they think—I have a little gremlin who rides along in my back pocket and writes? That's a popular perception.

Of course, anchor people in big markets do get their stuff written for them. I understand that. But the writing is still the basic building block, whether it's television or newspapers.

## PERSONAL LIFE

I suppose you never quite stop balancing, asking questions. You do it a little less frequently if things are working. You've got to be married to the right person. I'm blessed with that. My kids have grown up with my doing this. They're nine and eleven. There never was a time when daddy wasn't doing this. Even given the fact that what they perceive me doing is normal, there are times when they'll say "Enough" or "Watch it," things that make me think, "Wouldn't it be nice if I didn't have to make this trip?"

My daughter was about four years old when we were living in Buenos Aires, and my big story was all of the developments leading to the Panama Canal Treaty. People used to ask my daughter, "Where do you live?" And she'd say, "We live in Buenos Aires. My daddy lives in Panama." That said it. At that stage, I was commuting between Buenos

Aires and Panama—go up there for a week and home for a few days and go back there for a week.

I think almost everybody in this business who's out in the field will talk about the juggling act between travel and the demands of the business and the demands of raising a family. When you travel as much as we do in this business, raising a family becomes tougher. That's not to say it can't be done. There are a lot of successful marriages in this business and a lot that aren't.

It can really be tough when you have a private life that's based on the knowledge among everyone that when you leave for work in the morning, you may not be home for three weeks. You don't know.

I remember coming to work and in the course of the morning, Park Chun He, then president of South Korea, was assassinated. Since I had worked overseas and done stories overseas and was not at that moment working on any story that had to go on the air that night, the bureau manager got off the phone and said, "Dave—Korea." By 5 o'clock that afternoon, I was on my way to Korea.

I always carry a suitcase, but it's packed for coverage for our prime coverage area from this bureau—13 Western states—so it's two or three changes of clothes. But I knew I was going to be gone for a long time, so I did run home and change my suitcase.

We scrambled downtown and got ourselves a visa for Tokyo, and by the time we were done, the only flight we could get on flew out of San Francisco. We caught a PSA flight out of Burbank, flew to San Francisco, and then got on a China Airlines flight to Tokyo.

We got into Tokyo and went to the Tokyo bureau. It was a weekend. I'd never been to Tokyo. I'd never been to the Tokyo bureau. Before I had put my head on a pillow that day, I had done a story out of Tokyo. A volcano was erupting and the weekend newscast wanted a story on it. So we scraped up a bunch of video from Tokyo Broadcasting and I did a story out of Tokyo.

We got visas to go into Korea, and after we got there it became evident that there wasn't going to be war in Korea, so I came out after a few days and went back to Tokyo. Then I got a Thai visa and took off for Bangkok.

## COVERING THAILAND

I had never been in Asia. I had missed covering the war in Vietnam. I had missed an exposure to all the events that so many of my colleagues had covered that led to what I was seeing in 1979.

But the only experience you really needed was the ability to write a sentence and write a story. The story just came out and slapped you in the face. It was there. Human misery. Thousands and thousands of people of every nationality, of a people fleeing with nothing, people who probably had homes and families and stability, a value that we worship, reduced to rags. If they were alive, they were suffering from malaria, in many cases, walking stick figures. The story was there.

I was gone for a month. And before that month was over, I'd not only been to Korea, but I'd been to Tokyo and I'd been down on the Thai-Cambodian border, spending two and a-half weeks covering the refugees coming over the border.

## COVERING ANOTHER CULTURE

One thing you've got to learn is patience. We are an impatient people, and you're not going to get your story by rushing in, firing your questions and leaving.

I remember doing a story on the great coffee freeze in Brazil. To do the story, you have to talk to growers, the people who produce coffee and market it. And it took us two days to shoot a story on it. By the end of those two days, I had a terrible case of coffee jitters, because it became very evident that I just wasn't going to get the information I wanted unless I sat down and went through the simple rite of having a good cup of Brazilian espresso-style coffee before we got to the business at hand.

When you're out interviewing a rancher on what this disaster's going to mean to his economics, and you're going to ask questions about such delicate things as how much money he has lost and whether he's going broke, and his livelihood is coffee, you learn very quickly that you enjoy his coffee before you start asking personal questions.

Working overseas also makes you more resourceful. Communications in Argentina was really Third World. The televisions were all black and white. The telephone service was awful. I remember there were periods during the day when you could not get a dial tone.

There's this terrible, terrible waiting list just to get telephone service. So you look for an office with telephones in it, and the best we were able to find was one with a single line. That was our lifeline. We used to leave the telephone off the hook for a good part of the day just so we'd have a dial tone. To hang it up was to, in effect, wait in line until circuits cleared so that you could get a dial tone. Often the fastest way to check out a story was to just physically go there because sometimes the telephones just wouldn't work. You couldn't get the people you wanted on the phone, so you just go.

Periodically, there were bombs going off. Four of them went off within a one-block radius of my home in the last year I was in Argentina. If we got word that a bomb had gone off someplace and we had some vague idea where it was, we'd just go rent a car and chase off to find it, rather than trying to call the police, who weren't always very helpful anyway.

You also learn to place higher value on your contacts than you ever did before because with the cultural barrier and, initially at least, the language barrier, I was dependent on sources who spoke some English. That limits you more than you like to be limited. So when you find someone who is a good source, given the limitations you already have, culturally and linguistically, you value that source. You learn, living in police states such as Argentina when I was there, about protecting sources in a way that is much more immediate than you ever think about when you live in the nice, peaceful United States.

## ETHICAL DILEMMAS

There were plenty of situations where people wanted you to compromise your ethics. Dictators were always wanting lists of the questions ahead of time. That was so typical.

When you go to cover a place like Latin America for a network, revolutions seem to come out of nowhere when, indeed, there have been underlying factors brewing, festering for months or years or generations. So you always have the feeling of being parasitical—a guy who's going around looking for the action to happen. That has always bothered me.

You're just reacting to the big story of the moment. You're giving people an aberrant sense of an issue. Their sense of a country may be that it's a violent place because the only stories they've ever seen of the place are very violent moments.

In some cases, the information people were giving you, if you revealed the source of the information, could cost them their lives. I'll never forget this wonderful lady. She was the mother of a friend of my sound man, an aspiring and talented young playwright in Buenos Aires. He [the friend] disappeared. They came in, trashed his apartment, took him away, and he's never been seen since.

His mother used to come to our office and visit occasionally and she wanted to enlist us in the search for him. She was trying to get information, and she thought that being a news organization we might have sources that would have information about his whereabouts that she didn't have.

Well, it's a very typical story. Scores of people, hundreds, thousands were in the same situation as this lady. But I was trying to put together a story on disappearing people, so I needed somebody like her who would talk about what happened. She was, by this time, frequently being followed. She was getting anonymous threatening telephone calls because she had linked herself up with what became known as the Madres de Plaza de Mayo. So I asked her if she was willing to be interviewed on camera. And she said, "I've got to think about that."

Finally, it came down to a point where, if I'd have been in this country, I could have persuaded her to do it—pushed and talked her into doing it. But I suddenly had to tie my own hands because this woman's life, if she went on television to tell her story and point her finger, potentially could have been threatened. That's a pretty awesome thing to confront—do I want to be the one who, in the name of hotshot journalism, of getting a good story on the air, convinces this woman to do something that she may not in her heart be comfortable doing? Hands off. I let her make the decision and she decided not to, but she would have made a good story.

I've done a couple of stories in police states where I wondered whether the people being photographed and interviewed on television really understood the full implications of being on television. Even though my broadcast would appear in another country, the United States, his nation had an embassy in the United States and most assuredly had someone who either monitored American television or who had the responsibility of turning on a video recorder every night when the evening news was on.

Those questions have occurred to me. You always have a pang of conscience when you go into a place of misery and tragedy, and you shoot your pictures and interview your people. Then you retreat back to white sheets at night and a nice hotel and, ultimately, you retreat back to the safety of the United States of America. Unavoidably, that's the way it's done, but a little piece of me feels a pang of conscience every time I do it.

## FOREIGN GOVERNMENTS AND THE PRESS

I used to tell people I liked living in Buenos Aires, but I hated working in it. The first action of the Argentine security forces whenever there was a bomb explosion was to seal the area out of sight of the press and then, next, to worry about life, limb and property. I'm sure of it. They could always beat you to the site of one of these things and then deny you entrance.

One day I did a story and I needed some pictures—two exteriors and a shot of a location in a park where a man had been kidnapped. In the course of getting just those three shots, I was detained twice.

We had just started out for the first location and the cameraman remembered he needed a filter. So we went back to his house and he ran in to get his filter. Suddenly, from out of nowhere, at least six policemen leaped out with semiautomatic weapons and ordered us out of the car. They threw us against the car and shook us down, got our identification and then apologized.

*David Dow*

Then we got to the park to get our shot and almost immediately here came an air force vehicle. They had seen a camera and assumed we were spying on the air force, so they took us into custody. It took us two hours to talk our way out of that one. Fortunately, these guys were stupid enough not to confiscate our film.

Any shots that you wanted to get of police units in Buenos Aires, you were doing at your own risk because there were too many cases where they shot and asked questions later. The government was obviously intimidating local journalists. A number of journalists disappeared when I was there. An Argentine-born reporter for AP was kidnapped for 48 hours.

Aside from the incidents I described, I was never kidnapped or threatened, although toward the end of my stay there, a bomb went off in front of our apartment building. We lived on the third floor and the bomb blew out half the windows in my daughter's bedroom, set trees on fire outside our window and blew out some windows in our bedroom. My daughter was four. It made an impression on her, too. We didn't realize it at the time. Noises really bothered her for a long time.

---

## NUCLEAR WASTE IN MEXICO

This story had been covered and forgotten. There was an accident involving some [nuclear] waste [that was found] in a village in Mexico, and the story broke as sort of a one-day wonder. We saw a couple of small stories on it, but it just struck us that it was worth some more time. The consequences of nuclear radiation don't become manifest for weeks, months, years, generations.

We did a lot of work on the telephone lining things up—three or four days on the phone. We talked to lots of people in the scientific community just trying to make sure that the story, the accident, was as big as it was. We were trying to find out if, yes, this was the worst radiation accident in terms of possible effects on humans since Three Mile Island.

Then away we went to El Paso, spent two days in Juarez. Through our El Paso affiliate we hired a gem of a Mexican journalist who works for a television station in Juarez but who can serve his other clients from time to time. He saved us a lot of time because he knew where places were and knew where people lived.

When we got through in Juarez, we flew up to Oakridge, Tennessee, to interview Carl Hubner, who seemed to be the most knowledgeable U.S. scientist who had been called in as a consultant on the whole thing. Meanwhile, while we were doing that, I called Los Angeles and had one of our desk people get a shot of one of the machines that had provided the [nuclear] core. That proved very, very difficult, which also reinforced the notion that this was a machine that was obsolete from the time it hit Mexico. We finally found a next-generation machine like the one that had been involved in the accident and got a picture of it.

As in all successful ventures in foreign reporting, there was a lot of luck laced along the way. The man who drove the machine [nuclear] core to the junkyard and set off this whole bizarre chain of events just happened to be standing out in front of his little house when we got there. We walked up and asked if we could talk to him, and he said OK and we got the interview. Five minutes after we were through, his wife pulled up, saw that we were in the street, learned that her husband had been interviewed and reamed him out for being interviewed. If we had been there five minutes later, we never would have gotten the interview.

There was another stroke of luck with this one. The owner of the junkyard [where the nuclear waste was found] was a photography buff and he had shot his own home movies on half-inch videotape of the day they came to extract the [nuclear] core from his junkyard. So he had all these pictures, and we made a double of them and used them in the piece. Another terrific stroke of luck.

It was a classic case of how the creations of the most sophisticated men can visit their worst consequences on the least sophisticated people. This began with a man and his pickup trying to make a few bucks out of some junk. And there was a picture that we shot that seemed to symbolize the situation.

On the street where the man in the story lived, which was a modest, sort of run-down little street, through a couple of trees, you could see the skyscrapers of El Paso. Something about that picture symbolized the whole story, about the castoffs of our sophisticated culture—and this machine was, in effect, a castoff—and how a castoff could result in so much trouble for people who didn't understand the technology.

## CODES OF ETHICS

CBS has a guy whose job is to be sort of a referee, an ombudsman, to interpret CBS news standards. Lesson number one is that you let people commit their own news. You don't in any way try to skew or influence the news—the nonstaging rule. Back during the days of the Vietnam demonstrations, a lot of news organizations, including this one, had to deal with the dilemma of encouraging the demonstrators. To what extent does your presence modify their behavior?

People will do things in the presence of news people that they wouldn't do otherwise. They will act differently in the presence of news people, particularly television because it's so conspicuous. There's a running battle to try to minimize that. Politicians, of course, wouldn't act that way if it weren't for us being there. Protesters will do things differently than they would if you weren't there.

Then there's the story where you're profiling someone and you call the person up and find the person is very excited about being profiled. You ask him what he's going to be doing and he says, "What would you like me to be doing?" And I say to him, "I can't tell you that." And he says, "Well, I'm just going to be being me." Then you start saying, to get his mind working, "Well, what do you do for recreation?" "Oh, I jog." Jogging—I can get a shot of him jogging—physical fitness. "Well, when do you usually jog?" By this time he's getting media-wise and he says, "Oh, tomorrow morning." And I've had occasions when I arrive at the man's home at the crack of dawn to get him jogging and his wife is there and she says, "What did you get up so damn early for this morning? You usually jog at night."

I think most good reporters understand when that's happening, and also understand when somebody is trying to manipulate his way onto the 6 o'clock news. We have a set of danger signals that go off. You ask yourself, "Is the person telling the truth? Is this plausible? Is the person making claims to shock his way onto television?" You look for exaggeration. Journalistically, you always try to put the burden of proof on the other person to substantiate his claims. It's a plain and simple game of truth seeking.

I'm also amazed at some of the people who want to be on television. I interviewed a guy yesterday for this T-shirt story and he readily admits to counterfeiting T-shirts. He wanted to be on television. There's a "Hi, mom" element there.

## TELEVISION REPORTING AS A CAREER

Working for a network can be a lifetime occupation. Keep in mind that reporting is only one aspect of it. Plenty of executive positions are occupied by people in their late 40s, 50s and 60s. And there are plenty of people blessed with good health who are still out slogging through the mine fields at advanced ages. I think there are some stories that old men shouldn't spend too much time covering—the pursuit of battlefield stories, for example. But again, it's going to depend on one's state of health and how much one is willing to risk at what age.

There are limits beyond which this company won't go in probing one's motives for turning down an assignment and I've never seen anyone say, "You will go to El Salvador or you will lose your job." Never happen. I have the freedom to say no. I can remember at least once when I was asked to go somewhere in Latin America where I frankly thought I smelled a great deal of physical hardship in pursuit of a story that wasn't going to pan out. A certain sort of "I've paid my dues" instinct surfaced and I said no. No questions asked. Three other people in this bureau turned down the same story.

## WHY I LIKE WHAT I DO

I think it's variety, the same basic thing that got me started in the first place. Some people read about events in the newspapers. We go out and witness life in all its variety. I think there's a little boy or little girl in all of us who likes to be where the excitement is, where the action is.

Of course, having said that, it would be misleading to suggest that all of our lives are composed of one exciting event after another. There's a lot of dull stuff we do—a lot of dull drudgery on the telephone, of staking out places. In my first job at CBS, Watergate was breaking and those of us who were junior reporters in New York spent a lot of time staking out [U.S. Attorney General] John Mitchell's apartment, just standing there waiting for John Mitchell to come out and ask him a question. There were many times in those chill, terribly cold winter Manhattan days when I was thinking that this didn't seem like fit work for a guy who'd gone to college and envisioned himself being a big-time network correspondent.

I hope that the same people who were inspired by the Woodward and Bernstein Watergate story, who were inspired by the drama and excitement of breaking a story that changed the world, read the other words on the pages, which were the hours and hours of patience and drudgery and dead ends and frustration that would have turned average reporters off the trail long before.

## HOW THE PUBLIC PERCEIVES US

I think the public is ambivalent toward us. When the news doesn't affect them directly, people love a free press, they love the emissaries, they love the workers of that press. They certainly think that what I do is very exciting and glamorous. But when we're breaking news that's hard to take, a great part of our public gets very angry at the messenger and, in many cases, would like to have the heads of the messengers.

Then there's another part that worries me. That is reporters as celebrities. It seems like more and more, when you ask someone why they watch a particular station or a particular network, you're hearing, "Oh, I like—" and they name their favorite person. Less frequently than I would like do you hear, "I watch them because they do the best job of covering the news." It's usually a personality thing. And that bothers me.

It makes me wonder if we are putting ourselves ahead of the story. A lot of my mother's and my mother-in-law's friends say, "We see your stories. We enjoy your work. But we'd like to see a little more of you." And it's a lecture I've almost stopped giving. The story isn't about me. I should be there only if it helps me get the story. I am a messenger and nothing more. I am not the message.

*David Dow*

# Juarez Radiation Accident

d. dow/Neufeld/Gilman/various

EVENING NEWS

SOT—FEW SECONDS OF SPANISH AS DOCTOR EXAMINES PEDRO TORRES

continue exam

Pedro Torres says he feels all right— better than five months ago, anyway. But the check-ups may never end—not since he became a statistic ... a victim of a radiation accident far worse than Three Mile Island.

SOT—KARL HUBNER, M.D.
Oak Ridge Associated Universities

("IT'S ONE OF THE MOST SERIOUS ACCIDENTS IN THIS HEMISPHERE.")

SOT—VICENTE SOTELO
Ex-hospital worker

(COUPLE SECONDS OF SPANISH)

exterior hospital

exterior—dilapidated warehouse

scrapyard shot
shot of machine

shot of pellets with pencil to show tiny dimensions
workers in junkyard KDBC-TV material

Vicente Sotelo is still haunted by it. Someone at the Juarez hospital where he worked told him—he says—he could sell junk in its warehouse. He hauled it to the scrapyard, not knowing the "junk" included the highly radioactive core of a cancer therapy machine similar to this one.

Somehow the core was smashed open and hundreds of tiny Cobalt 60 pellets spilled into the bed of Sotelo's pickup.

Thousands more were scattered in the junkyard and eventually hauled off with other scrap to two Mexican foundries.

SOT—ROBERTO MOYA
Scrapyard owner
(cover to edit with preceding scene)

("IT WAS (edit) SHOVELED IN WITH EVERYTHING ELSE. AS FOR IDENTIFYING MARKS, THERE WAS NONE AT ALL.")

shots of junkyard and foundry workers

For six weeks, dozens of people worked around the radioactive pellets. Meanwhile, the pellets found their way into

---

*David Dow talks about this story on pp. 76–77. © CBS Inc. 1984. All rights reserved. Originally broadcast June 7, 1984, on the "CBS Evening News."*

| | |
|---|---|
| table bases—KTSP | 6,000 <u>tons</u> of table bases and construction rods shipped through the U.S. and Mexico. |
| rebars from KTSP and/or KDBC | |
| FILE SHOTS— Los Alamos gate ... to be provided by NY | The accident might never have been discovered had not the driver of one shipment taken a wrong turn into the Los Alamos/Nuclear Weapons Laboratory in New Mexico and tripped a radiation alarm. |
| NAT SOT— | (CHOPPER NOISE FOR SECOND OR TWO) |
| | With that the two countries launched a massive search for the other contaminated products. Most were located and recalled. |
| demolished building | Several structures built with radioactive rods were torn down. |
| street scene, showing where truck was parked | And when authorities tracked down Sotelo's truck, they found it had been parked outside his home for seven weeks exposing neighbors to a daily dose of radiation. |
| SOT—Dr. Juan Rauda, M.D. | (FEW SECONDS OF SPANISH) |
| possible folks in barrio or junkyard workers | "So far we've identified nearly 200 persons who've been exposed to the radiation," says Dr. Juan Rauda, a public health official. Most of them probably received low doses. But Pedro Torres and another junkyard worker have become sterile since the accident. |
| Torres | |
| microscope work and cell slides | Tests at the Oak Ridge Universities in Tennessee have revealed chromosome damage in at least ten victims. And there've been blood abnormalities, too. |
| ON CAMERA | A similar accident in U.S. territory just a few blocks away likely would have generated sustained, international headlines. |
| V/O pullback from El Paso | But here in the shadows of El Paso, radioactive exposure is a hard thing to understand. |
| SOT—XAVIER RIOS | (WELL, I DON'T KNOW NOTHING ABOUT ... UH ... COBALT 60.") |
| | Xavier Rios isn't alone in his bewilderment. |

| | |
|---|---|
| SOT—MARIA DE LA LUZ CALDERON-CHAVEZ | (COUPLE SECONDS OF SPANISH) |
| | Maria Calderon worries about the future of her children and dozens of others who played in the contaminated pickup. |
| SOT—GLORIA BARRA | (COUPLE SECONDS OF SPANISH) |
| | Gloria Barra was pregnant when she used to walk by the truck. Her new baby seems healthy. But she, like many here, wonders if everything is okay. So do doctors, who know that high exposures to radiation may lead to cancer. |
| SOT—DR. KARL HUBNER | ("I WOULD TELL THEM YOU WILL BE OKAY FOR A LONG TIME, PROBABLY FOR THE REST OF YOUR LIFE, AND THEN I WOULD, OF COURSE, HAVE TO TELL THEM ABOUT THE POTENTIAL RISK OF CANCER.") |
| conference material WWL | Today, Mexican and U.S. officials discussed the accident at a scientific conference in New Orleans—seeking answers. |
| file shots of core being removed from junkyard | The machine that wound up in the junkyard had been sold—legally—by a U.S. company to the Mexican hospital, which never used it. Yet, through apparent loopholes in laws and enforcement, it became a hazard. |
| RX SUPER—Date | |
| SOT—DR. HERBERT ORTEGA Pan-American Health Organization | ("SOMETHING WENT WRONG OR WE PROBABLY WOULD NOT HAVE HAD THIS SITUATION OCCUR.") |
| worker using geiger counter inscription being stamped on containers | Today, there are geiger counters at the foundry that made the table bases. Each shipment is now certified "free of contamination." |
| blue box in customs shed traffic lined up mountain of junk | Also as a result of the incident, other devices now check traffic for radiation at U.S border stations.

Outside Juarez, Sotelo's pickup and a mountain of other contaminated items await a proper burial. |

CU's as they're
mentioned

But that will not end the story.
Not for Pedro Torres...
Nor Maria Calderon...
Not for the others who can only wait
for the final chapter.

David Dow, CBS News, Juarez, Mexico

ABC News

*Don't believe that your success, your place in society as a reporter, depends on closeness, either socially or from the standpoint of power, with the people you cover. Be an outsider from the establishment.*

# SAM DONALDSON

"Bray It Again Sam," reads the headline in *Time* magazine about a recent White House press conference. *Time* says Donaldson asked an impertinent question. Donaldson is accustomed to the criticism.

"I have some sort of a reputation of asking flamboyant or aggressive questions," he says, "but I have never, ever attempted to do that. I have sometimes asked aggressive questions and needled guests, but it's because I want information, not because I want a show.

"Now, I'm no dummy. If I can get that information and it's interesting and it's interestingly presented, I think that's fine. I think, to get an audience, you have to not be dull.

"Presidents, like most politicians I know, call on people who are interesting. We like interesting people, whether we're going to have them over to dinner tonight or whether we're at a news conference and we're going to call on someone to question us. We don't like dull people, anymore than we like being dull."

Dullness is not one of Sam Donaldson's characteristics. He also does not lack energy. During the week, he follows the president. On Sunday mornings, he is a guest on "This Week With David Brinkley." Sunday evenings he anchors ABC's "World News Tonight."

Donaldson moves everywhere in a hurry. His conversation about himself has an even, practiced rhythm that indicates he is often asked about his work. When he is perplexed (rarely) or intense (often), his eyebrows knit in an upside down W. Sometimes in his voice are hints of his native Texas.

His father died of a heart attack before Donaldson was born, and he was raised by his mother in El Paso, Texas. She sent him to New Mexico Military Institute when he was 14. Then he attended Texas Western College and the University of Southern California. His first job was at KRLD-TV in Dallas, where he spent two years. He moved to WTOP in Washington in 1961.

Donaldson, 52, has been at ABC News since October 1967 and at the White House since 1977. He has covered every national political convention since 1964. *The Washington Post* has called him "Big Mouth of the Small Screen." His ABC colleague Ted Koppel has called him "perhaps the best White House correspondent ever." ❖

## SPECIAL PERSPECTIVES

*from Sam Donaldson*

- Covering the White House
- Challenging conventional wisdom
- Distancing yourself from your sources

# B̲EGINNINGS

Probably the one single episode that most prepared me had nothing to do with the news business or the techniques of the news business. It was the fact that I was sent to military school for high school and learned something about discipline, something about organization, and something about the give and take of competition in a setting that I had never had before. I look back on that experience as one that probably, apart from the news business, has helped sustain me as I go out and fight the good fight.

No one likes going to military school, it seems to me. I didn't like it. If you're not used to strong discipline, then it's a strong dose and you don't like it, you don't want it. But you learn that, like it or not, you've got to prepare your studies and you've got to clean your room and you've got to clean your rifle and shine your boots. The penalties are worse than the work expended to do that.

After a while, you learn that not only do you want to do that, but you want to excel, you want to win the best cadet award, you want to beat someone in swimming, you want to demonstrate your proficiency at the Queen Anne drill on the M-1 rifle that has everyone in awe. In other words, the first step is to learn that you cannot do it by yourself any way you choose, that society—in this case, military school—has rules and you have to learn to work within them, and you have to do your part within them.

*Sam Donaldson*  87

The next step is to excel by working within these rules and by doing your part and by learning about self-confidence. Today, I get a lot of mail that's very critical of my work. Actually, matter of fact, I get more mail that's not critical, it contains praise, but that's beside the point. People say some very mean things, very tough things. And they say them to me in person.

If I had a thin skin or if I was going to get upset about that, or if I didn't really think what I was doing, the way I was doing it, was the right thing to do—not just a personally satisfying thing or a thing that would bring me a reward, but the right thing—then I would get terribly upset about those letters and those criticisms. But because I have learned to have confidence in my judgment and what's right and how to conduct myself and to work within society's rules, then these things don't bother me that much.

I wanted to be in this business from at least middle teen-age years. The evolution of my coming into the business was just that—kind of step by step. I have never had and do not have any plan, a one-year, two-year, five-year plan—I'm going to be in this market when I'm 30 and when I'm 35 I'm going to have this beat. Nothing like that.

It's always been simple, I'd come to a fork in the road and I'd turn left or right. Looking back, you can see how if you turned the other way, it might have worked out differently. Opportunities have come along and I've taken them.

My advice to students is: First you give them the Horatio Alger lecture. If they've never heard of Horatio Alger, you ought to tell them who he was. Having done that, then you say, work hard, prepare yourself. And then you say, take every opportunity that comes along, even though it means more work, more responsibility—clearly you want that. Take the opportunity. Don't shrink from it, particularly in your early years.

When you get to be 51, then you can begin to pick and choose and say "No thanks" to this opportunity or that opportunity. But not when you're 21 or 31. Or for that matter, 41. Forty-one is probably the most critical year if you're going to talk about breaking out of the pack. Some people break out of the pack at 31 and we both know some people who are stars of various news networks who are not yet 30, but I think that they should not detain us for any serious inspection.

I didn't go to a network until I was 33, really a little late to go to a network. I worked for local stations until that point. And I did work at the network that I thought was good, and I think the network at the time thought so, too. When I was in my early 40s—I guess 41—I was assigned to cover Jimmy Carter. I covered two years of Wategate, and I thought I did excellent work—naturally I would—but nothing happened after that. Of course, in those days, nobody was watching ABC much.

## MY ROLE IN WASHINGTON

When I'm working as the beat correspondent at the White House, as apart from Sunday on the Brinkley show or some other enterprise for ABC, I try to answer one little, simple question: What's really going on here in any given day? Now, usually what's going on at the White House is something that the president and his aides have put forward as going on. They dictate the news agenda more than outside events dictate it.

Outside events can, on occasion, brush aside their preplanning for a day. The pope is shot, that's the story. If an event occurs of great magnitude, that may be the story. But normally, the story becomes what the White House projects it to be. If they make an announcement of some importance about, say, a tax reform bill and give some specifications of what the president is going to support, that is a story we all want to do. I might get up that morning and say, "I'd like to look at the latest wrinkle in the Nicaraguan policy." That's well and good, but the White House story on tax reform will take precedence.

It doesn't bother me. I'm a reporter assigned to report on the activities of the president. Why would it bother me that the president's activities, as he defines them, are the grist for my reports? Every administration attempts to manage the news and manipulate news reporting to its advantage. There's nothing immoral about that, let alone illegal. You and I do it in our daily lives.

So, it's simply that my job, in trying to find out what's really going on, is one part taking what they say is going on and one part taking what critics and others, who may not be critics but standing on a neutral ground, can contribute to what's going on, and then add my own experience and my own judgment.

ABC, just as the other networks in the case of their reporters, doesn't pay me to be an IBM machine or to have no critical judgment whatsoever. I've been in the town 24 years. If I weren't expected to make some use of that experience then why not hire a bright college student for a little less than they're paying me and let that person go over there and take notes?

## HOW THE WHITE HOUSE MANAGES THE NEWS

This administration is more effective than previous administrations, by and large, for a couple of reasons. The people themselves who are in charge of the news management know the business, certainly know television, understand our needs in the sense of deadlines, in the sense of material the particular medium can use, better than their predecessors.

The second factor, of course, is Ronald Reagan himself. He, on television, as well as in the prints, can project the kind of positive image and take the hard edges off problems to a far greater degree than any other president certainly since Kennedy, and perhaps including Kennedy.

For all his wit and for all the ability, verbally and the symbolism that Kennedy had that also made him more attractive to the press and to press coverage, it wasn't as all-encompassing as Ronald Reagan. Pat Schroeder calls Ronald Reagan the Teflon president, but I prefer my friend George Will's little description.

George Will says that Ronald Reagan is the only man he knows who can walk into the room, have the ceiling fall in on him, and walk out without a fleck of plaster in his hair. Now, that ability comes from his showmanship, and the ability he has to project one thing even though the facts are another.

I've never seen a president who has that quality and who can do that so well. I think it's true that his audience, meaning viewers, readers, are already conditioned to accept it. If Ronald Reagan appeared from nowhere, without any background, suddenly this man, 74 years old, appears with all the attributes he has, but we didn't remember him from the Gipper and from "Bedtime for Bonzo" and "GE Theater," it might be different.

But we are conditioned, now, to accept Reaganisms. He can say things which are obviously wrong—and I'm not talking about arguments over the merits of a policy, but I'm talking about facts. He doesn't have his facts right. He can tell stories which are clearly anecdotal, can't back them up and yet he insists they are true. He can call black white one day after calling white black, and it doesn't seem to matter.

That is a quality, back to the original question, which started this diatribe of mine, that no other president has had, including Kennedy, who came closer to it than, certainly, Lyndon Johnson, who was a disaster when it came to press relationships. Richard Nixon had his old, dark side which clouded everything. Gerald Ford was an amiable man and we all sort of liked him, but he was a transition character. Jimmy Carter, that feisty little devil, was far more interesting than Ronald Reagan as a personality because of the way his mind worked—his mind really worked.

Mr. Reagan has a mind which works, no doubt about it, but it's along familiar channels and there are no surprises as it wends its way slowly down the river of conservative ideology toward the sea of small government, small defense, no welfare queens on the rolls, and no abortions in the land.

Mr. Reagan, and it's a strength of his, has a unifying philosophy, unlike Jimmy Carter, who was the other president I followed very closely.

It becomes predictable. If you discover a bunch of communists in country X, you know where Ronald Reagan stands on it. Without any examination of the various foreign policy considerations that might really be different in the case of country X, it doesn't matter. Commies are dirty people and must be opposed. That's it. And down the line of litany of Reagan beliefs.

I'm not calling them all wrong. I'm simply saying, yes, I can predict to a far larger extent Ronald Reagan's reactions to events and issues and problems than I could Jimmy Carter's, although Carter did have some predictability about him. Carter tended to look at individual problems individually, particularly in the early part of his presidency, and try to come up with an answer to fit that problem. This was a weakness to the extent that by looking at every one of the trees, he missed the forest.

Ronald Reagan's never met a weapons system he didn't like. Now, that's a Lou Cannon-ism, but I believe it's quite true. Jimmy Carter—some weapons systems after analysis he thought were sound and ought to be built, including, in his day, the MX. He actually came up with a system for basing it that, had it been politically viable, probably would have made sense from the standpoint of a role and a strategic mission for that missile. But he didn't like the B-1 for reasons he set forward—not only cost efficiency, but the question of generation of weapons systems.

Reagan, however, you come to him and say it's a weapon system to fight the dirty commies, and he's bought it without much analysis. If you came to him and said, "I'm proposing this weapons system, but we—his people—don't think it's the right one," he would agree with his people.

I'm not trying to suggest that all you have to say is weapons and a light flashes on his head. But part of his presidency, a big part, as you know, is the delegation of the power, not only to analyze, but authority. So that he trusts his people. He has great confidence in them and he supports them. And when they come to him and say, "We recommend this," that's what he's for without great examination on his part.

## HOW TO ASK GOOD QUESTIONS

I asked Bert Lance, when he was on [ABC] a few months ago, if he had any current overdrafts at the Calhoun National Bank. I said, "If people in this country, beyond the politicians, remember you at all, they remember you because you resigned under fire in the Carter administration because of your banking practices. So I want to ask you, do you have overdrafts today, as you did in those days?" [He said] "Well, Sam, I knew you'd ask me a question like that." I got a bunch of mail telling me how rude I was on that.

But those are the questions that should be asked, I maintain, because people watching want you to ask, and I don't mean just for the theater. I have never asked a question with the thought that, "If I ask this, it will produce good theater, if I ask this it will keep me in the limelight."

Now you say, well, Sam, was it realistic for you to think that, no matter what his banking practices are, he would respond, "Yes, matter of fact, I have about $100,000 of overdrafts right now." I understand that. But to put them on record with that answer is worth something, when you go back and something comes up.

One of the ways guests prepare for the Brinkley show is—they're ready for me to start to interrupt, and they immediately say, "Well, please don't interrupt me. May I finish?" even though they know they have been going on, just diarrhea of the mouth, with no point. They know there's a certain element of the audience out there that sees me as rude and crude and hostile and that comment will immediately evoke a sympathetic response, even though they should be interrupted.

## THE IMPORTANCE OF PACING

I'm very conscious of the pacing. On the Brinkley show, I often will accommodate my questioning to what I perceive to be the best interest of the show from the standpoint of pacing. Each of us plays a part on this show.

David Brinkley is the gentleman. David Brinkley is the Gray Eminence. David Brinkley is everyone's favorite host, and he asks very general and friendly—I don't mean sellout—questions. George Will is the Philosopher King. There are three Gladstones, four references to "The Federalist Papers," and an underpinning of what's going on here in the context of the Holy Roman Empire. And I look for the hard news question. If the occasion merits it, I slash away.

As someone said to me the other day, I wouldn't watch an hour of Brinkley if you paid me, and I wouldn't watch an hour of George Will if you chained me, and I wouldn't watch an hour of you for anything in the world, but I'd watch two hours of the three of you on good days because the pacing is part of the combination.

## BEING USED IN WASHINGTON

There's sort of a middle place in journalism where you concentrate on the process, and in the process, if you're the White House correspondent, you go hear the press secretary give you the most rosy scenario of any situation possible, and he wants you to go and tell the American people that. Well, in a sense, you're being used. In another sense that, plus your own judgment, is the news of the day.

To say that people use us in Washington to get out a particular message is to state the obvious reason why we're in Washington as reporters. We are there to find out what's going on and tell everyone about it. So I don't feel used. Now, if the question had been whether I've been lied to, that is a different question. That's where you get even and you cut people off.

## HOW THE PUBLIC VIEWS THE PRESS

I think most people see the job of reporters, whether in Washington or someplace else, as it really is. They understand the press has a function they appreciate—I don't mean in terms of throwing garlands, but I mean that they believe it is important to their lives.

Naturally, newspaper readers or television watchers are not going to endorse every reporter's work or every story and they shouldn't, but I don't buy the idea that the vast majority of the American people has either great hatred or lack of confidence in the American press.

I think that generally most people in this country understand what we're about, they approve of our work in the sense that we ought to be doing it. They don't always approve of every individual, and that's exactly right.

## HOW THE PUBLIC VIEWS WHAT I DO

People are not sophisticated about my job any more than I am sophisticated about theirs. I think there are a lot of people in the country, for instance, who are intelligent human beings, who somehow think I'm on the White House staff.

I get letters from people saying, "I've written to Ronald Reagan and asked him to fire you from his staff." Well, you say that must be about 3 percent. No, I think some far larger percentage don't understand, really. They understand that I'm at the White House and I report from the White House. They think I'm on his staff. And, of course, there's some percentage who think I'm on Gorbachev's staff.

But if you leave out the fringes, the majority of the people don't understand the techniques that I employ in my business, and that I have to employ. They see the finished product.

## MY TOUGH REPUTATION

Take any series of press conferences with Ronald Reagan or experiences with Ronald Reagan and I can show you other people who have asked equally tough or tougher questions—by tough, we're talking about pointed questions, questions that require the president to actually come to the point himself or demonstrate that he refuses to do so. Others do the same thing. But there's this myth that I ask the tough questions.

Well, to one extent of course, that's flattering. To one extent, that is more than complimentary. It stands me in good stead. But to the other extent, it's a myth, just like any view that I am always rude and crude around the president, in my view, is another myth. It is not true.

But you get typed and cast, for better or worse. One of the problems of this business is that you get typed and people are loath to use you in another way. They think you do what you do, not that you can do something else. You have to try to convince them that it's not true.

In broadcasting, you specialize in what you report and what broadcasts you're on and how they use you. If they use you in a way that management and the public finds pleasing, then they want to keep you there and they don't want you to move on.

---

## HOW I WORK

Most days are boring for me. Most days are dull. A few are not and they're worth every boring moment in the business.

I go to the White House in the morning. I attend the briefing by [Press Secretary] Larry Speakes. It's fairly informal. He talks about the president's schedule. We ask him the immediate news questions that may have occurred overnight or since the last time we saw him. He either gives answers or "No comments" them or dances or weaves. Then the president's schedule develops during the day. Sometimes there's nothing on it that we can cover as reporters or photographers and other days there are three or four items that we cover.

Today, he had a leadership meeting with the Republican leaders of the House and Senate, after which, as they departed, we buttonholed as many as we could, including Dole and Michel—the two leaders. And they talked about Nicaragua and the budget, and Dole and Michel both told us that he pounded the table, that he was frustrated at the fact that 535 members of the Congress formed a committee that kept him from doing, in the field of foreign policy, what he wanted to do.

And we said, "Did he really pound the table?" And they got up there and went [pounds on the table]. Well, that's going to be on the evening news tonight, I can assure you. The most exciting 11 seconds this evening on any network are going to be Dole and Michel [pounds on the table] creating table pounding because Ronald Reagan was angry because of this awful system known as democracy, the federal republic that requires some checks and balances on the executive.

Then I saw Mr. Reagan later as he said goodbye to a man who is the president of Honduras—at least as we speak. When this book is published, God knows who will be the president of Honduras. After they spoke and shook hands, I asked Reagan—at a distance, therefore it was a yell—"Is it true you pounded the table in frustration over Nicaragua?" He said, "No, I was killing a fly." That was a Reagan one-liner, you see.

I said, "Oh, come on, we know you pounded the table. They told us." "No, I was killing a fly." I said, "Well, you really want to disband Congress. It's a bothersome, meddlesome thing, isn't it?" He has sense enough not to answer that, but a wicked grin told it all, and that was my exposure so far.

Later today, I won't see him because I won't be a member of the press pool, but he'll speak again on Central America. Today's the day that they defined around the Honduran visit, obviously, as a day when the story would be whipping on the Sandinistas of Nicaragua and those dirty, godless commies.

## SETTING THE AGENDA

Now you say, well, what about some other story today? Is there going to be a summit meeting, or this, that, and the other? Those are legitimate questions. We asked them to Speakes, but inexorably, since Nicaragua is a legitimate news story, it is the activity of the president today—going back to why I'm there and what I do.

Yes, that's the story I'm going to do on the air tonight at this moment. Is that manipulating the news? To some extent, they have set the agenda. I'll get to say whatever I want to say about this. If I want to take the view that pounding the table is a silly thing or not, then I'll have the last word, but it's their story.

Tomorrow he [the president] is going to Annapolis to deliver a commencement address at the naval academy. I'll go along. I'll listen to it. I'll report on that. We'll use sound, lights and the air of the address, and if he talks about the defense budget or defense matters in a controversial sense, we may have others speak out later in the day from Congress or elsewhere that I'll put in my report.

I try to cover the president's activities insofar as I am allowed to by the restrictions placed on the access in the White House and by my own ability to talk to enough people to find out what's really going on there. But I take a view by 6:30 Eastern time and whatever my view is—by *view* I mean what's really going on, not my own personal opinion of what people should think of the story or the issue or Ronald Reagan— I'll put that view on the air.

## FAIRNESS IN REPORTING

I try to practice my business using the clear lessons of journalism that I think work. And they're the obvious ones. I try to be fair from the standpoint of fairly reporting a quote so it's accurate, fairly including material in my reports so a viewpoint is represented and in context.

On the other hand, I am not there, anywhere, to report so that there are six pounds of material on one side of an argument and then I balance it with half a dozen pounds of material on the other.

If you're debating whether to build an MX or not, the truth has to be on one side or the other. It is not six of one and half a dozen of another forever. As reporters, we're trying to find out what the truth is. Is the missile any good? Will it perform a mission? Does it have a function? Will it scare the Russians? Will it work as a bargaining chip? Is the $24 billion they want to expend correct?

As a journalist, I ask you your view. I will fairly represent it in my report. To take an extreme example, if you take the view today that the earth is, in fact, flat, I may include it in my report. But I'm not going to be fair in the sense that a viewer who has no knowledge of the subject will come away not having any idea if the earth is flat or round. They would come away thinking the earth is round. That's my job.

My job is not simply garbage in, garbage out, and boy, I have been a good boy today as a reporter because I was fair. Horseshit. Excuse me.

My job is to find out what's really going on here. "All right, Mr. Allen, let me see now if I can recreate it. You took the envelope with the thousand dollars and you forgot it. C'mon, Dick. You forgot the thousand bucks? Well, it happens to every one of us." What is the fairness? The fairness is to fairly report what he says and you diligently seek out the truth by talking to people who have some knowledge of it. But eventually you're trying to present the facts to the public, and eventually the facts will sustain one view or another of what happened.

## WHAT PREPARED ME FOR THIS BUSINESS

I've done it by working hard. I am mindful of all the breaks I've gotten. And there are a number of individuals in my life, as there are in the lives of everyone, who have contributed to whatever success I've had. Without them, I could not have made it.

Having said all of that and acknowledged the truth of all that, I don't feel that somehow I have gotten to a point without having earned it. Nor have I been given something that I really don't deserve. I feel that I've worked hard to get where I am and I'm going to continue to work to get someplace else, too.

## MY FUTURE IN TELEVISION

I'm a reporter. I like being a news reporter. I intend to continue being a news reporter. I say that not because I have sampled all other careers and have made a considered judgment, but because I enjoy what I'm doing and I'm smart enough to understand that if I can do it well enough to command a job and a salary and all of that, I would be foolish simply to drop off the face of a cliff and see if I could grab onto a tree on the way down that would grow eventually even taller than the one I'm holding onto now.

Theoretically, what do I want? I want it all. I want more. *All* changes from time to time. Traditionally, in the last 20 years, principal anchor at a network has been considered, if not all, at least, most. But it's not going to happen.

There are two sides to a question like that. One side is, of course, you remain ambitious and you want more responsibility and you want more access to use the experience that you have and the ability that you think you've got. On the other hand, if it doesn't happen, I'm not going to be a frustrated, bitter, "Gosh, I've been a failure in life," individual. So there's kind of a balance there. Am I happy with what I have? No, I want more. If you don't get more, are you going to be happy with what you have? Sure.

There are many paths to God, and one travels one's own route. How do you define it in advance? I never did. You go along, not a road that you clearly plotted and conceived. You simply go on. You find a line of work that you enjoy, rather than one that you simply have to do because you have to pay the bills. And if you want to be in the news business, I assume it's not because you think you're going to make a lot of money. It's not the business to do that. There's something about it that you enjoy—covering news stories, reporting news stories, seeing new things, people, talking about ideas—whatever aspect of news you're interested in.

Having done that, start working and keep going and keep looking for opportunity and take advantage of the breaks when they come and work very hard. Then you look back, and you see the wake. You don't see the wake of the ship ahead of the bow. You'll see it from the stern. Where has it been? You can see the road that you've traveled, but you can never see the road ahead clearly. At least, I haven't been able to. So you make your own road.

## DON'T IMITATE ANYONE ELSE

There was a generation of correspondents at ABC that tried to sound just like David Brinkley. Well, there can only be one David Brinkley. I don't think they did it on purpose. I think it was just when you're around someone who makes such a strong impression, as Brinkley does with that voice and *patois* and the way he talks—well, [*imitating Brinkley*] it's. easy. to. just. fall. in. to. it.

But it was all to their detriment because no matter how closely they imitated him and how smooth they were, who wants a fake David Brinkley? So to say that someone's perception is that Donaldson's gotten where he's gotten by yelling at presidents and by being outrageous—it would be ridiculous for someone to try to pattern themselves after the way they perceive to be the way I've done it. Incidentally, that's not, in my view, the way I've done it.

## LEARN TO CHALLENGE CONVENTIONAL WISDOM

What I've learned is that the conventional wisdom is usually wrong. So whenever anybody in town says it's going to be this way or that, you seek out the few people who say, "Nonsense. It's going to be some other way." And you present their point of view.

Don't worry about a president having the ability to present his point of view to the country. Be fair to the president, give him a chance. They [the White House] can snap their fingers and command a 9 o'clock address to the nation. They're on the front pages of the papers any day they want. When they pound the table, they're going to be on "World News Tonight," maybe as the lead story.

It's not their viewpoint you have to worry may not get out to the country. It's the viewpoint of the little guy in the wilderness saying, "The MX. It's a turkey missile. It's not worth a penny." You get that guy, you get him on, too. He'll never command as much time as the president. But don't worry that you're counterbalancing as part of Gorbachev's team. Worry about the conventional wisdom going unchallenged.

Now, if the conventional wisdom turns out to be right, and it sometimes does, of course it will prevail. You will not have torpedoed it by putting on the few dissenting voices or other views. But if the conventional wisdom—"We'll take care of this little country of North Vietnam in three months"—turns out to be wrong, you will have done a service to the American people by not allowing it to go unchallenged.

Think if we could have reversed that war just two years earlier, maybe only saved 12,000 American boys. Well, every little bit helps. But 58,000 Americans died in Vietnam in a policy that was wrong. You can take the view it was wrong that we didn't go out to win or you can take the view it was wrong because we had no business there in the first place. But the policy was wrong. It was wrong because it didn't work. The situational ethics of results are such that if the policy doesn't work, we ought to try to know it in advance. We ought to try to figure it out.

Now, I'm capable of being misunderstood when I talk this way. I'm not advocating that you run out and disregard the facts and the quotes and the context and that you purposely withhold information or load your report to suit your own bias. I'm not advocating that. This is not advocacy journalism, which I do not support. The advocacy journalist starts out with a premise and then goes out to support it.

When I say challenge the conventional wisdom, I don't mean start out with a premise that it's wrong, but challenge it. It'll survive the challenge if it's right, and it may change from day to day, and you'll change with it as a reporter. But I think that's the most important aspect of why you try to find out what's really going on, what's really happening.

For my generation of reporters, the two cataclysmic events, Vietnam and Watergate, were such that some of us came to the view that I've just expressed. In the '50s, most reporters and publications were simply garbage in, garbage out. [Senator] Joe McCarthy said he could give a list of 205 communists to the State Department. It was reported uncritically, banner headlines. Not many voices said, "Nonsense. Show us the names and if you can't produce the names, we'll run you out of town because you're nothing but a charlatan."

Today, I hope I can say that Joe McCarthy couldn't exist. A senator could not stand up in Wheeling, West Virginia, and make those kinds of charges and have anyone pay attention to him. Part of that is the sophistication of the American people, but I think part of it is in the way journalists view it.

## ETHICAL DILEMMAS

When I first came to town, journalists wanted to be social friends of the people they covered, particularly the presidents. I think most of us believe today that we don't want to be social friends of the people we cover, and particularly of the president. That's not our job. If we want to make friends, there are other people in the world.

I'll tell you what happens to older reporters in this town. They begin to think they're part of the establishment. They begin to think they're part of the ruling class. We ought not to be part of the establishment. If we reporters are the ones who are trying to seek out what's really going on here and we're part of the establishment, then who is going to police us? Who is going to police the establishment? Who is going to stand outside and not really care if they get invited to a state dinner or not?

We are part of the power structure of Washington by virtue of the fact that we carry messages around town, publicly on the air or in print, and that we then carry to the country and to the world a view of what's happening in this town. We are players, no doubt about it.

We are players in the sense of being part of the decision-making process, but I ought not to have a vote or a view taken into consideration when people in government, charged with responsibility, make up their minds about something.

I wouldn't go to the Cabinet room because no one has invited me and I'm not a member of the Cabinet. I'm happy to give the president my views if he wants to watch the Brinkley show or listen to my reports on ABC News. But I ought not to be part of the direct process.

The main caution is, don't believe that your success, your place in society as a reporter, depends on closeness, either socially or from the standpoint of power, with the people you cover. Be an outsider from the establishment.

You will be successful and you will get all the rewards you can stand in the business and all the awards and the important jobs without once going to dinner in Georgetown, without once going to a state dinner, without once being patted on the back by a president who says you're just a terrific fellow. You don't have to have that. And in fact, in my view, it's a detriment because there are enough smart people around who will begin to question your objectivity.

If you're going to befriend someone, befriend someone who's taking it in the neck from the establishment, whether they're people who need assistance or someone who's been fired wrongly from the federal government. The powerful ones don't need your help. They get along very well without it.

---

# ABC World News Tonight—The U.S and Nicaragua

PETER JENNINGS: President Reagan is pushing again to get aid for the Contras trying to overthrow the government in Nicaragua. That is a foreign policy fight he has lost before. And today the President was blaming Congress for what he said was undermining this country's security. As ABC's Sam Donaldson reports, the President got very worked up on the subject.

SAM DONALDSON: The President of the United States and even the visiting President of Honduras lashed out at the U.S. Congress today over its recent refusal to renew aid to the Nicaraguan Contras. To begin with Republican congressional leaders reported that in a meeting with them President Reagan had literally pounded the table in anger and frustration.

SENATOR ROBERT DOLE: In any event he felt very strongly about the way Congress is horsing around on Nicaragua.

CONGRESSMAN ROBERT MICHEL: Well, he pounded it.

---

*Donaldson talks about his questioning techniques on pp. 94–95. Courtesy of ABC News.*

SENATOR DOLE: Pounded the table, took off his glasses, had a firm look on his face and laid it out there.

DONALDSON: The President reportedly told the leaders, "We've got to get where we can run foreign policy without a committee of 535 telling us what we can do." At the State Department today Assistant Secretary of State Langhorn Motley put it this way. "The U.S. Congress," said Motley, "can't make up its mind to go to the bathroom." And the President's visitor from Latin America, Honduran President Suazo, said the recent vote in Congress rejecting Contra aid was a victory for the Communist Party. "I think that everybody recognizes that," said Suazo. After this spate of Congress-bashing President Reagan tried to lighten the mood somewhat.

Mr. President, we understand you pounded the table in frustration over Nicaragua, is that right sir?

PRESIDENT REAGAN: Slapping flies.

DONALDSON: Every President, particularly in modern times, has slapped at that congressional fly, preferring to conduct foreign policy without such interference. But that is not the way it is. So for now the administration is hoping that its new push to win congressional support for aid to the Contras will succeed, that the House, chastened by the sight of Daniel Ortega flying to Moscow, will reverse itself and early in June vote humanitarian aid. Sam Donaldson, ABC News, the White House.

---

*Sam Donaldson*

WEAA-TV

*If we ultimately, as broadcasters, get to the point of trying to give the audience only what it wants to see, what we're going to end up with is a medium that transmits no valuable data at all, but only reinforces whatever values have been inculcated by the rest of the mass media.*

# BYRON HARRIS

Byron Harris believes in the media's social responsibilities. He is a reformer and a fighter. He quit one job in Oklahoma City because the station manager planned to let some car dealers preview an unfavorable story Harris had done about them before the story went on the air. Today, as an investigative reporter at Dallas's WFAA-TV, he says he sometimes receives threats because of his investigations, and he has been beaten up twice.

Originally he wanted to become a social worker, but he says he "didn't have the mindset." To Harris, journalism seemed to be a similar calling. Today, he worries openly about the future of local television news.

Harris, 40, worked at stations in Chicago, Milwaukee, Amarillo and Oklahoma before coming to WFAA as a reporter in 1974. For two years he was news manager in the WFAA newsroom before he returned to reporting. His title now is Senior Reporter. He also has written articles for *The Atlantic* and *Texas Monthly*.

With his special background as both news manager and reporter, Harris is critical of the manipulation of news presentation that is happening in many local television newsrooms. His voice intensifies, for example, as he talks fervently about the tendency at some television stations to feature sensational news.

"The murders and the rapes aren't necessarily the serious news," he says. "A murder, while it is certainly an important thing, is not necessarily the most important thing that happened in a city on a particular day. It's certainly less important in Los Angeles than it is in Wichita Falls because, simply, many people are murdered in Los Angeles and fewer people are murdered in Wichita Falls.

"Crime is anecdotal. The biggest questions might have to do with utility rates, medical costs, nuclear proliferation. Crime is only meaningful when it can be patterned. And you have to decide at what point the murders should be sublimated. It's a very difficult decision."

Harris attended high school in New Mexico. He graduated in 1969 from the University of Michigan with a B.A. in English and sociology. His master's degree in journalism is from Northwestern University. In 1978 he received a fellowship in economics from the Brookings Institution in Washington, D.C.

Harris has won more than 20 reporting awards from the National Press Club, the Dallas Press Club and the Texas Associated Press Club. In 1976 and 1977, he won two consecutive Dupont-Columbia Awards for outstanding news coverage.

He talked after work about his career and the future of television news, in the living room in his comfortable suburban Dallas home. He sat on the floor near the couch, after a home-delivered dinner of Chinese food. ❖

*from Byron Harris*

- The reporter as judge
- The effect of consultants on the newsroom
- The future of local television news

# Beginnings

I got drafted after I got out of college and I was in the Army and then I decided I wanted to go to journalism school. I was socially committed. For a long time, I was going to be a social worker. I ran a home for juvenile delinquents when I was in college, but I just couldn't do it. Journalism seemed to be along the same lines.

I got a master's in journalism. I don't know what made me pick TV. It just seemed to me what was happening. So then I found myself working for television stations.

I started as a film editor in Milwaukee. The only way to really move up in television is to move from one station to another. It's difficult to move from one job to another at the same station. I knew that I'd have to go someplace else, so I went to Amarillo.

When I got to Amarillo, the guy said, "You know, we work six and a-half days a week here." I said, "Yeah." I was thinking, "He's got to be kidding. He's speaking figuratively." Sure enough, the first week's schedule came out and it was six and a-half days. You got off about three days a month. You did radio news and you did television and you shot your own film.

Usually, in those markets, you had a Bell and Howell [camera] and a tape recorder. That was the way you did it. It's really better to learn the business at a small market like that because you learn how to think for yourself.

I remember doing a radio newscast. There's a town in west Texas called Muleshoe, and I came on this cold copy about the Muleshoe school system. When you see that cold, it's very hard. Of course I said "the Muleschool shoe system" and did several permutations. Then I just gave up.

There aren't many scoops in small town television news. It's not that the scoops aren't there. It's that the reporters generally aren't smart enough to recognize them, myself included.

I did find out that my news director was making political ads for the guy who was running for Congress. He was filming and writing these ads for this guy and it was totally unethical. First, I went in to see the station manager and he pretended he didn't know, but he knew. Ultimately, I left a very short time later.

## ETHICAL DILEMMAS

Ethics are what we're all about. When you're doing local news, you're really confronted with issues on a more regular basis because you do more stories, you're on the air more, you have to think more about what you're doing.

One story in Oklahoma City became a big deal. The story was about surcharges that car dealers were levying on people who had their cars in for repair. If you went in for repair, they would charge you a $10 surcharge. They said it was for rags and other things.

Car dealers found out about the story and they went to the station manager and said, "We want to see this story before it goes on the air." And our view and the view of the news director, Rick, was "That's wrong. That's prior censorship. Either you let us run the story as is or we quit." The manager said no, and so we quit. It was a big deal. It was in *The Wall Street Journal.* That was in about '74.

It's important to fight fights like that, not just because of the specific battles involved. It's important because you begin to know who you are and what you're about. And there have been lots of fights since then.

When you address controversial subjects—you don't get to do this very often at the network, but you do it all the time if you work in a good local newsroom—a lot of people don't like you. And they really make it hard for you. I've been beaten up a couple of times.

One story had to do with the Teamsters. Another time, a hospital in town got mad at me and sent out 5,000 circulars. The story had to do with malpractice. They had grievously chopped up somebody on the operating table. And I did some stories about it. They couldn't sue me because they knew I hadn't libeled them, so they sent circulars to all the doctors in Dallas and Fort Worth.

## THE REPORTER AS JUDGE

As a reporter, you have to remember that you're essentially judging people. Consumer reporting is very easy because usually you've got somebody who's been cheated and you can see it. But after you get out of that into other areas, it gets more difficult because you ultimately have to judge people. Whenever you're judging somebody, you have to understand how much harm you can do to people. Not many reporters realize that.

When you judge people, you have to always think, "I have the evidence of this person's behavior. Is there something that I didn't think about? What could I not have considered that could have led him to do that?" You have a conglomeration of information and it's often very easy to get swept up in that. Often it can lead you to an incorrect conclusion. There may be some secondary or tertiary fact you didn't think about.

Where do you cross the line from the anecdotal to the general? That's always the question when you're doing a story about malfeasance on the part of a corporation. How do I know that what the guy on the assembly line's telling me about where the wrenches are stored is a bad thing? He might have some ax to grind with the company that you don't know about, or there might be an entirely logical reason that he doesn't understand because he's where he is in the company.

## FIGHT FOR FAIRNESS

One of the reasons I get paid as well as I do is because sometimes I have to fight the people I work for. I'm an old guy. I have a lot of clout. I help run the newsroom, even though I'm not a manager. If I say we should not put this story on the air, a lot of the time, we don't do it.

What I'm there for is to say, "I'm the reporter. I know better than you do. We need to wait a day. I need to find this out." After Oklahoma City, I always said to myself, "I need to have $10,000 in the bank because I never know when I'm going to have to quit." Well, I don't have $10,000 in the bank today. But you've got to look at it that way.

You have to try to protect fairness. This [WFAA] is a good place. I love the people I work with and that's very important. But there are exigencies. Sometimes you just have to say, "We can't do this today." And that leaves a two-minute hole in the broadcast and that means the weather goes two more minutes.

What if you hurt somebody? Even if he's a bad guy, even if he's somebody you're not disposed to like, what if you hurt him? It's a terrible hurt for people to see their face on television for something they didn't do, or when some information about them is communicated incorrectly.

A lot of reporters, in fact they are in every newsroom, want to be on television more than anything else. I always wanted to be a journalist, that was my goal. Clearly, I must have wanted to be on television to some extent, because that's what I did. My goal still is to prove to the rest of the world that we're all not hair-sprayed yahoos. But there are many, many people driven in this business simply to be on television, simply to be famous, simply to have a famous face.

And that's one of the ways stories get on the air before they're fully researched. Sometimes it's totally accidental. There's no other business that makes a different product every day, but we do. Our parts don't come in until 6:30. Some of our parts are defective and we have to make decisions based on that. Sometimes mistakes are made in innocence. Sometimes we just don't think.

## THE ROLE OF CONSULTANTS

If you take a hard look at the kinds of data that consultants give you, it's really universally, statistically inaccurate. It's statistically unsupportable, if you look at it.

I think consultants in any business occupy a vacuum. If there's an intellectual vacuum, they will occupy it. If people don't know what they're doing, if there's a vacuum of knowledge or self-confidence, a consultant will occupy it just like a balloon or an inert gas.

Generally, where I work, the people know what they're about. The news director knows what his responsibilities are as a journalist and there's no vacuum that exists. The consultant doesn't work for the news director. The consultant works for the front office—the general manager. The consultant is there because the front office of our particular station—it's not that way at every station—wants to make a lot of money.

A consultant will come and say, "You're No. 3 now, and you want to be No. 1. Why do you want to be No. 1? You'll make a lot of money at No. 1." So the general manager will hire a consultant based on that. The news director's job is to beat 'em upside of the head and drive 'em out of the place.

Most news directors don't know what they're doing. How many news directors were ever reporters? Very few. All they know is sometimes they know numbers. I can't give you a statistical base on the origins of news directors. I know that they're generally not journalists. The journalists that I've known who were news directors were generally short-lived because they fought for journalism.

Journalism is certainly threatened. It's an endangered species. There are many, many threats. It's not just hairspray anymore. And it's not just animal stories. The latest thing is the meter spiker. Do you know what meter spikers are?

## METER SPIKERS IN THE NEWSROOM

Meter spikers look at lead-in programming and how a newscast can advantageously benefit from that. You'll see it in many, many stations now. If you have a 10 o'clock broadcast and your 9 o'clock entertainment program has to do with endangered elephants in Africa, you go out and do a story about endangered elephants in Africa and you promo that in your programming. In other words, you put a tease in the 9 o'clock segment that talks about endangered elephants that says, "At 10, we'll have a story about that." What you ultimately have, then, is programming determining news stories. Wholly illegitimate.

Meter spikers are another group of consultants who come in and say, "Consider this: If you put swim fins on all your reporters, you'll get the skin diving audience. And swim fins are big this rating book because ABC has a swim fin special." It's an insidious and terrifying business.

For news, this means only the worst. It means that [the movie] "Network" is just around the corner—meaning Paddy Chayefsky was a prophet instead of a playwright.

## HOW CONSULTANTS CAN AFFECT THE NEWS

The consultants are there to maximize the audience. Whether they do that or not, or whether they could if they were given a free rein, is an unanswered question. Most of the information they give is statistically invalid because it doesn't meet the methodological requirements of any statistically sound research.

Methodologically, their information is so anecdotal. They do focus groups or get 10 people together to talk about things. Well, that's just bull. It has no statistical validity. They don't ever reach statistical significance in numbers in their focus groups.

There is a larger question here about the statistical significance of the rating services. The city of Dallas now is metered. We don't have rating books anymore. We have 320 meters. How can you purport to assay the viewing habits of a statistical area of four million people with 320 meters? Well, you can't.

The consultants do even more spurious statistical evaluations to assay the opinions of people on things like anchor talent and reporters. I'm sure studies have been done about me, what people think about me, how I look and things like that. Sure, I worry. I'm expendable. I could be gone.

I do a lot more stand-ups than I used to because the consultants tell us that the audience likes to see that. They try to tell people how to write, but having never done that themselves, they don't know how to do it. I've been to their seminars.

The difference between the way I approach things and the way they approach things is that they have what they believe to be a science based on what they believe the audience wants to hear. Those of us who have been in this business have achieved what we've achieved simply by seeking to communicate well. And they're not the same thing.

Communicating well does not necessarily mean giving the audience what it wants to hear. It only means telling it clearly and effectively. Consultants are trying not only to dictate the manner in which the story's told, but the content of the story itself.

They would say, "Here are stories people like—dogs, snakes, children." We would say, "This is what they need to know—city council, told entertainingly, effectively, where the reporter says something and the message is communicated effectively to the audience." They would say, "It's another meeting."

But you don't have to cover the city council as a meeting. You can cover it in other ways. There are some things that are important in a democracy that cannot be told as entertainingly as Trigger jumping across the Grand Canyon.

---

## WHAT TELEVISION NEWS CAN DO

Television news can still do a lot of miracles that are astounding, the way you can tap people's consciousness. The combination of words and pictures together can be a very powerful medium. And sometimes when I'm just about to despair, something happens to indicate the way people think or to indicate the potency of what we do that is entirely refreshing to me.

Immediacy is certainly a quality I like. It's also a burden. I do both television and print and I feel that television is an order of magnitude more difficult to do. The immediacy of the medium can be as much of a threat to accuracy as it can be an enhancement to the event.

One time I was doing a live shot and there was a guy who had a child hostage who was holding a gun on the kid. The kid was the son of a woman he was trying to really get back at, and we were outside. At 10:01, we did a piece on the fact that he was still in there. Then at 10:06 there was a shot fired and my photographer went and got it and at about 10:20 we went off the air. And I had no idea—I had too many technical things to deal with—it turned out the guy had shot himself. He could have shot the child, which would have been more tragic, but by a matter of policy, we don't air suicide. It was also a very grizzly thing.

Another thing that happens a lot these days is gratuitous live shots, where you put a reporter outside of a non-event, and you have them reporting live on something that really isn't happening.

For example, they want to build a railroad from Dallas to Fort Worth that will whisk you from one city to another in 30 minutes. It will relieve traffic, of course. This other station tonight led their broadcast with a live shot of traffic. Well, that doesn't show anything. We've all been in traffic jams, we know what it looks like. And we've done similar things. The consultants tell us the audience likes it.

## DIFFERENCE BETWEEN PRINT AND BROADCAST

Broadcast can actually show somebody's reaction when you ask them a question. If you're quick enough as an interviewer, sometimes you can catch them off guard and ask them a question that they might not have expected and reveal a part of their character that you might not have been able to reveal as effectively with words.

Investigatively, it's a whole lot easier to do print. I do a lot of investigative reporting for television. I've camped outside somebody's door for 18 to 20 hours waiting for him to walk out of it just to get his picture for 5 seconds. I'd never have to face that if I worked for print. All I'd have to do is describe him.

The things we do for two seconds of tape are unbelievable. I've sat in airports waiting for felons to come through doors with their girl-friends. In fact, in that series, we flew to New Orleans just to get this guy with his girlfriend. I felt like scum sitting there. But I had to do it.

He was arranging his taxpayers'-paid schedule so he could see his girlfriend in New Orleans, but I had to make sure that's what he was doing. Of course, I had a great deal of evidence that he'd done that in the past, but I had to make sure that was still happening.

As I said to my photographer many times that day, "I don't want to know this stuff." But ultimately, I had to. Sometimes you learn things about people that you really don't want to know.

## MY ROLE AS A REPORTER

My role is to try to be fair and try to help people. I don't know what other people who aren't journalists do with their lives. I have no idea. We have to be here for some reason, and it seems to me that the only thing we can do is try to help each other, whether that's putting something on television, trying to tell it compassionately, or doing some-thing else.

I confess not to know why we're on this earth, but it seems to me that for some reason we have to help each other. When you see as much death and tragedy and dismembered bodies and souls as we do, either you become so cynical you can't do anything, or you try to do some-thing else.

When I go out on the street every day, I have to think that there are beneficial things in a democracy, and that a free press helps sustain those things. Fighting for what the founding fathers had in mind seems to be it for me.

## HOW TO BE A GOOD REPORTER

What you have to carry into every story is more knowledge than anybody else. And there's only one way you can get that, and that's read all the time. I generally get up at 5:30 in the morning and read for three hours before I go to work. That means today's paper, yesterday's *Wall Street Journal,* yesterday's *Christian Science Monitor,* and whatever else I can squeeze in.

If I'm in the newsroom and I see someone reading the paper, that's a bad sign. If you haven't read at least the local paper before you go to work, you're in bad shape. You've got to carry more knowledge into every story than anybody else if you're going to beat them, and it's a competitive business.

One of the reasons I like this business is the competition. I've generally beat the competition, but I do that because I work real hard at it. Intellect really amounts to very little. It's hard work that really makes the difference. So that means knowing more than the other guy. It means going to the library after work. It means going and tapping whatever databanks exist, whether it's the *Readers' Guide to Periodical Literature* or *The New York Times* on the computer.

Clearly, that's one thing that younger reporters don't seem to understand. Maybe being a face on camera is more important to them than transmitting a message. They should read, work hard, and be slow to judge—slow to make up their minds about what somebody did.

## THE ERROR OF THE STAND-UP

There's a myriad of things wrong with television, but nobody yet has written the definitive book of television criticism. That's the one I'm going to write. It would analyze the methodology of television, why television makes the mistakes it makes. For instance, there's the error of the stand-up. This is a big deal, but nothing's ever been written about it.

Print reporters never have to write the last paragraph of a story before they write the story. TV reporters do it all the time. That's what a stand-up is. And that's an incredible thing. It's the essence: We're going to make you decide, out in the field, after being on this story for an hour, what the final line is going to be. And you're locked into that. That's absurd.

That's why a lot of reporters do bridges instead of stand-ups. A bridge just says, "And then Joe went to the diner." It doesn't say anything. It gets your face on the camera, it makes everybody happy, but you don't have to draw any conclusions. A bridge just puts you at the scene and you say something and sail into the story, but it doesn't force you to draw a conclusion because it appears in the middle of the story.

A stand-up tag is the final thing. So it either forces you to make a conclusion you don't necessarily have the facts to make, or it makes you draw a namby-pamby conclusion because you don't want to get yourself into trouble. The worst part about television, across the board, is that it forces you into conclusions that you don't necessarily have the data to make—the typical, in one word or another, "remains to be seen" stand-up.

## THE IMPORTANCE OF DEADLINES

There's only one 6 o'clock in every day, and you have to be ready to move then. It's tough. I don't think I've ever not made a deadline, though, that I can remember, in the past eight years. You learn how to do it. You learn to be thinking and you learn what the exigencies are in terms of pictures and what you're going to have to edit.

You learn to discipline yourself about what you're going to need. You can sit down and talk to the guy for an hour, but ultimately, you know that what you're going to put on television is going to be between 15 and 45 seconds long. Granted, at 45 minutes deep into the interview he may set forth some revelation that's going to change the world, but chances are, he's not.

So once you get what you've got to get, you move on. We're like cartoon strips after a while—every quotable quote appears in a little balloon over somebody's head. Once you see that, you move on to the next person, being as polite as you can and not offending the person.

Sixty percent of the interviews you do, nobody says anything that dynamically quotable. The other 40 percent, you're lucky—somebody will say something really outrageous and then, 2 percent of the time, somebody will say something that's unbelievable.

## A GOOD TELEVISION INTERVIEW

Look for content. Some people are more relaxed in front of a camera than others, but just because a person isn't relaxed, doesn't mean that what he has to say isn't valuable.

A lot of times you run into people—especially people from New York public relations agencies—who think that everybody in the world has to speak in 20-second sound bites and they all have to wear blue shirts and they have to have perfectly straight, white teeth. And that just isn't true.

There are varying degrees of dynamism among people you talk to. Just because that dynamism is not necessarily photogenic or even if it's non-dynamic, it doesn't mean that it's not usable on television.

I try not to categorize interviews. I did a series a couple of years ago and I asked a guy a question and he just looked at me and said, "No." The words in the question and the word in his answer and the look on his face were just fine. Under any other circumstances, he wouldn't have been a good interview.

A bunch of people were illegally dumping chemicals and he worked for the state. He knew these people were doing it, and he knew another state agency was not enforcing the law. And I said, "Is the Texas Water Resources Commission correctly enforcing the law?" And he looked at me and said, "No." And the way he said it was just perfect, so that was a good interview. You could tell he knew his job was on the line by saying that, just by the look on his face. There was a peculiar melding of pictures and words that wouldn't have worked as well in print.

## HOW I WRITE

I almost always have the lead. That's a television-bound thing. I think television reporters are more accustomed to doing that, and they should be. You've got the guy sitting there in his living room and you've got to reach out of the television and grab him by the neck and shake him. Everything you do that day has to be aimed at doing that.

After you do this for a while, you see a picture and you think, "There's my lead sentence." And of course a picture isn't a sentence, but a picture combined with a certain sentence is going to have an effect. So, every time you're out on a story, you think, "That is it. That is the essence of what I want to say." I see pictures all the time that are sentences, and I have my photographer shoot them.

We were at a building today and we were on the 19th floor, doing a story on OPEC, about oil prices and gas prices. I looked across the road and there was a building and you could see the traffic reflected in the mirrored glass of this building. And I thought, "Gee, that's interesting."

So the sentence that went with that picture was, "Oil prices are usually reflected in gasoline prices," because you had a reflection there as well. Now, that may be too much. I don't know. But that's the way you think after you do this for a while.

## PERSONAL LIFE

It's fun. It runs my life, no doubt about it. It's everything I do. People ask me what I do on the weekends and what I do on the weekends is read. I work around the house a lot, but the weekends are pretty much the spacing between the rest of the time. Once you get into it, you can't get out of it. It's very addictive.

The urgency is very addictive. You create a realm of priorities that lead you to believe that everything revolves around what you do. The reality is, it doesn't.

Journalists have a certain arrogance about them in which they think they're smarter than other people. They also think that everything they do matters. They're wrong on both counts. I meet so many wonderfully fascinating people who lead me to believe we're not so smart and what we do isn't so important because they've very sagacious, these other people I meet, and they do very important things.

## THE FUTURE OF TELEVISION NEWS

If we're only going to give people what they want and most of the people get their news from television, then obviously all the major issues of the day are going to be circumvented. If we, as a profession, are worried about the hostilities that everybody levels at us, and every time somebody levels a hostility, we change as a result, it's a fairly dire thing.

Marty and I, my news director, were hashing this over a week ago. We are now in a world of instant ratings, where in the 10 largest cities in the United States, we get ratings every day from the night before. A producer, then, can look at what aired in his broadcast six minutes deep and get a minute-by-minute breakout of what kind of tuneout there was.

Now, if he changes the content of the newscast to jibe with what he believes the highest ratings were, or spikes—as is now the common term—think of what that means for news content. In Boston, there is a phrase—"If it bleeds, it leads." It may be the phrase other places, but that's where I heard it first.

After the producer evaluates where the tuneouts occurred, you will have, then, a newscast that could potentially consist of four murders, two adopted children and the latest animal at the zoo.

How are we to inform the public about public policy based on that content? It's a scary set of potentials. It's bad stuff. If we ultimately, as broadcasters, get to the point of trying to give the audience only what it wants to see, what we're going to end up with is a medium that transmits no valuable data at all, but only reinforces whatever values have been inculcated by the rest of the mass media.

Somebody has to stand up and say, "This is wrong, this is stupid." Stupid's too kind a word. This is tragically immoral. Unless somebody stands up and says that, look how far down the trail of irrelevancy we've already come. Unless somebody stands up and says something, what are we going to have left?

*Byron Harris*                                                                                   115

Here's another threat. There is, in my mind, a high potential that a lot of the United States doesn't want to know what's going on, that, indeed, they want to shoot the messenger. "If you guys are going to continue to tell us stuff that we don't want to know, we're going to say not only do we not want you in our homes, but when the pollster calls, we're going to say that you're biased."

It's clear to me, anyway, that some percentage of the people who comment about the media simply do not want to address the problems that the media set to them. There is a selective perception in all human beings. We hear what we want to hear and some of us train ourselves to hear more or less.

A lot of the negative feeling toward the press is, "We don't want to hear what you have to say. It's not that we don't agree with it. It's not that we dislike the way you're delivering it. It's simply we don't want to deal with these things." The reality is that, in a democracy, we have to deal with these things. That's what a democracy is.

Clearly, living in a democracy requires a degree of commitment. You have to care, to some extent, about what goes on, and you have to participate. They already say that less than 60 percent of the people participate in national elections. One of the messages we're getting now is that people don't want to participate in the news, either. Does that mean we don't give them the news anymore? I don't think so.

## THE ROLE OF REPORTERS IN A DEMOCRATIC SOCIETY

Reporters have to view their jobs as a trust. I won't get too dramatic here, but they have been entrusted with the communication of information. And society is only going to be able to continue to have the pillars that it has if that information has real content.

So it begins with reporters, the people who put the news on the air, and the producers and news directors. If it doesn't start with those people, nobody else is going to fight that battle. And it means producers as much as reporters, because producers are the people who decide what goes into the broadcast and who evaluate the reporters at the top.

They will have to fight the difficult fights. They will have to oppose the forces that want to make news a wholly commercial entity, who want the goal of news to be to make money at all costs and only incidentally to transmit the information that helps the democracy succeed.

# Quality of Mercy

start on family
pictures
super: Juanita Mefford

sound: Juanita Mefford: There's no amount of money that can bring my husband back, and there's no amount of money that can replace my husband. You don't measure love, companionship, by money. And I feel like he died for money.

stills on the wall

super: BH reporting

Jerry Mefford died last February. Technically, a heart attack set up by a degenerative heart disease took his life. But many say the cause was the stress the Social Security disability system put him under. And many people miss Jerry Mefford.

some coaching
pictures
let's dissolve

He coached boys and girls of all ages, in all kinds of sports. Although his cardiomyopathy, a disease that gradually destroys the heart, was diagnosed in 1980, he continued to coach as best he could. He could not return to welding, the only job he knew. He applied for Social Security disability and began receiving payments. He began taking vocational training, even though severe dyslexia kept him from learning to read.

full face

sound: Juanita: He never gave up hope of going back to work.

Jerry in a chair

But the coach could not go back to work; his health was deteriorating. His doctor even told him to quit going to rehabilitation classes.

sound: Juanita: He could never lay down to sleep for 8 hours. He slept for a couple of hours at a time. He'd get up and walk the floor, watch TV, he never went to bed.

document

Then, in November of last year, Jerry Mefford received notification that his disability payments would be stopped. Although he had received them for two years, the Social Security Administration

---

*This is the type of investigative story that Harris talks about on p. 106. Courtesy of WFAA-TV.*

another pic of his face

decided because he had not been going to rehabilitation, he was no longer disabled. He appealed. But on February 22nd he got word that his appeal was denied.

sound: He was sick by Friday. He had actually got sick. He laid on the couch all day. I called home from work. He said I'm real sick. (cut it here) On Saturday morning he got up. He acted like I'm gonna forget all of this has happened. He said three times that day, nothing's going to ruin today. We went to my son's ball game, we went out to eat, we went to Vikon Village and was walking around, and he just dropped dead.

font over full screen

In a terse letter to Social Security, his physician, Dr. Gordon Hosford, said Jerry's heart attack "was caused by the heart disease that your board decided was not severe enough to warrant disability payments."

comes in with his cane

David Daniels is still alive. But he suffers from a bad back, crushed in a construction accident, and a hip replacement necessitated by the same mishap.

super: David Daniels

sound: David at 9:19: It just hurts hurts hurts. And they want me to try and use a walking stick a little bit and I can't get very far on that.

But after receiving disability payments for more than a year David Daniels was cut off too. He is appealing his case.

let's dve their pix

David Daniels and Jerry Mefford are just two victims of a system gone awry. The Social Security disability system. A system which some say is no longer just but simply arbitrary.

super: bh 8

standup: Since 1981, the Social Security Administration has sent termination notices to 470 thousand people who were receiving disability payments. The goal was to save money from fraudulent claims. But the effect has been to rob legitimate claimants of what is rightfully theirs. The problem became such an

118

| | |
|---|---|
| exteriors of federal building | embarrassment in this election year that last month the administration announced that it would wipe the slate clean, and grant forty thousand disability claims that are on appeal. But the problem is deeper than that. The Dallas region of the Social Security Administration and its headquarters in Washington have been tampering with the legal system that decides disability cases, pressuring administrative law judges to make decisions that steal people's rights and save the administration money. |
| | It is a problem bad enough, that even taciturn judges are complaining about it. |
| Harry Holland administrative law judge | sound: Judge Holland: It's kind of like in Russia. I understand they have all this training for people who disagree with them, and they reeducate them, and that's how they train the judges. |
| Tomorrow: Justice Impaired | Tomorrow we'll travel to Arkansas to see how some judges are rebelling at what has been described as cookie cutter justice. They've taken the federal government to court. |

___

CBS News

*If I'm ever knocked off the air and I want to
continue to do this work, I can do radio. I'll
sound good forever.*

# MARLENE SANDERS

Marlene Sanders is a survivor. She was born in 1931 in Cleveland, Ohio, and attended Ohio State for a year, majoring in speech, before she decided she wanted to be an actress. She had some minor roles in Philadelphia theater and in one off-Broadway play before she decided to try another career.

In 1955, she met Mike Wallace, and he hired her to help him produce his newscast, which was just starting on WABD-TV [later WNEW-TV] in New York City. She then became associate producer of a new interview program that Mike Wallace started, called "Night Beat." Wallace left, and Sanders stayed until the program ended a year later. In January 1961, she joined Wallace to help with another program, and then in 1964, she was hired by ABC News as the network's second woman correspondent.

In 1964, Sanders was the first woman to anchor a network news broadcast. She had the job for one night. Seven years later, she took Sam Donaldson's place as an anchor for ABC when he went to Vietnam. Today, she is quick to note, there still is not a woman anchor on any of the weeknight network news broadcasts.

Eventually she would become a vice president at ABC, the highest position ever held by a woman in network news. She left ABC two years later to go to CBS and produce documentaries. Now at CBS, she is a general assignment reporter who anchors several television "Newsbreaks" each week and she often anchors CBS radio news broadcasts. She also teaches at Columbia University as an adjunct professor of journalism.

Four wood shelves, attached with metal brackets near the ceiling in her New York office, hold random books and scripts and a framed picture of her only child, Jeffrey, a New York attorney. Surrounding the desk are three filing cabinets full of story scripts. In the corner, a broadleaf plant and an orange watering can contribute color to the beige and blue room. Sanders speaks in a deep, self-assured voice. Her hair is close-cut, honey blonde. She has clear, aqua blue eyes, and she is dressed in a stylish, tailored maroon suit.

Sanders was once named Broadcast Woman of the Year. At 55, she says, it has often been noted that she is the oldest woman reporting hard news on network television.

"The challenge in this business," she says, "is hanging in there. Survival—not to be whimsically disposed of, which happens to a lot of people. They come and go. It's very risky. There is no guarantee. If people are really interested in security, they should not go into this business." ❖

*from Marlene Sanders*

- Women in network news management
- News trends
- The advantages of radio

# Beginnings

I fell into this business in 1955. The business was so new that I had no thoughts about it. It combined production work, which I had done in the theater, and news, which I was interested in—I was very political as a young woman, which was unusual—and I also had a certain amount of writing skill.

When I was growing up, I had no idea what I would do with any of these things because it was the '40s, the '50s—nobody thought about what women should do. I took speech and theater at Ohio State. There was practically no broadcast journalism to talk about. There was radio, but television was new so I had no goal in mind. There was no such thing as an anchor. There were 15-minute network news broadcasts. That was not a goal.

I moved ahead to writer, associate producer and then producer all within a local station, where I had a lot of opportunity to learn. They also knew that I could do just about anything, so that's what I did. I spent five years there, still not with any ultimate goal. I don't think you can do that—have A GOAL.

I find that sort of obnoxious, these people who say, "I want to be an anchorwoman." I feel absolutely hostile and resentful against them because they don't know what they're talking about.

There's been far too much emphasis on these five-year plans and goal setting. It's too wacky a business. I don't know how you can do that. It's just not possible. I think these people are limiting themselves.

How do they know they're not going to find something they like better? Or that just as their plan is unfolding, somebody who likes them is going to get fired? You can't control all these things. It's not a nice, neat business. And I just look at these people like they're a little weird, frankly.

You learn as you go along. You stumble into jobs or you find yourself in a happy confluence of events that gives you an opportunity. That's how it works. Lightning doesn't suddenly strike.

The only thing in my career that qualified as an accident was when I was a correspondent at ABC. I was there, I think, three weeks when the other woman who was doing a program called "News With a Woman's Touch" got suspended because she got involved in local politics and they threw her off the air. Since it was called "News With a Woman's Touch," I had to sit in and anchor for her. I was the only other woman. Ultimately, she was fired and I inherited the show. So you can say, yes, that's fortuitous.

## FIRST WOMAN NETWORK ANCHOR

The other thing was when the evening anchorman, at the same time, lost his voice and they had me sit in. And that was the first time a woman had ever anchored an evening news show. Ever. I did it for that night. That's it. Jack Gould wrote it up in *The New York Times.*

Then, when Sam Donaldson went to Vietnam, I sat in for him for three months. Nothing happened, by the way, as a result. The fact that I sat in at night didn't cause anybody to say, "Now it's time for a woman to do this."

It was '64 the first time and '71 the second time, when I sat in for Sam Donaldson. Both those times, there were articles saying it was the first time [a woman anchored a network news broadcast] because so much time had elapsed between the first time in '64. Even in '71, nothing happened. I think it was legitimate to make a note. It was breaking old patterns.

## HOW TO TRAIN TO DO WHAT I DO

Someone should do what I did, work their way through the system. The big problem is everybody wants to have their success in five years. I've been in it 30 years. I'm old, but I'm not that old. I started as a commitment to work. I assumed I'd be supporting myself. I did get married in the interim, but I never changed that idea. I was going to work in this business somehow. And I just sort of slogged along.

I think in a funny way, it's been more satisfactory making the steps in a gradual fashion because I see some of these young anchorwomen, 28, making big bucks. Doing that, what have they got to look forward to? Getting fired is the only thing they can look forward to. Because they don't last.

That's how it works in local news—the general manager changes, the news director changes, the studies of the demographics change. I've had a lot of interesting jobs. I've learned a lot and I just think it's a better way to do it.

## WHAT THE NETWORK LOOKS FOR

The networks are becoming less demanding, looking for local types, rather than people with credentials—young, attractive, inexperienced, decisions based on star quality or charisma or presence, based on what they think will get ratings. I don't think they're right, but that's what they decide.

I think people prefer to get the news from credible people, rather than blow-dry hair and all that garbage. I think it's also reflected in the kind of news you're doing—more animal stories, more features, fewer documentaries. Forget about documentaries. I spent half my career doing documentaries. I'll probably never do another one. They're doing magazine shows. So it's all short, more entertaining, more audience-grabbing. It's all part of the same idea.

## WHAT MAKES A GOOD TELEVISION REPORTER

Good writer. Fast, quick mind for television and radio. Someone who's fast, puts pieces together, synthesizes a lot of information, presents it well. This would also mean someone who I hope would be well-read and generally well-informed. If you go into a situation where you haven't had a lot of time to do research, you should be able to put the right pieces together. Obviously you have to have some ability to communicate verbally and to look passably decent.

## WHAT QUALITIES ARE BEING HIRED

Some of these same qualities are being looked for, but the order would be different. Appearance is important. They're always looking for people who have some kind of presence—which is the catchword now—somebody who lights up the screen, somebody who has a certain show business attractiveness.

I think that if you're a very straight person, that's a liability. That's one reason I've never made it big. I'm very straight. I speak very well. And my manner is direct, no crapping around.

I like good speech. I think it's really important. My mother, who is no longer young, says she can't understand a lot of people on the air. They don't speak well. I think that we used to set the speech standard.

There was always a standard American radio voice sound, and I like that. I think that's important. A lot of people don't have it.

Most people in this business would want people who are well-read, who have studied economics or political science, who have had some practical experience on a newspaper or at a radio station in school, and who use their education that way. There's no way that any degree is going to guarantee anything. There's no harm in it, but most of the people who filled this business the first 20 years didn't have any of that.

## AGE-ISM IN TELEVISION NEWS

The age thing is yet to be decided. It's not a drawback for men, although a lot of the men are worried about age discrimination now. If they're not the stars, they're worried about it. Although you look at Irving R. Levine on NBC. He doesn't fit any of the stereotypes. He sounds sing-songy, he's bald. Kurault is bald. Whether the people who are 30 years younger could get away with that in the future, I don't know.

My husband died a year and a half ago, and so I have increasing concerns about economic survival. Our management says, in published statements, that age will not be a problem for women. It's just that none of them has been in the pipeline long enough to get old. All the articles that have been written in the last two or three years always mention my age and that I am the oldest woman doing hard news on the air.

I'm very visible on the air. I don't know what will happen. We have women anchors on the weekends now. We will see a woman anchor during the week when we have a woman president—around the same time.

But I don't think that's the crucial issue anyway. The issue is decision-making power. Top jobs in management. Top executive producer jobs. It's not all what's out there on the screen. The entry-level jobs are there and women can get hired in almost all lower-level categories and work up to a point, at which time it becomes very difficult when the good jobs are available, such as producer of the evening news.

There are some women in all these jobs—bureau chiefs—there are some women now. Our vice presidential level is almost 100 percent male, one woman. It's not so much overt discrimination as the old boys' club. The men hire the guys they feel comfortable with. They feel more ready to do that.

## WOMEN NETWORK CORRESPONDENTS

As far as on-the-air is concerned, that's a very iffy proposition for women. You can do it locally and in some network jobs, but there's a lot of travel in network. It really kills people. It kills the men, too. The hours are bad, and it's very difficult to have family life at the same time. Unless you are extremely driven and ambitious, I think it's a bad choice.

I have a son and I have a family. Somebody who's a White House correspondent has a much harder time. I'm not saying it's impossible. It's very tough. A woman with a family who's also a correspondent is going to end up with two jobs, until a more perfect world emerges. Sure, you have a good housekeeping staff, but you still have the basic responsibility. There is a man here who is a field producer and he just took an office job because he said he didn't see his kids. So a lot of men don't like it either.

I work here three nights a week, and some women work midnight to 8 a.m. and then there's 4 p.m. to midnight. How do you have a social life? You're out of sync with everybody. Or you work weekends and have Monday and Tuesday off—it's lousy.

## PEOPLE'S VIEW OF WHAT I DO

People's view of my job is totally unrealistic. They're sitting at home at night and they see me come on for those Newsbreaks. I'm very careful about my clothes and what I look like, and I come in the middle of a lot of big entertainment shows. I'm sure it looks very glamorous. But it isn't glamorous at all.

I mean, dragging around a really cruddy newsroom all evening, waiting to do this. The studio is dirty and just a few technicians are in there swatting flies. You can get a certain kick out of being on the air. It's very easy for me to do. I'm very comfortable. But it's not glamorous.

Shooting stories on the road is usually very difficult, pressured. Travel is extraordinarily arduous. You just cannot believe how tough these trips are. I did a story which we had to shoot at St. Lawrence University, which is practically in the St. Lawrence River. It was winter and you can't get there from here. You have to fly to Buffalo, I think. Someplace. Then we were supposed to pick up a commuter flight, which was grounded because of snow. So then we had to drive for three hours through a blizzard, which got us there much later than we wanted.

We were exhausted. We had to shoot all the next day and then had to get back. It's running around and a lot of pressure. Editing and writing—that part's easy for me. I like that part. But it's the trappings. I'm burned out on the travel.

## THE POTENTIAL OF THE MEDIUM

The medium's potential is so fantastic. I've done a lot of documentaries and some of them, I feel, have been very good. Usually my favorite is the last one I did—"What Shall We Do About Mother?" I think you can do really important problems very well and analyze things, if you're given enough time. The medium can be a terrific educational tool. It's just that a lot of the potential is unused.

It's very suited to my personality as a worker because I'm very fast, very glib. I'm a good synthesizer. I can take a story and reduce it to 10 seconds if I have to. I'm absolutely unflappable on the air. I've gone on when things have been a total disaster around me.

I had written a Newsbreak. We had two pieces of tape in there and a lot of visual, and the producer thought I mistimed it and she took three pages out, which changed all the graphic order. And she was wrong. About a minute before we went on, we had to put everything back. The script had to be in the right order, in my hand, and on the prompter.

Ten seconds before we went on, everything was in order. And I went on, just as cool as you can be and it was perfect. But you could've just blown up, absolutely blown up.

## HOW TO GET PEOPLE TO TALK

There's no rule. It depends on the situation. I do not ask those questions—"How do you feel?"—when somebody is dead. But there's a way to get the same kind of material by more sensitive questioning.

Basically, if you're a sympathetic person in that kind of situation, people will talk to you. If you become hostile and demanding and obnoxious, you're not going to do as well. Sometimes you have to be very tough with people who harangue you. I don't have any special recommendation, except be a human being and not a machine.

I remember the mine disaster at Farmington, West Virginia, in '68. One woman's husband and her son both worked in the mine. When I was talking to her about it, I think her son was still down there. Her husband had come up. He was all right. When I started to talk to her about her son, she just fell apart. And I thought, "OK. A little of that is all right, but I don't want her to just go to pieces."

So I said, "But your husband was down there. What happened to him?" And she perked up a little bit, that he had escaped. I kind of pulled her out of it. I just didn't want it to be entirely maudlin. You have to have a sense of how far you want to let people go.

## TRENDS IN NEWS

I hated the trend that made reporters part of the story. I had to do a little bit of that. I had to jog with Dustin Hoffman here in New York as part of a long piece I did about him. It was not my idea. I sort of caught up with him and continued the interview. It was so stagey. I just didn't like it at all. I felt so stupid, and I just hated that. I find it totally obnoxious. I think you're a reporter. You're not part of the story.

## ETHICAL DILEMMAS

With dying patients, and stories like that, I felt that we were going to handle it well, that we weren't forcing it on anybody, that we weren't doing anything without somebody's permission. I felt there was a valid purpose for doing the story. So I didn't feel anybody was being taken advantage of. If people don't want to participate, they don't.

At the mine disaster, I think people felt somewhat reassured that they weren't being ignored, that people were paying attention. Those who didn't want to talk, didn't talk to us. I don't feel much of a conflict.

I know what makes a story, and no matter how devastating it is, or how much I'm affected by it, I am never that affected that I am not able to stand outside and watch. Never.

## JOURNALISM IN TELEVISION NEWS

A person who was hired and doesn't know how to write and is going out and doing stand-ups at fires, may be fast on his feet and a glib talker. But that's not journalism. I don't know what it is—something else.

Serious people don't depend on television news anyway—the intellectuals. Most of them don't watch it much. They'll watch MacNeil/Lehrer and they'll turn to books and publications. But they don't take television too seriously.

What really bothers me is the people out there who depend on it entirely. They are not getting as much depth as they should. That's dangerous because they're not going to know anything. They're going to be dummies out there very vulnerable to shoddy leadership of all kinds. News is, I think, becoming more entertainment-oriented. I don't think that's its function.

Television news is supposed to inform, supposed to tell you what's happening, tell you what something means and do some interpretive work. The problem is, as soon as it started making money, the entertainment aspects became too dominant—the attractive, young, blow-dried types, more features, less depth and more show biz.

## THE CASINO STORY

The story that I just got an hour or so ago is how the gambling casinos are doing in Atlantic City. By the time I do the story, I'll know a lot about it.

The system here is that you work with a producer. The guy I'm working with came up and said, "Would you like to work with me on this story?" And I said, "Great." So we talked about it and decided what we were going to examine: Are there too many casinos? Are they making money? What's happened to the city?

He left me research material and I wrote down when I was available. I said, "We have an air date. We should back-time two days—we need two days for editing. Based on that, here are the days I'm free." We'll do one interview in New York, one interview in Philadelphia, and the rest in Atlantic City.

In the meantime, I'm going to read all the research material while he gets on the phone and tries to set up the logistics—the interviews in different places, and so on. Then we will coordinate all this. We'll go shooting, in a collaborative fashion. He was talking to me about high shots, and I said, "Well, the buildings are not very high. I happen to know Atlantic City. You might want a helicopter shot." What you do is make suggestions rather than issue orders when you're not in charge. I think I get along very well with most of the producers because I do that. And they want to look good. The better the piece is, the better it is for everybody.

I'll say, "What is the point? What are we trying to find out?" We're going to say, "Tomorrow morning, a new casino opens in Atlantic City." Then I imagine we'll do something like, "Since 19 da da, when gambling came to Atlantic City, everybody expected that the community would be transformed, that it would get a shot in the arm in terms of business and the money from gambling would rehabilitate Atlantic City." Then we would say, "Has it?" And we would try to answer that question. I don't know whether it has or not. I'm just saying this is one way we can set it up. And then you talk to a couple of stock market people to say the promise has or has not been fulfilled—that there are too many hotels or there are too few or that they're trying to split up too little business or that it's run by the gang, or whatever.

When we get everything shot, we'll talk about the structure, the screening, and then I'll write it. Then we get the script approved by the producer of the weekend news before we start editing. When I write the script, I've seen everything and I indicate the pictures in the script. Then we'll finish it.

Your role is to see if there's a story. You find out what it is, the best way to tell it, who the best characters are to tell it. You shoot more than you use. When you put it together, that's when you really figure it out. You say to yourself, "What is the point?"

## HOW I FEEL ABOUT RADIO

I do like it. What's not to like? It's good. It's fast. You do it yourself, nobody else. Almost all of radio is written by the person who does it. A lot of people listen to it. I listen to it. It's also my secret backup for aging. If I'm ever knocked off the air and I want to continue to do this work, I can do radio. I'll sound good forever.

I'm not young. Maybe three, four years from now the toll will really be taken. They might be smart enough to keep somebody who still looks pretty good but is definitely older on the air. Some friends have said to me, "You're not a good test of the age thing because you don't look your age." Well, I don't. And also, if you're attractive, you can get away with a lot. But what if you had Dan Rather's bags and gray hair and you didn't do anything about it? Would you be on the air? I don't think so.

There is some gray there, but I don't let it show. Hell, anybody can do that. But you really do make an effort to keep glued together.

## WHAT MAKES A GOOD STORY

Conflict. One story I did, "Dilemmas," was a prison story, a story about a woman with a program to rehabilitate prisoners and keep them from becoming recidivist. What came out of that was (a) her determination and dedication and that she'd established a terrific program and (b) that these women were real tough cookies, really hard to work with and it was a real challenge and (c) that your expectations are not always fulfilled by these programs and (d) that overall, it was a good idea and there should be more of them. You can't call it conflict, exactly, but dilemmas.

## REWARDS OF THIS BUSINESS

The reward is feeling I've done a good job—a certain self-respect and satisfaction in feeling that you've done something worthwhile. I'm pretty well paid and have a certain amount of stature and respect.

The disadvantages at this point are that you suffer a certain amount of burnout after a while. I look for stories I haven't done. A lot of them, I feel I've done 10 or 12 times. I did a story on moose in Maine and I loved it. And I had never done a moose in Maine story. I learned and it was a different setting and it was a lot of fun. The rewards are when you learn something.

Other disadvantages are having to do boring stories, being out of the mainstream, which people fall in and out of, not getting stories on the air.

The reason I like Newsbreaks is that I do them, they're live, they're over and nobody can mess around with them.

## A ROLE MODEL

I think that probably, if I look back on 30 years in this business, the major thing that I contributed is being a role model for other women.

Because I had none, and I've been told by many of them who are in the business today that I was a role model for them. There's a certain amount of respect for being outspoken for women, which I have done. So I think that's a plus.

I've done a lot of good work. I've done a lot of good documentaries, but whether that's made an impact, they probably don't. Here and there, but you wouldn't want to overrate that.

People write in and you get requests and people rent the tape, so you know you may have made a difference. I ran into somebody not so long ago. She said she had just run a show I did on child abuse. I can't remember the name of it. It was half an hour. I did it at ABC in about 1973. It's still out there being circulated. And it's still valid. So I thought, "That's nice, that's great. This thing is still kicking around and people are going to get something out of it."

---

## Casinos in Atlantic City

| | |
|---|---|
| casino construction | v/o<br>Trump Castle is the eleventh casino to open in Atlantic City since 1978. |
| buses arrive | The customers appear to be out there . . . nearly 29 million came last year. The problem is, most of them drive or come by bus, and almost all of them are from a radius of 150 miles. |
| interior casinos | The casinos' lure is there, but overnight accommodations are not. |
| super: Stephen Norton, VP Resorts | Norton o/c<br>Our biggest problem now is getting more non-casino hotel rooms so that we can accommodate that secondary market in Pittsburgh and Detroit and Cleveland that right now we can't accommodate |

---

*Marlene Sanders talks about this story on pp. 129–130. © CBS Inc. 1985. All rights reserved. Originally broadcast July 2, 1985, on the "CBS Evening News."*

*Seven*

because they can't drive in and out the same day.

Marlene o/c bridge (on boardwalk)
Many of the tourists who come to Atlantic City are day trippers. Casino operators say they spend too little time here and not enough money.

set—tourists re: come by bus, how much they spend, etc.

boardwalk folk

v/o
Casinos are trying to attract bigger spenders. They offer high rollers free hotel suites ... and free transportation to Atlantic City. One big obstacle—Atlantic City's two airports are inadequate. Few commercial airlines fly in.

dinky airport

airport shots

v/o
The city has studies under way on how best to expand airport terminals. More hotel rooms are being built. Recent legislation will provide casino money for upgrading roads, housing and other needed improvements.

hotel bldg.

super: Steven
Eisenberg
Leisure analyst
Bear Stevens

Eisenberg o/c
If city govt., local govt. really wakes up, the opportunities are that within 3 to 5 years Atlantic City will be supporting at least 10 thousand first class hotel rooms, maybe as much as 12,000 with maybe 13 or 14 hotels, that is hotel casinos operational, as opposed to the 11 we have now.

convention hall repairs

M.s. v/o
Convention hall is being remodeled. The hope is to attract more convention business and traditional vacationers, along with the gambling trade in them. And the city wants to see families as well.

boardwalk folds

super: Mayor James L.
Usry

Mayor o/c
We're just now going over and approving the plans for the rebuilding of Steel Pier. (edit) We find that at last the gaming industry is recognizing the fact that there must be some type of activity and some program for those who are not going to go sit at those tables, I mean for any extended length of time.

beaches

new hotel

v/o
The beaches are still wide and beautiful ... the boardwalk still an attraction. Much more is promised. And with the opening of every new hotel and casino, the city's boosters are betting on a rosy future.
Marlene Sanders, CBS News, Atlantic City.

---

ABC News

*In my opinion, the most valuable attribute for a journalist is the ability to write the English language.*

# DAVID BRINKLEY

David Brinkley is not an equivocator. Very seldom will you hear "perhaps," "maybe" or "might" in what he says. Is he really that certain about everything? "Yes, I am" he says. "I think it's because I've been around long enough to think about things."

Brinkley, the son of a North Carolina railroad worker, began his journalistic career at the (Wilmington, N.C.) *Star-News*, where he worked for two years during high school and after he graduated. He joined the Army in 1940, and when he was discharged in 1942, he was hired by United Press (before it became United Press International) to cover four cities in the South—Atlanta, Georgia; Montgomery, Alabama; Nashville, Tennessee; and Charlotte, North Carolina. He studied English at the University of North Carolina and Vanderbilt University, but he did not graduate.

In 1943, he went to work as a radio writer at WRC in Washington, D.C. In 1947, Brinkley and John Cameron Swayze delivered a 15-minute NBC television newscast to a very small Washington, D.C., audience. There were only a few hundred sets in the city.

Brinkley's wider notoriety began in 1956 when NBC decided to team Brinkley with Chet Huntley for the first time to anchor the national political conventions. After the conventions, Huntley and Brinkley stayed together to anchor the NBC News, which was re-named "The Huntley-Brinkley Report." Brinkley often referred to himself as "the other side of the hyphen." Huntley reported from New York and Brinkley from Washington. In 1963, the newscast was expanded to 30 minutes.

Huntley and Brinkley anchored together until 1970, when Huntley retired. Brinkley stayed one more year as anchor, and then NBC shifted him to his own public affairs program, "NBC Magazine with David Brinkley." In 1981, after 38 years at NBC, Brinkley surprised many people when he left to join ABC, which was beginning a new program to compete on Sunday mornings with "Meet the Press." Today, "This Week with

David Brinkley" often has an audience twice the size of the audience for "Meet the Press." David Brinkley, 66, has covered every political convention since the first one that was covered by television in 1956. He has won 10 Emmy Awards and two George Foster Peabody Awards.

Brinkley, who has been called "one of the two or three gigantic figures in broadcasting history," is a surprising man. In 1959, when he was the distinguished co-anchor of Huntley-Brinkley, he owned a white Corvette. He makes furniture. His last project was a poker table.

"I'm good at poker," he says. "One night I had a poker game with Jack Valenti, Art Buchwald, a lot of supposedly smart people, and I was one player short so I invited my son John to play. He was about 25. It was the first time I'd played with him. He was the best goddamn player. He won all night. I was very proud of him." John works for Scripps-Howard in Washington, D.C. Another son is a history professor at Harvard. Brinkley's third son is a Washington reporter for *The New York Times*.

Brinkley also designed and built a brick dollhouse for his daughter when she was young—"the world's most beautiful dollhouse," he says—an eight-room replica of their house, complete with a stereo system and fireplaces. He glued on the one-inch bricks individually.

"You smooth the wood, you glue the brick on and put the cement in," he says, "and it looks perfect. What I do during the day is always gray—somewhere between the whole story and part of it. Maybe not all of it is true, and I have no way of knowing," he says. "When you're working with wood, it either fits or it doesn't. It's either perfect or it's not. And when it's not, it's very easy to see that it's not, so when you finish it, you're very satisfied."

For someone who makes his living talking, Brinkley is unusually quiet and taciturn. He is taller than you would expect—over 6 feet. And he swears often. His conversation reflects the familiar punctuated timing, as he places invisible periods after every important word. He likes to laugh, and when he does, he smiles widely and his shoulders move up and down with enjoyable, deep humor. He is circumspect, gracious, and a little angry that the world isn't quite as perfect as his daughter's dollhouse. ❖

*from David Brinkley*

- How to write for television
- How to conduct a good television interview
- The importance of a sense of history

# Beginnings

At UPI, I worked in four towns in the South—Atlanta, Montgomery, Nashville and Charlotte, as a so-called bureau manager. I was a one-man bureau. They give you the title of manager so they don't have to pay you overtime. Very few stories in those cities ever got beyond the Southern wire—the legislatures and the governors. But I learned a lot. I learned to get by with nothing—no help, no information. After that, everything has seemed easy.

When I left United Press, I came to Washington and I was told—this was radio days—an O & O [owned and operated station] in Washington had a job opening. In fact, they told me they had a job opening. So I came to Washington to go to work for CBS, reported over there and they pretended they'd never heard of me. So I've hated the bastards ever since.

I walked four blocks to NBC, I asked for a job, and I was hired on the spot by the manager of the NBC O & O, called WRC, as a writer. I sat next to a man who was an outstandingly good writer and he taught me to be a writer. I had been doing wire service and newspaper writing, which is different. His name was Leif Eid. I was writing scripts for announcers to read. I wasn't on the air for a long time.

When television came along in about 1947–8—this was one of the first stations in the country—the big-time newsmen of that day, H. V. Kaltenborn, Lowell Thomas, did not want to do television. It was a lot of work, they weren't used to it, they were doing very well in radio, making lots of money. They didn't want to fool with it. So I was told to do it by the news manager. I was a young kid and, as I say, the older, more established people didn't want to do it. Somebody had to.

By that time, I had been on the radio some and was doing very well with it and nobody knew anything about television yet anyway. They figured if you could do radio, you could do television. An interesting point is that all of the big names in radio news later tried to get into television and every one of them failed. Not one of them ever made the transition. We had no idea it would come to be what it is.

The news business is all I've ever done, so I never had any idea of being in any other business. But of course I didn't anticipate all of this. When I started, there were newspapers and radio and that's all there were.

## EARLY TELEVISION BROADCASTS

The early broadcasts were extremely primitive by today's standards. It was mainly just sitting at a desk and talking. We didn't have any pictures at first. Later we began to get a little simple news film, but it wasn't much. The pictures were black-and-white, or that kind of bluish color that television always had. The editing was very primitive, picked up from the movie industry. All the equipment we used was Hollywood stuff, and Hollywood never was interested in speed. It took forever to do anything. The sets were very simple—usually a piece of painted plywood.

In the very beginning, people would call after a program and say in tones of amazement that they had seen you: "I'm out here in Bethesda, and the picture's wonderful." They weren't interested in anything you said. They were just interested in the fact that you had been on their screen in their house.

It was all new and no one had ever seen it before, selling television sets on the installment plan, and screens about 5 or 7 inches. A TK630 was made by RCA, and they made the best television set that has ever been made, up to and including this day. General Sarnoff, who pretty much started television in this country, said that this first set was the one by which television would live or die—630 means that it had 63 tubes in it, glass, looked like light bulbs. A couple of engineers at NBC still have them as novelties and they still work—terrific pictures.

Finally, they started a network news program with John Cameron Swayze. Swayze was also an interesting case. He was on the radio and NBC said to him, "You're going to do television." So he was sent over to television because it was thought of as Coventry. He went over there and became famous and began making lots of money.

## HUNTLEY JOINS BRINKLEY

About the time of the [1956] convention, they hired Huntley because the thinking then, if you call it thinking, was that a network must have an Ed Murrow, as if you can go find an Ed Murrow on a street corner. They hired Huntley because they thought he was similar to Murrow.

Then the '56 convention came along and we had both done a fair amount of television by then. They figured that whoever did it [the convention] was going to become famous—by '56, television was perking along pretty well. They didn't want to use any of their older people because they wanted somebody they could get some years out of. I was 36 and Huntley was 46, so they put the two of us on and it worked beautifully and I've done every convention since.

As a result of the convention being successful, they decided to put the two of us together doing the news. Interestingly enough, Huntley and Brinkley was a flop at first. For about a year, it didn't do anything. It seems to me that they didn't do ratings as much as they do now, maybe because it wasn't so competitive. NBC was the first, the biggest, the best, had all the big stars, and they really didn't have any serious competition until much later.

At first, Huntley-Brinkley wasn't much good. The critics didn't like it; I don't know about the audience. In fact, they were thinking of getting rid of Huntley. They told him they were going to take him off, and he had gone across to New Jersey and bought a horse farm, which he was going to run when he was off television. Then suddenly it just caught on and it dominated the news for 14 years. Don't ask me why. I have no idea.

## COVERING THE CONVENTION IN 1956

The thinking was that, since we were going to be describing events for the public, we should always see what the audience saw and nothing more. So they put us in the studio with no view of the convention floor. All we could see was the television picture. By the standards of the time, it worked. Since nobody had ever seen it before, they didn't know how bad it was.

The most memorable thing was being there at all, being on the air at all in 1956. There is one thing that I would like to claim credit for. NBC decided their news programs were not spiffy enough, and they hired a man named Barry Wood, who once was a dance band singer. He once sang on the "Lucky Strike Hit Parade" and tap danced. They brought him in to jazz it up.

And they called me in one day along with the president of news, whose name was William R. McAndrew, and he had a red blazer, and on the pocket was an embroidered NBC symbol with three chimes, like xylophone keys. He said, "Put this on and see how it looks." And I said, "I'm not going to put this on. And if you have any idea I will wear that on the air, forget it." And they said, "Well, we'd like you to put it on." I said, "I will not put it on. If that is a condition of employment, I quit. I refuse to wear it." And I was even slightly vulgar.

And I believe that if Huntley and I had started wearing those goddamn things, they would have become acceptable and part of the scenery of doing the news on television, and people would be wearing them today. I think I saved them from that.

---

## "THIS WEEK WITH DAVID BRINKLEY"

We put people on who are as close as we can manage it to this week's news. Some weeks there's no news. But we don't do soft subjects. Most of the people I deal with are accustomed to being interviewed. Because they are public people, they know if there's anything nasty, I'll ask it. They don't expect anybody to be sweet to them.

In a news interview, the purpose is, first of all, to explain the issue to people who don't do what we do every day. To a degree, I'm a teacher, not because I'm so smart and I know so much but because that's what I do. Other people do other things, and don't have time to keep up with what's happening in 250 countries around the world, so we do it for them.

At least half or more of the people we have on the air I already know. The others I don't know but I have talked to before, like tomorrow we have a member of the Politburo from Moscow. It's a very difficult interview because I know what he's going to say and the answer to every question. Every answer will be a lie, but I can't do a thing about it.

I can't get it to be a debate, such as why they shot down a Korean airliner. I know why they shot it down, but he will lie and say it was on a spying mission. I know it was not on a spying mission, but I can't prove it and pull out a document and wave it in his face, à la Mike Wallace. There is no such document. So he will lie, and I can't do much about it. All I can do is say, "No one in the U.S. believes that, and there's no evidence to support it." That's about all I can do.

What we think we are doing and what we hope we are doing is exploring a subject of general public interest, in this case, American-Soviet relations. I am not trying to hang anybody. We really don't do that. Suppose you succeed? What have you done? That's policeman's work. What I am trying to do is to expand, explain, illuminate an interesting and important topic. This sounds very grandiloquent, but to increase the public's understanding of it. We're not trying to prove anyone's a crook.

If somebody wants to filibuster, we interrupt. If they don't like it, too bad. We haven't got them on there to deliver a sermon. We've got them on there to answer questions, and give their views and whatever information they're able to give. Once they've done that, I don't want to hear any more about that. I want to hear another question. So we interrupt.

There are very few subjects that we can deal with. We can't deal with a water bond issue in Dayton, Ohio. We have to deal with something that presumably is of interest to 50 states. Despite what we pretend, there isn't really that much news most weeks. U.S.-Soviet relations has been a subject of discussion and public interest for 40 years. It isn't something that started yesterday. But it's worth returning to every year or two because there are developments and changes and new people.

The world's greatest interviewer cannot get blood out of a stone. That is another reason why I've never been all that crazy about interviews as a journalistic device, particularly on the air. In print, if it's not good, you just forget it. On the air, you're stuck with it. If the person has no interesting thoughts, no interesting information, or is unwilling to give you whatever thoughts or information he has, you're stuck. You really can't do a good interview without a good interviewee.

## TYPES OF INTERVIEWS

What kind of interview is it? Is it an interview with a movie star, some glamour queen, and you ask her what her hobbies are, which is entertaining? Or is it an interview with someone who is being tried for selling narcotics who is, of course, out to defend himself, unlikely to answer any questions you might ask, but you have a camera in his face and a microphone? What do you ask him?

There's the interview with somebody who is in a position of power, the prime minister of France, say, who is in a position to do something about his opinions. There's the interview with some routine politician who's full of opinions and not necessarily able to do anything about them. There's the interview with John Q. Public standing on the sidewalk who has just watched something and hasn't the faintest idea what he's seen. Everything he tells you will be wrong, you can count on that. If the eyewitness was there and you weren't, about the best you can do is try to find three or four and distill from the three or four some version of the facts because they'll all differ.

## KNOW ABOUT THE PERSON

The first requirement is that you know the subject and you know as much as possible about the person. I'll tell you just as an incidental footnote, I've been interviewed a thousand times by journalism students. It is very annoying to have one sit there and say, "Where were you born?" It is a waste of his/her time and my time. They should have found that out before they came. And sometimes I lecture them and tell them, "If you want to be an interviewer, that is the first thing to learn. Don't waste time with those silly questions. Look it up before you go."

The more you know of the subject being discussed the better. You should never interview anybody, except in extreme circumstances, without first having gone through the morgue and the clip file and having read it all and found out what he has said before and try to advance it beyond what is already in the morgue.

There's the matter of tone, personality, attitude. You try to get him/ her relaxed and talkative, particularly if you're in a situation where you can throw away the first half and use the second half. If you have the time, you might try to start with a few soft, nice questions to get them to relax, if it's not somebody who's been interviewed before, who is not accustomed to it, somebody you don't know, doesn't know you. If you have some zingers, save them until the last.

## COVERING DISASTERS

Then there's somebody whose family has been lost in a flood and the silly ass reporter sticks a microphone in her face and says, "How do you feel?" Well, that is silly. But what the hell do you say?

I've been doing this kind of stuff all my life. If I was there, and the woman is crying, her babies have been washed away, what the hell do I say to her? What is the question? Everyone says that question is terrible, you people should stop doing it. Well, then, what is the question? I don't know.

Thank God I don't have to do that, but if I did I would ask a question that I could then cut off and just use the answer because I don't have a question to ask somebody who is suddenly in some indecently tragic situation. They always say, "How do you feel?" It annoys the audience. It annoys me. But what is the right question? I don't know.

## CELEBRITY INTERVIEWS

I wouldn't do a celebrity interview if you held a gun to my back. I've never done one and I will never do any because I don't care about them. I have no questions to ask them because I don't care about their answers with the possible exception of maybe half a dozen—Clark Gable, Groucho Marx, John Barrymore, Charlie Chaplin, someone like that—seminal figures who are intelligent and literate, articulate. That might be kind of OK.

*Eight*

## THE JOE PINE INTERVIEW THAT DIDN'T HAPPEN

Years ago there used to be a man—I think he was in Los Angeles—named Joe Pine, whose specialty was having guests on and insulting them and he invited me to be on. I could hardly wait to get on because beneath this sweet and lovable exterior is a nasty SOB.

I mean, I have the nastiest, most cutting tongue in the eastern United States. And I wanted to take that SOB apart and leave him bleeding on the rug, which I could have done. NBC would not let me do it. They said it was beneath me, and they didn't want me talking to that crazy bastard. I would have so loved doing it. I don't know why other people went on the program, but that's why I would have gone. Because I was going to cut him up. I would leave him bleeding. The first question was, "If you're so smart, then why are you doing this tin-horn program?" And then I would have gotten nasty.

## TWO GOOD INTERVIEWS

I'm not very high on interviewing as an art form. I think it leaves a great deal to be desired as it is practiced. Television and print on that score are very different. In print, you can interview somebody for an hour and you can use a minute of it, which is normally what you do, use a paragraph of it. On television, it all gets on, if it's live. And of course you can do a taped interview and cut it. All the interviews I do are live.

I've done very few interviews that I felt were worth a damn. It may be that I'm not a great interviewer, but I've seen others do very few that I thought were worth a damn. I did one with Richard Nixon about two years ago, which I thought was excellent. A little bit of it got on the air, but very little. I did one with Admiral Hyman Rickover, who has never been interviewed on the air before or since, and that didn't get on the air either, but it was terrific. There wasn't anywhere to put it.

I talked to those people two or three hours. I was there long enough to be able to get them relaxed, and to joke with them and to make fun of them in a nice, mild way. Rickover always comes across as being a piece of granite. I had him giggling like a schoolboy. He finally figured that I was not trying to set a trap for him. He has some rather crazy views. He would shut down the Pentagon, for example. I have heard worse ideas.

## COVERING WASHINGTON

As for very interesting people, this town is full of them. Whether you like them or not isn't the question. It's been full of jerks and rogues and liars and thieves and brilliant people and a few who were interested in public service, rather than themselves, which is rather rare.

Sam Rayburn, Speaker of the House for a long time, was a total public servant. He never made any money, never wanted any, never cared about it, never got anything for himself, lived very modestly. He was probably the member of Congress I have known and admired most, probably one of the best members Congress ever had in its whole history.

There haven't been that many. Most of them have been routine, ordinary, sort of OK. Some, of course, have been rogues, thieves. This is just a wild guess, but I would say there have been maybe 30 since Congress began who were truly able, outstanding, honest public servants. I'd say 30 was probably generous.

## THE IMPORTANCE OF WRITING

Good writing is like a painting or a flower. You know that it's beautiful, but you can't say why. Can you tell me why a rose is beautiful? E. B. White is my all-time favorite writer. He's the best writer in the English language today. He writes the cleanest prose I know of. It's simple. *The New Yorker* has not been very good since he left.

In my opinion, the most valuable attribute for a journalist is the ability to write the English language. That is what did it for me. I ain't good lookin'. I can't do many things any better than anybody else. But I am a very good writer. That's the only thing I'm really any good at.

You can't talk until you learn to use the language and put words together clearly, unambiguously, vividly. Writing is what got me into journalism in the first place. I liked to write, I was good at it, and I still am. That's the only virtue I will claim. I do write well.

Anyone who wishes to be successful in broadcast news must write his own stuff. Otherwise he will never have any style, any individuality; no one will ever recognize him/her as anything more than some voice. If you don't want to write it yourself, you should go and sell insurance. If you can't write it yourself, don't go into this business.

In some journalism/communication schools, they put excessive emphasis on talking. I have met their graduates because they come looking for jobs. And I don't say this to them, because it's too rough for some young kid, but the question is, "Fine, you've learned to talk. Have you learned anything to say?"

I hear them on the air, and I can tell if they know about what they're saying or if they're just reading words. It's very easy to tell because the emphases are always wrong. They speak beautifully in nice, round tones. But when they say a sentence, they emphasize the wrong words because they don't understand the sense of it. They are reading words. They will never know why audiences don't find them very appealing.

The primary tool of journalism is writing the English language, writing a clear sentence. There is remarkably little of it, I must say, even in the higher levels of journalism. There are people in this building who can't write worth a goddamn.

I haven't done the news for a long time. I did it for 25 years. I'm sick of it. I don't want to do it any more. Once in a while in various emergency situations, I've had to do it, always unwillingly. I've always written everything I've ever said, but occasionally something happens while we're on the air and somebody has to write something for me. So someone will write it and hand it to me. It is so awful that it is unsayable. John Barrymore couldn't say it.

## GOOD WRITING FOR TELEVISION

The language is the spoken language. Written language, prose, is the spoken language on paper. If you read a paragraph in *The New York Times* and you don't understand it, you can go back and read it again. On the air, if the news person says something, you can't go back.

You can use more complex sentence structure on paper than you can in spoken English, but when you are writing material to be spoken on the air, the best way I know to do it is to read it aloud as you write and see if it can be said clearly, simply, directly, vividly. If it can't, then change it, rewrite it. Write it the way you would say it if you were talking to someone, with slightly more care.

My favorite little anecdote is about an actor named Charles Boyer. He was helping some young woman who wanted to be an actress and he said, "My dear. You're on the stage before an audience and you say, 'Please come in for dinner before the mashed potatoes get cold.' If you can say that line and not get a laugh, you're an actress."

As you write it, say it aloud. See if it comes out right. See if it's easy to say, easy to understand. You avoid lots of dependent clauses. It's not all simple, declarative sentences, but most of it should be. You certainly never put a dependent clause at the end of a sentence, which newspapers always do. It is always, " 'Blah blah blah blah,' he announced today." Don't ever do that. Newspapers shouldn't do it either.

## IMPORTANCE OF A SENSE OF HISTORY

History is the second-most important attribute for a journalist. If you don't know what has happened before, you cannot evaluate what is happening now. History and English, I think, are the basis. You can learn to add and subtract if you want to.

How can you decide if a story is important if you don't know what happened before it? I think it is an act of (a) laziness or (b) selfishness, or self-centeredness, to think the world began the day you were born, that nothing is important except what has involved you directly. It's stupid. Anyone with that attitude may get a job at KTRQ somewhere, but they'll never do well.

A knowledge of history is absolutely essential—it's indispensable, second only to English. What you are as a journalist is a sort of daily historian. What I do today is what my son [a history professor at Harvard] may be teaching 20 years from now. Essentially they are the same work. I deal with events that are of no great historical importance, plus a lot of others that are.

I wrote a story here the day the atomic bomb went off. I didn't know what the hell I was doing because I didn't know what the atomic bomb was—I mean, I knew what it was, but I didn't know what it was. Usually I know when a story is something of permanent and enduring interest. I also know when it's not.

## HOW PEOPLE PERCEIVE THIS BUSINESS

Almost all their perceptions are wrong. Usually they think you sit in front of a TelePrompTer and read, which I don't, never have and never will. Very often, people will say that I said something on the air that they disliked, "but of course I understand that those were not your words, but what you were told to say." I don't feel like striking a pose of righteousness and saying, "No, no one tells me what to say," but that is the fact.

I wouldn't call it glamorous. Sometimes it can be annoying to be recognized when you're trying to do something, but it's not a serious problem. People are always very polite and very nice. In Washington, everybody thinks he is a celebrity. Everybody thinks he's important. There were times during the [political] conventions when it was quite embarrassing—I would draw a bigger crowd than the candidate. So I would disappear.

## THE ROLE OF MANAGEMENT

I've worked at two networks, and the management in both cases was decent, fair, enlightened and, in about 40 years, nobody has ever said to me, "You cannot put this on the air, you cannot say this." No one has ever done it once. I've probably led a charmed life, and I don't know how many others would be able to say that.

## TELEVISION NEWS TODAY

It's all mainly hair and teeth and TelePrompTer. They all look alike and they put on essentially the same material. A good deal of that is inevitable because if it's a big story, obviously everybody is going to put it on. But for that, and other reasons, they come out looking very much alike.

They [reporters] try to get too much into 90 seconds to the point where, if you already know what the story is, the story becomes unclear and fused. They feel it necessary to jam every possible word and picture into the short time they have, which I think is a mistake. That's the main fault I find with it.

Plus, there's a kind of herd instinct, and everyone feels that they must do what the competition is doing. I don't agree with that at all. I would do what I thought was right and wouldn't give a goddamn what the competition is doing. Let them look at us. We don't have to look at them. It requires a degree of confidence in yourself that maybe not everybody has.

## HOW REPORTING HAS CHANGED

Basic journalism has not changed 5 percent in all the years I've been in it. Reporters are better educated now, I think. But as for journalism, the dissemination of information and ideas, I can almost not think of any changes at all. The technology has changed the methods and the appearance and ability to gather it and the ability to bring it in, but I don't really know that there's been any change in journalism.

There's been some change in reporters' attitudes. I kind of think it began with Watergate. It began to appear that an adversarial relationship was necessary, and it was important for success and promotions and Pulitzers, and so on. And while in some cases that probably is true, I think it's overdone.

Another thing I think is that a substantial part of the public dislikes us, all of us. I think the reason is that they find us to be excessively cynical. We're never willing to grant anybody a free pass. Reporters always look and see if he isn't really a crook beneath it all, always look for a negative factor, some nasty little line to put down in the middle of the story. The criticism of that is valid.

It is true that a great many members of the public dislike the news media altogether, probably without exactly knowing why. My guess is that is why—they find us cynical. They think we're negative and we're always looking for something nasty.

## THE EFFECT OF DEADLINES

It has made me compulsive. It has made me impatient with fooling around, wasting time, taking an hour to do what can be done in five minutes. It has affected me in that way because I've had to spend my whole life being ready at a set time with no nonsense. You can't be one second late. I guess when you do anything that long, it becomes part of your genetic structure. I'm very impatient with wordiness, tedium, repetition. I'm very impatient with it.

## PRIVATE LIFE

I guess I have become a public man, in a way. I never intended to be, but it seems to have happened. Again, that's not such a problem in Washington anyway, less so than any other town I know of. One of the virtues of this job is that it pays well, and with enough money you can have all the privacy you want. I have a house in the country, which I'm going to tomorrow afternoon, and it's totally private.

This job can take all your time because you're not working just when you're working. You have to work all the time because you have to keep up with things, and you have to do a lot of reading, and you have to see a lot of people. It takes all of your time, if you're serious about it.

## THE ROLE OF JOURNALISM

There isn't really anything in life except doing something that you think is worth doing and is of some use. If you don't think that, I don't know any real reason to be alive. So I think what I do is of some use and I do it because I like being useful. You can say that I do it for myself or for whatever public benefit it may have. I really don't think there's any great difference.

I wouldn't say so much of what I do makes a difference, but certainly journalism makes a difference. Where would we be without it? How could we get along without it? People have never gotten along without it. Back to and including Rome, they had what they called newspapers. So I think journalism is extremely important. It's a very satisfying kind of work to do, and it does matter. It clearly does matter. The country couldn't operate without it. How could you run a democratic political system without journalism? You can't.

# Commentary on the Russians and the Press from "This Week with David Brinkley"

It is interesting and maybe encouraging even to see that the Russian leadership has moved into the age of television and is trying to manipulate the news like Western politicians we have known for so long. We saw it in Paris Friday when Mikhail Gorbachev, on a visit, stood there and took reporters' questions for an hour on live television. In the past their leaders have behaved very much like our Herbert Hoover, who would never take a question unless written in advance, and he said, "The President of the United States will not stand and be questioned like a chicken thief." Well now, Gorbachev, in a first for his country, has moved beyond that. He's learned the tricks. A question he does not want to answer he turns aside and says he has already answered it, even if he has not. And when he does have news to put out, he spreads it out over several days so he will get into the papers and on the air more than once. He behaves as if he were running for office in a country where offices are not run for. And he's trying to put the United States on the defensive, making it appear the Russians want arms control and we don't. He may not succeed, but if not it won't be because he hasn't learned all of the politicians' tricks. At least they're tricks we know how to deal with, because we've seen them all our lives.

For all of us at ABC's This Week, until next Sunday, thank you.

---

*David Brinkley talks about his writing on p. 147. Courtesy of ABC's "This Week with David Brinkley."*

CBS News

*There's no room for shoddiness or mistakes or half-hearted work. There are no excuses. When 6 o'clock comes, the story has to be done. It has to be complete; it has to be a good news story every day.*

# BILL WHITAKER

Bill Whitaker, who grew up near Philadelphia in Media, Pennsylvania, graduated from Hobart College in upstate New York in 1973 with a degree in American history. He attended Boston University to study Afro-American studies, and spent a summer in Liberia, West Africa, as part of that program. At Boston University, he mentioned to a professor that he had an interest in journalism, and got a job working for the university as a production assistant, making films for the Bicentennial.

In 1976, he moved to San Francisco to attend journalism school at the University of California, Berkeley. A year later, San Francisco's public television station, KQED, hired him to work on a series geared to black teen-agers, "Up and Coming." He finished his courses at Berkeley, but still needs to write his thesis to get his degree. "My mother hounds me today," he says. " 'Have you finished your thesis yet?' My mother, my sister—nobody lets me forget it."

KQED produced its own local 30-minute nightly news show. Whitaker started in the newsroom as a production assistant—"You did everything nobody else wanted to do," he says—then he became field producer and, for six months, producer.

"In public television, you don't have the best equipment in the world," he says. "There were things that folks in the local commercial station took for granted. During a program we'd cut to city hall where the reporter is standing by and the reporter is all distorted and his voice isn't coming through. We'd say, 'OK, we'll go back to that later.' And all through the broadcast, our lead story couldn't run because we couldn't get it back from city hall, just seven blocks away."

In 1981, Whitaker moved to North Carolina and joined CBS affiliate WBTV to do general assignment reporting and, eventually, to cover the legislature. In 1984, WBTV assigned him to cover the Jim Hunt–Jesse Helms race for U.S. Senate. Helms and Hunt spent $20 million running against each other, and Whitaker says that during the campaign North Carolina was "the most politicized place I've ever seen. Nobody had no opinion. There was never a public opinion poll with 20 percent who said 'I don't know.' "

In November 1984, two weeks after the election, Whitaker was hired by CBS as a network correspondent, based in Atlanta, to cover the Southeast. Whitaker, 35, is eager to do well in his new job. He works in the CBS bureau in an office building 15 miles from downtown Atlanta. The bureau, with a reception area and a 30-foot-long series of desks and cubicles, looks like any other business office. The only sign that this is a television bureau is the large blue backdrop painted on the far wall in the back of the office, behind the cubicles, in case someone needs to do a quick stand-up.

Whitaker spends very little time in the office. Working in a network bureau like Atlanta usually means that he gets on a plane to cover most of his stories. "It's demanding, but it is more than worth what you give up," he says. "If it gets to the point where I say, 'I don't want to get on another plane, I don't want to have my whole weekend ruined by a phone call,' it's time to get out. If you want total stability and want to know what you're going to be doing in the next 24 hours, this isn't for you. If you can adapt to change immediately, then you've got a chance." ❖

*from Bill Whitaker*

- How public officials use "free media"
- Working as a network correspondent
- Minorities in journalism

# Beginnings

The first time I remember even seeing anything about television news, I was 12 or 13. There was a commercial that ABC used to run with Howard K. Smith. He came out and sat in front of a bookcase in a wood-paneled room and he said, "I'm a broadcast journalist, and I deliver the news every day." That was the first time I'd ever heard what it was these people were called.

My mother has since reminded me that I said, "That's what I want to do." I don't remember being very dogged about it. I worked on the high school newspaper and dabbled in writing in college, but I didn't go into journalism in college.

I've always enjoyed writing. Whenever I did term papers in school, it was never a problem. I would make everybody else angry because I could wait until the last minute and I would write something and the professor would say, "How profound."

I finally decided to apply to journalism school and I wanted to go to California, so I just applied to [University of California] Berkeley because I knew it was a good school in the Bay Area—terrible reason for choosing a school.

I moved to California in the summer of '76, and loved it. It was a wonderful place to go to school. Right off the bat, I had a real tough Journalism 101 teacher, just like everybody says you're supposed to have, who would take your stuff and say, "What kind of trash is this? What are you doing here?"—who made you feel real bad and pounded you into somebody who could see a story and make some sense out of it. I look at the stuff I used to write, and it was very flowery, very grandiose. I used to have "therefore, we see" in my history papers. I got rid of all that.

## WORKING AT KQED NEWS

I was in the second year of Berkeley's TV program when I got a job at KQED, the public TV station in San Francisco. My primary interest was news and KQED had a very good news program. In 1979, I became a production assistant, which was low man on the totem pole.

It was one of those jobs where, in the morning, you could take a breather. And starting around 2 in the afternoon, you started running around like a chicken with its head cut off—grabbing tapes, hounding people—"Is this tape done?" You were the obnoxious person in the newsroom. And you had to type it all up and make sure everybody had copies of the sheets and knew what was going where and when and how and what the tape number was.

We had real news of the Bay Area. While everybody else was doing blood and guts, we were doing city hall and corruption and crime and talking heads, a lot of talking heads. It was a terrific newscast. I still have a hard time looking at Bay Area news because it's so glitzy. We were proud that we were doing news of substance, news that mattered.

Then I got promoted to associate producer. I did field producing on pieces, produced the program twice a week to relieve the producer. Basically, I read over scripts and came up with story ideas and went out and produced some stories. After about a month, the producer left to do a couple of documentaries. He was gone for about six months. In his absence, I became the KQED news producer.

I had the full load of whether it was going to be a great broadcast or a horrible broadcast right on my shoulders. You lived and breathed KQED news.

## SOME MISTAKES

When I was production assistant, I had grown up in the East and I wasn't familiar with all those Spanish names in the Bay Area. I remember typing *Monterey* [to be keyed in on the screen] as *Monterrey*. And people would call up in a second. The phone would just go off the hook over what I thought was one little tiny mistake.

I told my mother that I was having spelling problems and she sent me this book on typing and spelling. She was real concerned. From then on, I looked at a map. Even in such a low level as typing in names, you have to be absolutely sure because you're broadcasting—in our case—to thousands of people.

The federal government cut back funds to public TV after the '80 election, and KQED didn't have money to produce a nightly news program anymore. All through this, I had been in touch with CBS. This friend at CBS told me about the CBS minority training program. With this program, you would go to work at one of the CBS affiliates for six months. After six months they would say, "He's terrible, fire him," or "He's got potential, keep him for six months more." So I went for an interview at WCCO in Minneapolis, but I didn't get the job.

I went through all these doubts—is this what I really want to do? I thought for a second of law school and said, "Are you kidding? You don't want to go to law school." I began to realize that yes, I really did want to do this, even though it wasn't falling out in front of me as I'd hoped.

## MOVES TO CHARLOTTE, NORTH CAROLINA

So I went back to KQED as a free-lance producer for the rest of the year. Then I called CBS back again and said, "If you miss it the first time, do you get another chance?" And they said, "Sure, no problem. We've got one right now in Charlotte, North Carolina. Why don't you send a resume?" So I sent a resume and I went down to this interview in Charlotte in October 1981, and I got the job.

I moved to Charlotte in two weeks and started working. By then I was 30, which was a little older than just about everyone in the station. Everyone else was a youngster. I figured, "This is it. This is my opportunity. I'm 30 and I have to make something of this."

So I read everything I could about Charlotte—books and atlases—and I just devoured newspapers. WBTV was the first station in the Carolinas and it's the largest station in the state, so everyone respected WBTV. It was just a very, very good place to learn—small enough, yet large enough. After a year on the minority program, BTV hired me.

## HOW TO REPORT FOR TELEVISION

Reporting for television doesn't come naturally. There's a certain way of projecting yourself and making yourself the center of attention, to make it seem that what you're saying is worth listening to. When I first started out, I didn't naturally have that. That had to be developed.

BTV at the time was going through this idea that meetings are boring, meetings will not dominate a story. So the way to do it was to get pictures of what they were talking about in the meeting. If they were talking about sewers, then we'd go get pictures of the sewer treatment plant and make sure there was some action in the picture, then go back to city hall to get a response from one of the politicians.

I learned to wisely use the pictures, to use the technology and the medium well. I can see how using the pictures to tell a story along with your words is the best use of the camera and the journalist. It's not just an electronic notepad. It broadens your scope.

All the stuff you think about when you're in school—oh, this is fun, exciting—yes, no doubt, that's what keeps a lot of us here. But it's hard work. There's no room for shoddiness or mistakes or half-hearted work. There are no excuses. When 6 o'clock comes, the story has to be done. It has to be complete; it has to be a good news story every day. And you don't know until you do that daily how demanding and draining it is.

Some days I would get up and say, "Oh, God, the last thing I want to do is go trudging around North Carolina in a van and go knock on somebody's door and ask them questions." But even when you're feeling your lowest, you have to do it. Sometimes I envy people who have office jobs who have a project due next week. They know that if they work real hard tomorrow, they can catch up and take a little time off today. There's none of that. You're called to put out 100 percent every day and you have to. I think that's the main thing I learned.

Another thing you learn is to just do it. If you sit here and worry about it, you're using up precious time. Once it's done, if you have a little bit more time, you can say, "I could have done this better." But the demands of the clock are constant.

With daily news, you don't always get the kind of creative satisfaction you get with documentaries. You get the satisfaction of doing a good job and getting it done on time. You don't always get, "That was the absolute best way I could have said this. Those words were the best that my brain ever produced." That's not a daily satisfaction. But there are others. And when those things do mesh, you say, "Boy, that was terrific writing and those were the best pictures." You just walk out the door feeling that's what it's all about.

## A MOVE TO COVER POLITICS

My fiancee from California had come to North Carolina and we had gotten married and were living in Charlotte. And we had just moved to a new apartment. The apartment was just what my wife wanted—with a big porch. The day we were moving in, they came to me at the station and said, "How would you like to go to Raleigh?" The Raleigh bureau was 150 miles from Charlotte.

So I came back to the apartment and my wife was sitting there, looking at all the boxes, and I said, "Well, dear, how would you like to go to Raleigh?" It didn't go over real well, but we talked about it and it just proved to be too good an opportunity to turn down. Jim Hunt was going up against Jesse Helms in the election [to the U.S. Senate], and it was the center of politics. A whole lot was going on in North Carolina politics at the time.

To anybody who's interested in history or politics, North Carolina is fascinating—new and old, progressive and regressive. The cruncher was that the Helms race was going to be the big thing in '84. So we left everything in the boxes and told the moving van to pick them up and we moved to Raleigh. I was the Raleigh bureau chief. It sounds terrific, but it was a photographer, an editor and me.

## COVERING JIM HUNT AND JESSE HELMS

I think the Hunt-Helms U.S. Senate race was probably the most interesting political race in the country in 1984. The back and forth got to be so rude that we were never at a loss for a story. Never. One candidate would say one thing on Tuesday. On Wednesday, the other would respond. Thursday, it would go back. You could literally have done a whole campaign of "he says, he says." You really did have to learn to be judicious because they dominated the news, but they could have dominated it more. Very colorful.

They pumped a lot of money into campaign commercials that didn't tell you anything about who they were or what their position was, for the most part. They were very attacking kinds of commercials—attacking the other person and not saying anything about the candidate's positions.

I remember doing a piece or two on these commercials and then I went to talk to political scientists to round it out, saying, these folks aren't telling people anything. They're just attacking each other, and it isn't contributing much to the advancement of the political process.

It was a media circus with national folks and newspapers. We followed along in our van and our folks would hire a plane or have a helicopter pick us up at the airport and whisk us back so we could sit with the anchor and say, "Well, Bob, I just got back from the campaign trail. . . ." Then we'd go back out that night and catch a plane. Very good experience.

## COVERING POLITICS FOR TELEVISION

It helps to like it. I like the give and take and the fight. You learn that there is an almost symbiotic relationship between the press and politicians. They seek you out and you seek them out and they need you and you need them. You always have to be on guard against being manipulated.

Politicians want to be on television. It helps their constituents to know they're working on something, that they have an issue that's important. The candidates would talk openly about the "free media." They were spending so much money on paid campaign commercials, but they had to take full advantage of the "free media," which was a couple of minutes on local news across the state every day—"Here's the governor saying this" or "Here's Jesse Helms saying that." They were very, very good at that.

## GETTING FREE PRESS

These candidates would hold press conferences to introduce their new commercials. They would hold press conferences to accuse each other of something underhanded that they couldn't really prove. It was constant. There were press conferences that weren't absolutely necessary, to keep them hot, keep them going in the press.

Jim Hunt did more photo opportunities because he was there in the state all the time. Jesse Helms was a true politician who wouldn't come into the state a whole lot. He would make statements from Washington and appear very senatorial—he was doing his duty in Washington and couldn't come down and reprimand Jim Hunt, who was lying about him.

They were both very smart about the use of the media. After a while, it becomes very obvious that a press conference is called for the news value and not for the importance it has to the general outcome of the campaign.

## MOVES TO CBS NETWORK

I stayed with the campaign through the '84 election. Then I started with CBS two weeks later—a week off and I started the next week. Being a network broadcast journalist has always been my goal. They sent me down here [Atlanta] on January 12, 1985.

Since I've been here, I've done lots of trials. There was a man in Florida who killed his wife because she had Alzheimer's disease and she begged him to put her out of her misery. A woman in Oklahoma killed her husband because he was abusing her. One night following what she says was a big fight, she shot him and killed him. Oklahoma put her away for life. The trial this past Friday was a civil rights trial in Alabama. Blacks in Alabama were saying that the Justice Department, which was investigating voter fraud in black-controlled counties, was racially motivated.

Very little of what we do actually takes place in Atlanta. There's a plane trip involved 99 percent of the time. You have to keep a bag packed. They told me that when I first got here and I thought it was just a way to frighten you. But no, they're serious.

Working for the network, the scope changes from working in local television. The impact and the import both change. There's a little more time both to put it together and the amount of time you have on the air. The average is around one minute-45 or two minutes. You can even get two-30 or so. Local television would be a minute-30. I would try to squeeze out a minute-35 and they would cut it to a minute-30.

## CHARACTERISTICS OF A GOOD REPORTER

You must be a good writer. You must be tenacious in that you don't let somebody say, "Oh, we'll call back." Never allow that. Say "I'll hold." Or call them back in half an hour.

You must have an ability to organize because the time constraints are so tight that you have to be able to get the story just bam, bam, bam. You have to be able to zero in on the essence of the story—what the story actually is about—and say it. That's not always the most satisfying thing.

You also have to be a generalist at the level where I am. There are lots of places in the State Department where you can become knowledgeable about the State Department, but for someone who's in the position I am, you never know what you'll be called on to cover. So you have to read everything—newspapers, news magazines, fiction, anything that will help.

Reading is very important, and just being an interested, involved person. By involved, I don't mean you have to be a member of a club or group, but you do have to be aware of what's going on around you and care about it. That's probably as important as all the technical things.

I've had to cover tobacco. The death penalty. Nuclear waste. Cancer. The law. When you're covering trials, you have to know what motions they're going to make. If they do it at 3 in the afternoon, you don't have time to go to the library and find out what that meant.

High technology. Computers. I was in the Research Triangle area of North Carolina. There were lots of high-tech stories, there were farm stories. Yams, farmers, that sort of thing. Agriculture, pollution. Just a wide range. You have to become an instant expert on everything.

I'm a sports fan, but not a sports fanatic, and one of the first things I had to do in Raleigh was cover the NCAA championship with North Carolina State, and they won. We had to go live—"Bill Whitaker live at the Arena"—and the pep rally lasted an hour. And my knowledge of sports could probably fill up 10 minutes, talking slowly.

I knew I was going to be there, so I'd done all the research and I got all the information on each player. But I'm sure I repeated myself. I remember saying a lot, "Listen to that crowd roar," or "As you can see, the crowd is enthusiastic about the returning champions."

## WHAT I LIKE ABOUT TELEVISION

I like and I don't like the same things. The technology. You can do things with television that you just can't do with print. Someone in print would have to take several paragraphs to describe a scene, but you can let the camera do that for you. That's one thing people have problems doing—letting the camera do what it does best.

At the same time, the technology is cumbersome and intrusive and it takes three people to show up to talk to one person, whereas a newspaper person has his pad and it's much more personal. People have to get used to the fact that the camera is on, and that's not something everybody feels comfortable with immediately. So you find yourself taking a lot of time talking to somebody, getting them to talk to you, asking them a few questions that have nothing to do with what you're there for, just to get the person to feel relaxed with the camera.

But if you're going to a tornado and you've got this camera and you see people walking through the weather and hear people cry, I'm sure someone could write a *New Yorker* article that would evoke the same response from a reader that a TV picture would for a viewer, but the immediacy of it and the impact of it are undeniable.

## DISADVANTAGES OF DOING STORIES FOR TELEVISION

Time constraints. In following the campaign last year, the newspaper political reporters were able to have half the front page and half the back page to tell what happened. If we were lucky, we could get two minutes. So you have to try not to do with television what you would do with newspapers. There's a difference, and understanding and accepting that difference is basic. But it's not limiting, it's challenging.

When you read *The New York Times* and you watch the "CBS Evening News," I'm sure you'll be able to get more in-depth coverage on the subject from *The New York Times*. But as far as seeing who the person is and hearing how the person talks and making some contact with this person—there's no comparison. You have to understand the limitations and the benefits, and not lament the restrictions. Go out and do what television does best.

## HOW I WRITE

For me, it's important that I keep updating the story as I go through it—which lead is the most important feature—just keep updating myself. Even if it's not written down on paper, I have to keep that story churning, so when I do sit down, it's not, "Now, what is this all about?" If I have the lead, I can go from there. But if I have the lead and how it ends, then I'm on easy street. The rest of it just falls into place. It doesn't always happen, though.

I try to write to the tape—see what the pictures are, what is best said by the pictures and the natural sound and what is needed for me to say. But sometimes you get back and there's no time for you to spend 15 minutes looking at that tape. You have to sit down and start writing. So you work very closely with the producer. He's fully aware of the pictures, and if he finds a picture that's perfect and must be used, he runs in and says, "We've got a picture that says this. You don't need to say that."

## HOW STORIES CHANGE

The story when you get there is never what you thought it was before you got there. Never. There are often times when you go out expecting an interview that's the *pièce de résistance*. This person's gonna sock it to ya. You get there, and they're scared of the TV cameras or they realize that their words are going to be heard by lots of folks, so they're more circumspect than they were on the phone. That happens a lot.

As for stories that change when you get there, I can remember a story when I first started out in Charlotte and a new mall was opening in Shelby. It was supposed to be, "Go over to this new mall opening in Shelby and come back." Well, when I got there, I wanted to do something to break out of the pattern, to not just be a 30-year-old reporter doing mall openings. So I made it into more than that—the downtown was dying and everything was moving up to this new mall, and the folks downtown didn't like it. We did the story about the fall of downtown Shelby and it turned into a pretty big story.

## ETHICAL DILEMMAS

During the campaign in North Carolina, a Helms supporter—an independent newspaper publisher—accused Jim Hunt of being a homosexual. I really do think it had an impact on the election. The polls that were done afterward say that people felt Jim Hunt wasn't tough enough, man enough. Jesse Helms said, "Of course, I don't support this type of journalism."

The press jumped all over it and everybody knew what this little tiny newspaper in Chapel Hill had to say about Hunt. We almost all went out of our way to say what the newspaper said without saying it. But there was no denying what this guy was saying about the governor—we just didn't use the crude language he did. I just felt uncomfortable repeating this. If it's libelous for this guy to say it in the first place, why is it all right for us to pick it up and say it again, which everybody did? I called the station attorneys and they assured me the way we handled it was legal and appropriate.

It did raise questions of how far we should go. If I had to do it again, I'm sure I would still cover it. I think if everybody had to do it again, we wouldn't have snapped it up as quickly and played it up as big. But by then, the campaign was so down and dirty. By then, this was just, how low can this go? It was just another potato in the stew. There was something about the story that was newsworthy. But it didn't sit right.

## INTRUDING ON SOMEONE'S LIFE

Someone who is suffering from a natural calamity or is the victim of a crime or hostage situation, we intrude on their lives and their grief and expose that to TV. In the beginning, I did feel uncomfortable, but I came to terms with it, figuring that I wouldn't go in there and say, "Hey, this is my story and I'm gonna make them cry with this old woman crying on camera."

I can't feel that I'm just snatching this person's image and their life and making something out of it that will benefit me or my career or my station more than it does them. I have to feel I'm there for a purpose, and the purpose is larger than getting me a story that I put up in the local Emmys or something. It's got to be bigger than that, more important than that.

## THE ROLE OF A REPORTER

You are a conduit. You are a relayer of information, and it's inappropriate for you to put your beliefs in this transmission process. If Jesse Helms said something that I did not agree with, it was important that I keep my beliefs out of it and say, "Jesse Helms said this," and present it. At the same time, there were things that Jim Hunt said and did that I felt were foolish or incredibly politic, but I'm not an editorial writer, I'm a reporter. I don't think everybody manages to do it at all times, but I think it's very, very important.

There were times when Jesse Helms would make a statement that bordered on being racist, things that he did in the campaign that appealed to people's bigotry, and I was unable to stand up and say, "This reporter believes . . . " That's just not the way it's done.

When I was at Berkeley, one of the big topics was reporter objectivity. And the teacher was saying that not only are all reporters to be totally objective, but that's what the whole thing is about. I remember I wrote a paper which he liked, saying that it's not possible for a person to be a television camera. Even with a television camera, it's subjective as to what it focuses on, what you see.

I am a transmitter of information. I am the eyes and ears of people who can't be there. As best I can, I give them an idea of the total picture. I just lay the issue out. As I said, I majored in history, so it's all very important in the sense that we have a big role to play in American democracy. We keep that dialogue going, we make sure people are aware of what's going on in their country, that they can see and be aware of the issues—abortion, crime, drugs—the whole range of things that affect us all and that we need to talk about, need to make decisions about.

We allow folks in a little hamlet, little towns to know what's going on with wife abuse in Oklahoma and with blacks in Alabama saying that we've got to protect voting rights. That's part of the mix, an increasingly important part of the mix, of the dialogue of democracy. And if that doesn't sound corny—

## HOW PEOPLE PERCEIVE WHAT I DO

I think most people think it's glamorous and exciting and fast-paced and fun. And it is. But what they fail to realize is how demanding it is, how much it requires of you. CBS can call you at any hour of the day or night and ask you to get up out of your bed, catch a plane and fly to nowhere, USA, and stand in mud and rain and talk about a flood.

You're counting on a two-day weekend, you and your wife are planning to go to the lake and everything's fine, and Friday night they call and say, "Nope. Catch a plane, go to Florida, go to a forest fire." So you spend the next four days smelling like smoke and trudging through the fires. That really happened about two months ago. Friday night, ready or not, you're going to Florida.

## ONE STORY THAT MADE A DIFFERENCE

In Charlotte, I had the social services beat, and the county used to give out fans in the summer to the elderly. But because of budget cuts, they didn't have the fans to give away this one year. So we did a story using one woman as an example, and I swear I couldn't have made up a better person to do this story.

She was a 60-year-old woman with her 80-year-old aunt, and the aunt was blind and had diabetes and both her legs were amputated. We got there just as the Meals on Wheels was arriving, and she was taking the food and she was saying, "I don't care so much about me, but it's my poor old aunt who really suffers from the heat."

We put that story on, and the fans came rolling in. She called me up the next day and said, "Mr. Whitaker, please. I've got more fans here than I know what to do with. And when people get here and see that

I've got all these fans, they get mad. They drove all this distance and I've already got a fan."

Well, the station just loved that. So we had to go out the next day and do a story about the reaction. And we took all the fans over to the social services building so they could distribute them to everybody else, and people were still sending in fans.

In a local station, you get that immediate response a lot. It's gratifying, but it's also problematic. Because these folks you are using as an example of a general problem may get their problem solved, and everybody thinks, "Oh good, we did something for this one person." But it doesn't alleviate the problem. It does alert people to the fact that there is a problem out there, and politicians start talking, and maybe they'll do something.

## HOW PEOPLE REACT TO BEING COVERED ON TELEVISION

We usually have a producer, sound man, cameraman and a reporter riding in CBS cars. Then they all jump out and tell people, "Don't worry about the camera and the lights. Be yourself." But it seems to me that America is getting so used to TV being everywhere that we rarely have people who out-and-out refuse to talk or who get so shy they can't speak.

People seem to accept that the camera is going to be there for good or for bad. I'm not sure what I think about that. I've been in places where people are talking in a group and we walk up and stick the camera in their faces, turn on the lights, put the microphone over them so we're picking up everything they say, and they sort of look over their shoulders and say, "Oh, TV's here," and they carry on.

I'm sure people stand up a little straighter because mom might see them on TV, but it's not like, "What are you doing here? We're having a private conversation." I find that, more and more, people accept and expect our presence.

At the same time, people are becoming savvy. We were down covering the teacher's strike in Mississippi, and the teachers sent the word out about which schools we were going to video. When we got there, there were all these pickets. A great protest was going on—50 pickets at this school. We'd go to the next school and there'd be 50 pickets there. We'd see some of the same signs and some of the same faces and realize these folks were one step ahead of us.

They wanted America to see that this strike was big stuff down here, which it was. We tried to tell them, "You don't need to manipulate it like this. If there are five pickets there, it'll make the point." And they said, "Fine, fine." And we'd get to the third school and the same group of picketers was there. So the way we had to do it was to say we were leaving town, tell everybody goodbye, and then go back to one of the schools where we were before and get the number of pickets who were actually there. The average American is becoming very TV-savvy.

## NEWS NEEDS A VARIETY OF REPORTERS

As a black male, I'm going to approach the story differently than a white male or an Asian female. It's not that it's bad, that's just the way it is. All of us try to keep ourselves out of the story, but the emphasis may be different, what you think is important in the story may be different.

I think it's important that a news operation have that mix of people so that the audience gets those different points of view—even with everyone trying their damndest to be totally objective. The approach that the reporter brings to the story is valuable to the readers or viewers. It's important that in America, blacks, whites, Asians, Hispanics, everyone be able to communicate their experiences through their reporting of the news to the community in general.

It's important in a pluralistic society like the United States that everyone be represented, be acknowledged, through this most powerful of communication media. Everyone brings something different to the presentation—the delivery, the gathering of the news. For a society such as ours, it's important that it be representative, that it have all of these voices participating, and that no one be excluded from presenting the information of the day to the rest of American society.

You do not get to present *your* news. I write it and there's a producer who goes through it with me, and we send it on to New York and there's a whole slew of producers up there who go through it. There's just no way that a personal presentation of the news is going to get through that whole process. A black reporter has to be as accurate and as factual and as objective as a white reporter. There's no difference.

We all bring something different to the job. And it's important that I be able to ask the questions I would ask and put them in the form that I think is important, just as it's important for a white male to go gather the information and put it in the form he thinks is important. Because no two of us seeing the same thing are going to report it the same way. It's important that we all participate.

# The Jesse Helms–Jim Hunt Campaign

CAM/
CK:
    Last week WBTV reported on the substantial sums of money Senator Jesse Helms and Governor Jim Hunt are raising from out of state contributors for their senate campaigns. Bill Whitaker reports from Raleigh the matter of out of state contributors is becoming a controversial campaign issue.

NATSOKC COMPLETE _____
SUPER: February 28 (upper left)
(CART :22)
    A fifty dollar a person fund-raiser for Jim Hunt in New York City, sponsored by the New York Committee to elect Jim Hunt. At this and two other such affairs, candidate Hunt raised some 130-thousand dollars for his senate campaign from New York supporters.

    In the past, Hunt has criticized Jesse Helms for soliciting out of state contributions. And in a stinging commercial now airing across the state, Helms charges Hunt with hypocrisy.

(SOKC :15) (sound bite paraphrased)
    SUPER: Helms for Senate commercial (upper left)

Jim Hunt is running commercials saying: the governor of North Carolina should represent the people of North Carolina. He's not the governor of California or New York. So what's Jim Hunt doing holding a fundraiser in New York City? Something's not right here. Where do you stand Jim?

(CART :01)
    Today, Jim Hunt struck back.

(SOKC :06) (sound bite paraphrased)
    SUPER: Jim Hunt
        Candidate for Senate

That's absolutely false. Negative. The worst kind of ad.

(CART :08)
    While many at the New York fund-raiser, like Mayor Ed Koch and feminist Gloria Steinem, were prominent New Yorkers, most, said Hunt, had North Carolina connections.

(SOKC :14) (sound bite paraphrased)

The real events that took place in New York were organized by people from North Carolina. Graduates of North Carolina State and the Uni-

---

*Bill Whitaker talks about this story on pp. 159–160. Courtesy of WBTV.*

versity of North Carolina who live and work in New York now. That's
who put on this event.

(CART :   )

A spokesman for Senator Helms says Jim Hunt is trying to have
his cake and eat it too.

(SOKC :06)

SUPER: Claude Allen    (sound bite paraphrased)
        Helms spokesman

But what is Jim Hunt doing criticizing Senator Helms for raising
money out of state when he is doing that himself?

(CART :   )

The truth is that both Hunt and Helms raise a considerable por-
tion of their campaign funds out of state. So far Helms has raised
three times more money out of state than Hunt.

(SOKC STAND-UP :16)
SUPER: Bill Whitaker
        WBTV NEWS

The Hunt campaign dismisses this and other Helms commercials
as negative and distorted. But if recent polls, which show Helms
closing in on Hunt, are an accurate indication, negative or not, the
ads appear to be effective. Bill Whitaker, WBTV NEWS, Raleigh.
        NATSOKC OUT _____

Photo by Geoffrey Cathers

*People think this business is glamorous. I have to laugh, as I'm spilling cold pizza on my lap in the back of a truck. I eat so many meals in moving vehicles. There is nothing glamorous about it.*

# SUSAN WORNICK

Susan Wornick started in broadcasting in 1974 selling advertising time at WFEA radio in Manchester, New Hampshire. When the station manager offered her $5 a newscast to do the news three times a day, she sold time and did the news until she was hired at WGIR radio in Manchester to do just the news.

She moved from WGIR to WKBR—there were only three stations in Manchester—where she worked as radio news director during the week. On weekends she commuted an hour to WBZ radio in Boston, working part-time. From WBZ she went to WHDH, and she worked weekends at WCVB-TV. In 1981, WCVB-TV hired her full-time to be a general assignment reporter. Her husband, whom she met at WGIR, is now a television sports anchor at a Boston station that competes with WCVB.

Wornick attended Emerson College in Boston, but never took a communications class. She majored in education and psychology. She has learned her broadcasting skills on the job, she says, and from her husband, Bob Lobel. Wornick, 36, has a flamboyant, friendly manner and an easy, engaging smile. She combines street smarts with a quick sense of humor.

She says she likes local television because she stays close to the people she covers. What she reports affects them, and she likes that sense of community. "Nine out of 10 people recognize Bobby in Boston," she says. "Maybe three out of 10 recognize me. I used to feel that just because somebody recognized me, I had to be their best friend. Bobby did, too. We'd be out for dinner and people would come over to the table. Bobby would feel that he had to invite them to sit down. It would get to the point where I'd have to say, 'OK, everybody, back to our house for coffee and dessert.'"

Wornick seems a very unlikely candidate for jail. Yet, in May 1985, she faced a possible sentence of 90 days in jail because she would not reveal the name of someone she had interviewed for what seemed a rather routine story.

Wornick works nights at WCVB, which means that she often covers crime and police stories. One night in February 1985, she was assigned to cover a story about police who were suspected of looting a pharmacy. State police were investigating the local police in Revere, Massachusetts, who were suspected of looting businesses and then covering up their crime by pretending the businesses had been burglarized.

In the process of investigating the story, Wornick received a phone call from someone who said he had seen police at a pharmacy, loading goods into their trunk one night. He agreed to go on camera with his identity disguised to describe what he saw. Wornick agreed to keep his name a secret, did the interview, and put it on the air.

As the investigation proceeded, this man proved to be the only one who could corroborate other testimony before the grand jury that the police had loaded the stolen goods into the trunk of their police car. Wornick was the only person who knew his name. She was called before a judge in May 1985 and threatened with 90 days in jail unless she revealed the name. She wouldn't. Only when the witness came forward and identified himself to officials was she spared the jail sentence.

Wornick found herself on the other side of the camera as a newsmaker instead of a reporter. The press camped on her lawn for an entire day as they awaited a phone call from the judge, and she and her husband ended up inviting the crowd of reporters into their house for spaghetti. "We got criticized for that," she says, "but what am I going to do? These are my friends."

Even though she was frightened by the prospect of jail, "You can never expect to be a reporter anywhere in the country again—ever—if you go back on your word," Wornick says. "The decision was made when I gave this guy my word that I'd protect his identity. That was it. There was never anything else to think about." ❖

## SPECIAL PERSPECTIVES

*from Susan Wornick*

- Reporters and their sources
- What happens when a journalist becomes news
- Agents and salaries

# B EGINNINGS

I absolutely fell into this business with my eyes closed, really. I suddenly woke up one day and I was doing it. It's almost that accurate. I went to college, Emerson College in Boston, which is a big communications and broadcast school, and I never took a broadcasting course.

I got married in '72. I was 22. I moved up to New Hampshire and I went to work as a secretary for a mobile home insurance company. You're gonna think I'm making this up. It was a one-man office; he had one secretary and you're looking at her.

Then a friend who was selling radio advertising for WFEA said they had an opening. I must have been about 24, 25 now. My husband then—now my ex-husband—was also working at this radio station as a news reporter and news anchor. I didn't know much about it.

Back in those days, there were no women on the radio in New Hampshire. Very definitely because I was a woman, the job was probationary. My ex-husband left the station just as I was starting and they began to tease me—"Your husband could do news. Can you do it?" As a joke.

The news director gave me a chance and a lot of guidance as well. He said to me one day, "Listen, I think you should do the next newscast." And I said, "Oh?" I had been there about six months, selling advertising. I said, "I should?" He said, "Yeah. I'll write it. All you have to do is read it. I want to hear what you sound like." So I said, "Fine. I'm a big shot. No problem." So we go into the little news booth and he says, "Now this is how you turn on the microphone and this is how you turn it off. When I point to you, just turn on the microphone and start reading. You'll be reading for three and a-half minutes, and then say, 'WFEA news time is 3:15. I'm Susan Wornick. Good afternoon,' shut the mike off and that's all you have to do."

I said, "Sure. No problem." I went in there and I sat down, I put on the headset, I looked at the clock and there were about 30 seconds till I was going to go on. He was ready to point to me, and I took the headsets off and I went running out of the room like a maniac, screaming, "I can't do it! I'm scared to death! I can't do it! I'll never do it!"

And he said, "OK, I'll do it this hour, but you do it next hour." Sure enough, I did it the next hour and I've been doing it ever since. WCVB hired me full-time in March of 1982. In November 1982, I was married to my husband. Now I work Monday through Friday, 3 to 11—nightside, general assignment.

## DIFFERENCES BETWEEN WORKING IN RADIO AND IN TELEVISION

I'll never feel like I have totally mastered video. For so long [in radio], I took a great deal of pride in being able to describe scenes, and now I don't have to.

You're a master of your own destiny in radio. You go out, you have a tape recorder and a microphone, and you can be a one-person radio station. You can go live from anywhere in the world, as long as you have a telephone. You need no one.

It was wonderful to have that kind of autonomy—get in the car and go. In radio, I like the immediacy. Something could be happening this minute and I could be on the air this minute talking about it. More and more with live television, that's also possible, but in radio, all I'd have to do was dial the phone. In television, you've got to get the live crew there. Then the live crew's got to set up the microwave.

At Channel 5, we have a real state-of-the-art piece of equipment called Newstar. They are trucks—they look a little like garbage trucks, to be quite honest—and they're equipped with satellite equipment so we can beam right up to a communications satellite. All you have to do is be able to see the sky and you can go live from anywhere in the world. Then they order a down-link back to the station. Please keep in mind that I have absolutely no idea how any of this works, and I have no desire to know. It's, "Get that baby over here, give me the microphone, we'll go on the air." That's all I want to know.

Also, in radio, you could get six or seven different angles on a story because there were so many newscasts. In television, for the most part, it's a minute-45, two minutes for something exceptional.

In radio, you can sit on your behind and do it. You can just use a telephone and interview people. A television reporter really has to be there because you're using video. In radio, it's not as easy to miss a story. If we heard a story on another station that we didn't have, we'd just pick up the phone, make a call and get the story.

If an accident occurs on the highway and you don't know about it and you hear about it on another radio station, all you have to do is pick up the phone, call the police, roll the tape and have the police tell you what happened. In television, if you miss it, man, you missed it. There's no way to make up the video, whereas in radio you can make up for it.

One of the big frustrations of television, too, is that in my experience there are few people running the news departments who actually have been reporters. As a result, they don't always know what we're doing. They don't always know how to get it done. In radio, so many news directors get there by having been reporters first. In television, our news director right now was not ever a reporter. That's a real major difference.

Television is a much more compelling medium simply because people don't have to imagine. They can really see it. On the radio, if I say "spectacular," you may think of one thing and I may mean something else. But if I show you a fire, I don't have to say it's spectacular. You can judge for yourself. In radio, to describe, you have to use adjectives. The more words you use, the greater the possibilities for miscommunication because people hear words and define them differently.

In television, you have to be a better writer because you have to make sure you don't play Show and Tell. If I'm going to show you a picture of a big red house burning, I don't need to say, "And the big red house burned down." You have to be careful that you're as familiar with your video as you are with the written word.

## TELEVISION AS A BARRIER

Sometimes people are a little intimidated by the camera and also the microphone in their faces. The microphone that's attached to the camera picks up a lot of the sound around us, so you really have to put a microphone in someone's face.

If you can talk to someone and ease their fears on the phone, fine, but if not, meet them in person without the camera. The one thing I've learned that's very important in this business—and it doesn't matter what kind of reporting you're doing —is trust. You've got to have the trust of the people you're covering. It's obviously ridiculous to think that you can develop a personal relationship with every person you cover, but hopefully you will have developed a reputation that speaks for itself so that people you're covering will know *of* you before they know you.

Usually, though, the first thing people say is, "Oh, God, I look like hell." You try to explain that the little flaws they see don't show up on camera. They say, "Come back after I've had my hair done." They are either slightly reluctant and easily calmed or they just don't want to talk and you never talk 'em into it.

People are more impressed with television than they are radio. The newsmakers pay a lot more attention to you when you've got a camera. Their priority is to be on television, I think. They realize the importance of radio, but their priority often is to get their message on television.

## FIRST TELEVISION STORY

I sure do remember my first story. East Boston people were upset that Proposition 2½ [a tax-cutting measure] was taking effect, and they were going to lose their fire station. They demonstrated out in front of a tunnel that led to the airport. They blocked the tunnel, and that was my first story.

They gave me very little direction. They simply said, "Come in at 9," and I got there [at the station] and the assignment editor said, "There's a demonstration going on and you are going to go. Larry Weisberg will be your photographer." I met Larry and I said, "OK, Larry, now what?" And he said, "Well, I'll shoot it and I'll tell you what I shot, and then you just write your story." And he shot it and he told me what he had, and then he said, "Now just write a radio report and put video to it." Basically, that's what I did the first time.

## HOW THE PUBLIC VIEWS WHAT I DO

I don't think that most people understand how much goes into finally getting a story on the air and how many people are involved. Most people realize that you've got to go with a photographer and you've got to edit the videotape that you shoot, sometimes a 20-minute tape down to two minutes. But I don't think that they fully understand all the ways it can go wrong.

First of all, somebody decides that we're going to cover the story, then somebody decides who's going to cover the story and who the crew will be, then how much time you'll get for the story. Then you edit the story with yet another person. Then you get the story done and the technical people are responsible for getting it on the air. I don't think people really understand the numbers of people involved in getting that story on the air. People think that you go cover a story and you come back and put it on television.

People think this business is glamorous. I have to laugh, as I'm spilling cold pizza on my lap in the back of a truck. I eat so many meals in moving vehicles. There is nothing glamorous about it.

## THE IMPORTANCE OF APPEARANCE

Sometimes people criticize us for the cosmetic aspect of television. But the truth is, people are not going to watch something that they don't find appealing, point one. Point two is that I look a lot better with eye makeup than I do without it, and if I go on television without it, I look real tired. It's hard to concentrate on what I'm saying because people may be thinking, "God, she ought to see a doctor."

Television reporters, mostly women, but men, too, are very careful about their appearance because we don't want to offend in any way—by being too flashy or not flashy enough. We want to be appealing because that's the name of the game. People want to like what they see.

Let me clarify something. Just because you look good doesn't mean you are a good television reporter. Somebody might like the way you look, but there's no way you can maintain a career on your looks. I believe that. What I'm saying is that it's a lot harder to get people to hear what you have to say if they can't stand the way you look.

You can't be totally unattractive. You can't be someone people look at and gasp. I'll tell you something really perfect. We have a weekend anchor at our television station who is bald. Happens to be a man. He's also the first bald man to be anchoring television in Boston. He's a very handsome guy and very attractive in every way, voice and everything else. But still—how many bald men do you know on television?

## WHAT MAKES A GOOD TELEVISION REPORTER

A good reporter is so many things. A good reporter is open-minded. A good reporter is analytical. A good reporter has command of the language, the simple language, the ability to communicate, to use words that everybody knows. It's one thing to talk about "noxious fumes." People know what you're talking about. But not a "conflagration."

A good reporter can communicate with anyone. A good reporter must also have the ability to coordinate events and present them in a way that anyone can understand. A good reporter is competitive. A good reporter is loyal. Loyalty is an important factor, I think, because you want to do the best you can for your employer, not just for yourself. You have a responsibility to the rest of the team, from your boss on down, because Channel 5 doesn't get to be good just because of one reporter. Channel 5 is good because it's a whole team effort.

## THE ROLE OF CONSULTANTS

Management really never lets you know the effect a consultant is having. But you always know when the consultant has been in town because things just happen. All of a sudden for no apparent reason you're told, "You're not wearing red on the air anymore." These things happen and you say, "What's this all about?" Then you know that it's probably the work of the consultants.

One of the people Channel 5 uses, for example, is Magid Associates. Now, I want someone to tell me, who is he? Where did he work? How successful was he? What gives him the right to tell me what my audience wants when he's never even lived in Boston? You just wonder about it.

I believe that every market in the country is different and what works in one place does not necessarily work in another. One of the big complaints we have with consultants is that they'll do something in one market that will be a smash, and then order the same thing for us. And you fall flat on your face.

Periodically we'll be told to do more stand-ups or stand-up bridges, or be told to walk in our stand-ups, be more animated, do more interviews, do fewer interviews—those kinds of things. Mostly, when it comes to the on-air product, it's in terms of a reporter's stand-ups.

I'm sure they have a lot more to say about the anchors, telling the anchors how to sit or how to look. I did some fill-in anchoring a couple of months ago and the man I was working with was the full-time anchor. I said, "Jimmy, what can you tell me about anchoring? I've never done it before. Give me some tips." Well, they sent him to anchor school and he related some of the things they told him. For example, don't ever start a story by saying, "Well, Jim." Why not? "Just don't say 'Well.' It seems to trivialize what you're going to say."

Prove it. I'm not sure I buy it. The other thing is that when you pass a story back and forth to the anchors, you're supposed to look at each other. That was another thing that he suggested. Sometimes they tell you to put your hands on the desk when you're not reading, or get your hands off the desk. Sit up straight. The consultants are the so-called experts in the look of the show.

What happens is that things change fairly regularly. And just because something's good today, it doesn't mean it will be good tomorrow. The producer of the 11 o'clock show will say, "This week we're doing stand-up teases," as it comes down to her from upper-echelon management. Next week, we're not doing stand-up teases. It can vary that much.

I had a kind of bad experience myself, though, and I think it was the result of a consultant. A year or so ago, my boss came to me and he said, "I don't like the way you look on the air." I said, "OK, what is it you don't like?" Well, he not only didn't like my voice, he didn't like my hair, he didn't like my makeup, he wasn't wild about my clothes, and he had some vague complaints about my reporting, but nothing really specific.

I found that once I changed my eye shadow from blue to brown, suddenly he was very happy. I figure a consultant probably said, "Blue's out. Get it off." I look at that now and I laugh. I mean, that little incident is a mosquito. It's a momentary battle, but then you can get beyond it.

## REPORTING VERSUS WRITING

Reporting I like better, just the challenge to get the whos, whats, whys and all that stuff. There's no bigger challenge in life than to arrive on the scene of a breaking news story and get it covered. Getting the information is truly the challenge.

It's a little frightening when you stop and think that for so many people, their only source of news is television. My court case was a good example. The governor's office was flooded, they said, with phone calls and letters, people so incensed at the thought that a reporter might go to jail.

## STORY AT CVS PHARMACY

In February 1985 one of our photographers said he had some information that state police were doing an investigation in Revere [Massachusetts] about allegations that Revere police officers looted a CVS Pharmacy. The people who make the decisions in the newsroom said, "Go see what there is."

First we had to confirm whether or not there was an investigation and we did that through sources at the state police. I broke the story. We had the story on the air, every newscast, for two days.

Then one night, after the 6 o'clock news, I got a phone call from a man who said, "I think I saw the activity at the CVS store and I want to know who I should talk to." And I said, "You really ought to talk to the police," and I gave him the phone number and he said, "I'll call him first thing in the morning."

Then I said, "What did you see?" He said, "I was going to the bank"—there's a bank in the shopping center—"and I saw the police with their cruisers backed up to the store with their trunks open. I really didn't think much about it, but then I saw your report on television. Maybe I saw something. I think I should tell the cops. I want to talk to the investigators, tell them what I saw."

I said, "I'm sure they'll be very happy to hear from you. How about doing an interview with me tonight?" He said, "No. I live in Revere and you don't know these cops. I would be really afraid that there would be harm that would come to me and my family."

And I said, "I tell you what. I'll conceal your identity. We'll do it with your back to the camera and no one will ever see your face." Eventually, I convinced him to do it in time for the 11 o'clock broadcast.

My crew and I met him on his way to work. He put a big jacket on that belonged to one of the crew members, with the collar up, and there was no way you could ever identify him. The camera was trained on the back of his head and me. He described for the camera what he saw that night. The whole interview took maybe four minutes.

I promised him anonymity and said to him, "You've got my word. I'll never tell anybody who you are." As I look back on it, I never had any thought that the next day when he called the state police that he wasn't going to tell them who he was. As it turned out, he never told anybody who he was. Suddenly, I became the only one who knew.

The next morning, I called the police and I said, "Did you see the story last night at 11?" And he said, "Yeah." And I said, "Did you get a call this morning? Was he helpful?" And he said, "Yeah, he was. I'd like to see him but he won't meet with me." And I said, "Why not?" And he said, "Because he doesn't want anybody to know who he is." And I said, "Oooooo."

I told him I couldn't tell him who he was because I promised I wouldn't. But I said, "What I will do is talk to him and try to convince him that he's got to come forward and talk to you in person." I tried to do that, but unsuccessfully.

When the case went to a grand jury, they decided that he was a crucial part of the state's case [against the police officers]. They subpoenaed me before the grand jury at the end of May [1985] and I refused to give them the name. We went back to court a week later and the judge ordered me to reveal the name. Again, I refused, so he ordered me to jail, 90 days in jail. We immediately appealed through the state appeals court. Within a couple of hours, we had a hearing before a single justice. To be real honest, we never held out much hope. I really thought I was going to jail.

In that appellate court session, we asked that the state Supreme Court hear the case and that my jail sentence be stayed pending that consideration of the case. The judge took it under advisement for 24 hours. He said, "I'll make a decision tomorrow."

There's just no question I was absolutely scared to death. Everybody kept saying to me, "Well, don't worry. Governor Dukakis knows what's going on. He's not going to let you rot in jail. Don't worry about it. He'll get you out." It wasn't the fear of the 90 days that bothered me. It was the fear of being locked up. It was the fear of the first time they closed the door and I couldn't get out. I wasn't worried about the conditions in jail. It was the confinement.

My husband has a great sense of humor. That was the only way we could keep it in perspective. If I went to jail they were going to send me to Framingham State because it's the only facility for women. He would say to people, "She'll go to jail until the first sale at Bloomingdale's and then she'll sing like a bird."

The next day the source started to make the decision that he was going to come forward. And a few things happened simultaneously. He made that decision late Wednesday, June 5th, and he met with the district attorney on the 6th. And it was all over. They brought him before the grand jury. All of the police officers were indicted. But his name has still not been made public.

## SOME LESSONS FROM THE EXPERIENCE

I wouldn't do anything differently. I'd do it again, given the same set of circumstances. I wasn't going to give the name. Just because they're threatening to put you in jail doesn't mean that they're going to control the media. If you have to go to jail, you have to go to jail. The press would be vulnerable if it consisted of journalists who didn't believe that. I can't think of a reporter in Boston who wouldn't have done the same thing.

Sure, I didn't want to go to jail. I was scared to death to go to jail, but I was going. There was no question about that. No matter how much we joked about it, the bottom line was that I was going to jail.

There are a lot of questions that were raised, some of which I still haven't answered in my own mind. One is, are we, as reporters, to be considered an extension of the investigatory process at the whim of investigatory agencies? Apparently we are, in my case. And it's up to us to say, "Hey, we're not."

## BEING A REPORTER WHO BECOMES A NEWS ITEM

It was also interesting to walk out of the courtroom and suddenly, there were a dozen cameras. You were pinned to the wall. I said, "Hey, fellas, I'm not going anywhere. Back off." I've thought a lot about that and how and why we do that. We do it not so much because we're afraid that people are going to get away from us, but because we're competitive.

Every photographer wants the best angle. And so they don't really mean to rush the newsmaker. What they're doing is jostling each other, and everybody's trying to get a better position. I think unfortunately very little attention is being given to the feelings of the newsmaker. So sometimes, I guess the criticism is valid.

You figure if you hang around longer than the next guy, you'll get something the next guy didn't get. If a reporter leaves the scene before you do, maybe you'll be there to see something he or she didn't see. If we're accused of being vultures, I assure you it's not because we want to pick the skeleton to death, but only because we want to do a thorough job.

The next week when I went back to work, there was a story where somebody was being held against their will and a relative lived in a nearby town. I went to the relative's house to try to get a comment, and the woman said, "I'm sorry. I just don't want to speak." And I said, "OK. No problem. See ya later." That didn't last. I've gone back to being as persistent as I can in a polite, friendly sort of way. But I could understand what she meant when she said "No." I knew exactly.

## AGENTS AND SALARIES

I know a lot of people in my position who don't want to be bothered with negotiating. We just want to do the job and we want to get paid as much as we possibly can. So it's good to have an agent because I have no idea what other people in town are making.

I've taken a particular interest in it. I've done a lot of asking around. Channel 5, I'm told, pays the least of the three stations. Channels 4 and 7 pay considerably more. An average television reporter at Channel 4, general assignment, I'm told, is paid about $75,000, $80,000. Some of their veteran reporters are making well over $100,000. I think that the average reporter at our place is probably making $65,000 or $70,000.

If an agent is taking care of John Doe and John Doe is coming from another station and his new employer is going to pay him $100,000 for making that switch, and the same agent is taking care of Jane Smith, who's coming from another market, the agent knows what they're paying John Doe, so that can help her.

Yeah, it is too much money. But I think professional athletes make too much money. I'll never turn it down. I'll never say, "$25,000—not a penny more." It's all relative, and if the market can sustain it and that's what the rates are, then that's what the rates are. Never in my wildest dreams did I think the job would pay this much money or that television anchors would be paid hundreds of thousands of dollars.

## THE BURNOUT FACTOR

The other side of the question is there is a tremendous burnout factor. You can't pay me enough to kill myself the way I'm killing myself night after night. Last Thursday night, for example, I was down on the Cape covering a political story. Halfway back from the Cape—this is about an hour away from the station—they tell us there is a general alarm church fire. This is 8:30 at night. The fire is on the other side of Boston by about 40 miles and they want me to get there and they want me to go live at 11.

I don't get there till 10 o'clock. Once I get there, I've got to do interviews, I've got to do a whole story within half an hour so it can be edited and get back on the air, plus I've got to line up guests for my 11 o'clock live shot. Not only have I got to do it all in half an hour, but I've got to do it in the pouring rain.

So the emotional factor, the tension, the stress is incredible. And you have to say, "Well, how much is that worth?" That's worth a lot. You know, on that side of the coin, however much they pay me isn't too much.

I'm not so sure that print reporters have that kind of stress. First of all, print reporters don't have to worry about the way they look, they don't have to worry about running around in the pouring rain in terms of their appearance. I've learned some tricks with the camera—"Shoot me from half a mile away, fellas."

I gotta tell you, as I'm running down to the control room, clutching the script in my hand, 30 seconds before 11 every night, I say to myself, "I'm getting too old for this crap." And I don't use the word *crap*.

But you never get too old if you love it. If they say, "We've got a general alarm fire at a church," and you say, "I don't feel good. I'm tired. Send somebody else," you're not tired of the story. You're looking to get out of the business.

## WHAT TO REMEMBER ABOUT LIVE REPORTING

If a fire burned something down yesterday, we may show you video today from when it was burning, but we're not going to stand in front of the building just for the sake of a live shot. The management at our station has had the good sense to steer away from that crap. You're fooling people. That's show biz.

The most important thing that you have to learn about reporting live is concentration. The minute people see that television camera, they're transformed into maniacs. I'm not talking about the news-makers. I'm talking about the onlookers. Suddenly, people who appear in every other way to be stable individuals with responsibilities, when they see that camera, they turn into raving lunatics who want to wave and scream and jump up and down and look ridiculous on television.

It's also some kind of national sport, around here anyway, to try to make the reporter laugh or in some other way take attention away from what they're supposed to be doing.

Just a couple of weeks ago, I was doing a live shot in Copley Square. It was the hottest day of the year, and it was a story about weather. And we were really having some fun with the story because, let's face it, the weather's not death and destruction.

So I did the live shot at 11 o'clock in Copley Square and there was a man standing not three feet away from me with an ice cream cone. And I knew I was getting that ice cream cone in the face before I went off the air. I absolutely sensed it. That man was going to stick his hand over and put that ice cream cone square in the middle of my forehead. I spent the entire time thinking what I was going to say when that happened.

The way I handled it was I said on the air that, "People have been wonderful. As a matter of fact, I've had offers of free ice cream from people"—so that, if in fact it happened, people would almost be expecting it. But then once he heard me say that, the effect was gone for him, too.

You've really got to be able to concentrate because people come by and they scream or honk or do all kinds of things. I was once doing a live shot at a food line. Vice President Bush had said there weren't hungry people in the country. So, of course, we set out to prove him wrong. The general feeling at our station was that there were hungry people in Boston so we set out to see what their reaction to the vice president's comments were. I found myself doing a live shot at a food line at the Salvation Army.

In the middle of my live shot, a man goosed me. And it was nothing that was obvious on the air. The only way it was going to become obvious was if I made it obvious by saying, "Ooooo. Somebody just goosed me. Well, I'll be darned." So it was one of the biggest challenges of my career. I had to continue. I made this little deal with God—he could make it up to me another time, but please don't let me laugh. Just not now.

## PERSONAL LIFE

Some days the news drives my life, some days it doesn't. The news has as much effect on my life as I want it to have. If they beeped me right now and said, "We want you to come in and do something," it would depend on the story. If a big one went down, I'd have to say, "Come with me."

My husband, Bobby, is in sports and I'm in news, but we work for competing stations. There are very few mornings that we really just lie around and do nothing. We both have responsibilities between 6 p.m. and 11 p.m. Sometimes he's got to do an update at midnight, sometimes a game will still be going on. So the latest he's home is at 12:30. If I've done a live shot, I'm not going to be home much before 1 a.m. But if we're both home and I have to say, "I gotta go to work," he understands, because he does it more.

## BEING KNOWN IN THE COMMUNITY

In a lot of ways, you're a goodwill ambassador. When people recognize you, it's a compliment most of the time because that means you've had enough of a presence to have an impact on them so they remember your face or your name. You must try to be as pleasant as you can. You even try to be pleasant to people who are abusive, and now and then that happens.

I don't like the word *celebrity* because I don't do anything. I do a job and I do my job the best I possibly can. I've tried often to think of a word that I prefer instead of celebrity, and I really don't have one. I guess I want people to respect me and to believe me—credibility is very important—but I don't want people to feel I'm important just because I'm on television. That's garbage.

My job is to inform the public—to be the eyes, the ears, the nose, the voice and, in some regards, the mind of the viewing audience. I don't want to make up the audience's minds for them, but I am their minds in terms of digesting everything that's happened over three or four hours and spitting it back so they'll understand it. That's my job.

*Susan Wornick*                                                                                185

CVS

the scene of the revere investigation shifted to the suffolk superior

courthouse today... state police detectives met with officials ~~of~~ *from*

the district attorney's office ~~to request an investigative grand jury~~

~~to continue the probe into~~

*detectives* ~~have~~ asked *district attorney* to convene

~~the~~ state police, ~~are asking~~ the ~~d a will order~~ an investigative

grand jury to continue the probe into allegations that ~~8~~ revere

*in the overnight hours of February first.*
police officers participated in a burglary at the local cvs store,

*but* *to convene the grand jury* *secret*
the decision ~~apaprently~~ rests on an eyewitness ~~written~~ account

*So far, that man has refused to identify himself to investigators.*
of the robbery. ~~that man who has requested annonymity detailed~~

*He first told*
his story to newcenter 5. ~~told newscenter 5~~ he was at the all-

night banking machine nearby when he saw revere police putting

merchandise into a cruiser. bank statements and deposit slips

~~at the time the breakin~~
verify the man was there ~~at the in the early morning hours~~ . ~~.when~~

*at the time* breakin
~~of the crime.. of~~ the ~~robbery~~ occured.

altho he has talked to police ~~but~~ this eyewitness refuses to go

public .. because ~~probably~~ he is afraid of ~~the possible~~ retribution ...

he disguised his voice this afternoon in a telephone interview..

[sot... ]

the final decision on whether or not to convene an investigative

grand jury will be made by district attorney newman flannagan.

late this afternoon first assistant Paul Leary said there are many

*week*
factu[~~y~~]ds to be considered .. and it will be next before the matter is

settled.

*Susan Wornick talks about this story on pp. 179–181. This is a close reproduction of the script from one of the follow-up stories about the CVS Pharmacy burglary that was aired on WCVB. The story that was aired the night the witness phoned Wornick is part of the court file and cannot be duplicated. Because the original script is difficult to read, a transcript of the story follows. Courtesy of WCVB-TV, Boston.*

# Follow-up to the Revere Police Investigation

The scene of the Revere CVS investigation shifted to the Suffolk Superior Courthouse today. State police detectives met with officials from the district attorney's office.

State police detectives asked the district attorney to convene an investigative grand jury to continue the probe into allegations that Revere police officers participated in a burglary at the local CVS store in the overnight hours of last February first.

But the decision to convene the grand jury rests on a secret eyewitness account of the robbery. So far, that man has refused to identify himself to investigators.

He first told his story to NewsCenter 5. He was at the all-night banking machine nearby when he saw Revere police putting merchandise into a cruiser. Bank statements and deposit slips verify the man was there at the time the break-in occurred.

Although he has talked to police, this eyewitness refuses to go public because he is afraid of retribution. He disguised his voice this afternoon in a telephone interview.

The final decision on whether or not to convene an investigative grand jury will be made by district attorney Newman Flannagan. Late this afternoon first assistant Paul Leary said there are many factors to be considered, and it will be next week before the matter is settled.

NBC-TV

*I have not arrived at a party in years without finding the host and hostess still in their underwear. Because of my conditioning to deadlines, if they say 8 o'clock, I arrive at 8 o'clock.*

# DON OLIVER

After more than six hours of talking about his broadcasting career, Don Oliver turns and says, "But that's enough about me." His eyes begin to wrinkle in the corners. "Now let's talk about what *you* think about me."

Don Oliver is an imp. His colleagues have nicknamed him "The Devil," and he uses the name for himself. His wry view has helped him through 30 years in broadcasting, 20 of them as a network correspondent for NBC.

He began as a graduate of the University of Montana School of Journalism in 1959. In 1985, he returned to Montana to help celebrate the opening of new campus studios for the broadcasting students. When Oliver attended the school, he says, they had only a tape recorder and a microphone.

From 1959 until his return to Montana in 1985, Oliver worked all over the West in radio and television at five local stations before joining the NBC network in 1966, covering the Midwest from Cleveland, Ohio. He transferred to NBC's Los Angeles bureau in 1969, where he has been based ever since, except for two years when he worked in Tokyo.

Oliver, 50, has covered political candidates since 1968, and in 1984 he was one of four NBC correspondents on the floor of both the Democratic and Republican nominating conventions. When he is not covering campaigns, he works general assignment.

Among Oliver's assignments in the last 20 years at the network: the assassination of Martin Luther King Jr., the Charles Manson trial, the Patty Hearst kidnapping, the Alaska pipeline controversy, the wars in Vietnam, Cambodia and Laos (Oliver was the first American television correspondent allowed back in Vietnam after the fall of Saigon), the peace talks in the Middle East in 1977, and the riots in Manila following the assassination of Benigno Aquino. He has reported from most of the countries in the world for NBC, and says he travels about 100,000 miles a year.

189

Oliver prides himself on his ability to get a story accurately and quickly. He talks in a rich baritone voice. His manner is self-confident and engaging. He likes to tell stories, and he can remember details from reporting adventures that took place 20 years ago as easily as he remembers yesterday's news. He loves a laugh, even if it's on himself. He begins his story with characteristic self-deprecating humor. ❖

SPECIAL PERSPECTIVES
*from Don Oliver*
- Covering diplomatic stories
- How to meet a deadline
- New television technologies

# BEGINNINGS

I was born at an early age. I got interested in journalism when I was in junior high school. I applied for a job writing for the junior high school newspaper in Billings, Montana, and I got it.

When I got into high school, I kept taking journalism courses. I thought people needed to have the benefit of my cleverness, so I decided that I'd write for the school paper, where they could all see how clever I was. I also was a stringer for the local newspaper, doing school sports—the *Billings Gazette*. They paid me 11 cents a column inch.

When I graduated from high school, I decided to go to journalism school. I knew that people made a lot more money in radio and TV because I had talked to people in the business. And I figured, well, hell, I might as well get into this television—whatever it was. We didn't have television in Billings until I was a junior in high school. I never saw it at home. I had seen it for the first time in Los Angeles on a trip when I was about 11 years old.

## ENROLLS AT THE UNIVERSITY OF MONTANA

So I went to the University of Montana and enrolled in the radio and television sequence. That was 1954, and I was 18. Good school. I learned a hell of a lot. About 80 percent of the journalism classes were regular writing classes and 20 percent were geared toward radio and television.

They really had nothing other than a tape recorder, as I recall, and a microphone. By the time I was a junior, they had put in a small broadcast station. It made my mother happy because she got to hear me on the radio once. When I graduated, I had a double degree—a degree in journalism and a degree in history and political science. University of Montana, Missoula—1958.

Finally, I got a job working mostly for United Press, which was in the same building as the radio station in Helena, Montana. The manager of the radio station and the United Press bureau chief split my salary between United Press and KXLJ. I wrote copy for the radio station, but I didn't do it on the air. The general manager of the radio station would come in and read it.

One night he called in sick and wondered if I would do it. I was not great, but I guess I was adequate because he came in the next day and offered me $5 more a month—I started there at $310 a month to do the program as well as write it.

After two months, I went to work for the radio station full-time, writing copy, learning to run the board, and doing a little bit of television. Then I heard they were looking for a radio announcer in Great Falls, paying this magnificent salary of $415 a month. I was hired in May 1959 at KFBB as a disc jockey. I sat there and spun those stacks of wax.

After about three months, there came an opening in television at the same place. We had United Press news film that arrived anywhere from a week to two weeks after something had happened. We would string it together and say, "You might remember that earthquake that happened last month." It was always film. We had the Ed Sullivan Christmas Show around Easter.

## MOVES TO SPOKANE

I decided after nine months that I had to find a real job somewhere. And a former professor of mine dropped me a note saying that a major market was looking for TV newsmen to write radio news and 11 o'clock television newscasts. It was in Spokane, Washington, which may or may not be a major market, but from my perspective it was. It was Mecca.

I started at KHQ in May of 1960, writing afternoon radio news until drive time—although I'd never heard of drive time. I was the evening news editor and writer. It paid very little, but gave enormous titles. I was making $500 a month. I began to do some television work in the afternoon—go out and cover stories, do stand-uppers, pretty exciting things like that.

I never learned to really run the sound equipment, but I learned enough to know what you can do and what you can't do. In later years, at least I knew when a cameraman was telling me he couldn't do something and I knew damn well he could.

## THE CONSEQUENCES OF THE NEWS

One night, the cameraman shot an accident, nobody really hurt or anything. A little while later, we got another one. This one had a really good injury, and I said on the two-way radio to him, "That's really great. We'll put the two together and that'll make something interesting."

He came back and said, "Well, that may be great for us, but I don't think the people involved were too thrilled with it." This was the first time I really felt that you are making your living off other people's misery. To me, it was something that would make my news program fresher. To the people involved, it was something that may have ruined their whole lives. Maybe it took every bit of money they had, maybe the guy lost his job. That was the first time in my embryonic career that I really realized that you feed off other people's problems when you're in the news business.

## OPENING UP KIFI

After about a year there, in 1961, I learned of a new station opening in Idaho Falls—KIFI—looking for a news director. So they hired me.

I got there the day they were to have their gala grand opening program. I arrived in the early afternoon, I had driven down with my wife—we had one baby then—and went in for the rehearsal. Nobody knew their lines, they didn't have the sets built. As it turned out, of all the people they'd hired, I was the only one who had ever been in television before. So I was the first one on the air for the station, sitting on a stool in the middle of the studio, saying "Welcome to Channel 8, KIFI."

We had a 15-minute newscast. I started off with a Polaroid camera, which took slides of train wrecks. You stuck the slides in a rear screen projector. I would stand there and this wreck or a dead body would pop up behind me. I was it. Every once in a while the station photographer would help me and shoot some film, but we had to send it to Salt Lake City to be processed.

So I thought we really ought to have our own processor. He and I built one out of three galvanized tanks, an old turntable motor and a bunch of bicycle chains and pulleys. Then we had a real film dryer. We put it in my office. My office was underneath the stairs back in the storeroom, and I found a place on top of a balcony in the storeroom to put the film dryer. That lasted for nine months.

## ATTENDS COLUMBIA UNIVERSITY

One day I got in the mail an application to apply for a scholarship given by NBC to the graduate school of journalism at Columbia. It was open to all employees of NBC stations—this was an NBC affiliate. So I applied. This is 1961, now. I'm not sure why, but I won it. I spent September of '61 to June of '62 at Columbia. My wife went to Montana and stayed with her parents. I lived in a converted hallway—it was about 800 feet long and 3 feet wide.

I felt I needed to know more about how journalism worked in the big city and how it applied to social, political and economic topics of our day. It was a fascinating experience for me. I learned a hell of a lot. Never regretted it. I got a master of science in Journalism.

## WORKING AT KCRA

I went around to a variety of stations and finally, I got a call from KCRA in Sacramento. This was now July of 1962. When I was being interviewed the news director asked me what my goal was, and I told him it was to become a network correspondent. He said, "Well, I wouldn't tell the owners of the station that, because they'd like to think that you want to make this your career." When I had my first lunch with the owners, I said, "I'd like to settle down here."

I was at KCRA from 1961 to 1965, a long time for me. I'd never been anywhere for more than a year before that. By 1966 I was in Cleveland as a Midwest network correspondent for NBC. I wound up doing a lot of things for "The Today Show."

## PERSONAL LIFE

It became increasingly difficult once I went to work for the network because I was gone birthdays, wedding anniversaries, children's birthdays, little important events in my family's lives, graduation from kindergarten and that sort of thing. I was invariably somewhere else. I think I spent my wedding anniversary three straight years, sitting in airports somewhere, catching a plane.

It put a strain on our relationship, I suppose, on many of them. I know very few network correspondents who haven't been married at least twice, or at least divorced once. The year 1967 was bad enough. We had only one car, and so in the middle of winter, I'd come back from a story, my wife would have to bundle the children up at 11 o'clock at night and drive down to the end of the rapid transit line and pick me up and take me home.

I remember going to work one day and they said, "Go to Pittsburgh." Some story of minor significance. I went to Pittsburgh and that story didn't pan out. They said, "Get to Detroit immediately. Ford Motor Company has just been struck by the United Auto Workers." Twenty-one days later, I got home, without having packed a bag—no clothes, no shaving kit. I had to buy all these things along the way. Wore the same clothes most every day.

But there was never a point at which I said, maybe I ought to give up my career. I was doing what I wanted to do. I felt we'd weather it somehow. I was making more money than I'd ever made before. I was enjoying it. I liked the pace, liked the idea of having a reputation of being able to go into an area, size it up quickly, get the story done and get it on the air. It's a heady feeling. I was 29 when I went to work for the network. I was eager. I was ready to go anywhere, anytime, any-place. Phone calls in the middle of the night—great. Leap out of bed and grab a suitcase and head for the airport. I knew every airport in the Midwest—intimately. It gives you a sense of satisfaction. You say, "Gee, I'm having such a good time doing this, and I'm getting rewarded for it as well." The business was everything I'd really hoped it would be.

## A MOVE TO LOS ANGELES

After the '68 campaign, I wanted to leave Cleveland. I always knew when I was arriving in Cleveland by looking out the window of the airplane. If I couldn't see anything, I knew Cleveland must be some-where nearby. And my wife was once attacked by a large ball of flame in the sky, which she hadn't seen for so long, she failed to realize it was the sun. Shortly after the first of the year, 1969, I packed up my furniture and my family and moved to LA.

## A MOVE OVERSEAS

In '72, I did not do the campaign. Then in '74, I was getting a divorce and I moved to Tokyo, knowing only two words of Japanese—"Good morning" and "Thank you."

I'd been there three or four months and there was a demonstration in front of the Korean embassy. The Japanese were mad at the Koreans for something. And they had all the riot police there, water cannons and all that. The camera crew and I went to find out what the hell was going on.

I got separated from the crew—I was on one side of the police lines and they were on the other. So I thought, how do I say, "I am an American television reporter?" So I said, "Oh, hell." I went up to the riot police and said, "Wataski-wa NBC. No America-teribi Densha-desu." And he gave me a sort of blank look, and I said it again. He said, "Dozo," which means "Please," and let me by. So my crew asked me, "What did you tell him?" I told them and they rolled on the ground laughing. What I had said was, "I am an American television electric train."

I liked doing stories that compared and contrasted what went on in Japan with what goes on in the United States. Then at the end of 1974, I found myself in Southeast Asia. I spent almost all of the first six months of 1975 either in Cambodia, Laos or Vietnam.

## REPORTING IN SOUTHEAST ASIA

Had I been prepared, I might have been so scared all the time that I couldn't function. Other than the riots I had covered in the United States, a few shoot-outs with police, I wasn't really prepared to be in combat a lot. That was at the end of the Vietnam War. I was in situations, as I look back on them now, where I think I would have been frantic had I realized the level of danger that was involved.

## COVERING THE EVACUATION OF NHA TRANG

During the evacuation of Nha Trang, I was scared, but I wasn't as scared as I should have been. It was a town along the coast, about 150 miles north of Saigon. Everybody had cleared out because they knew the NVA [North Vietnamese Army] and the Viet Cong were moving in. We decided to go back for one more story about how they were evacuating the town.

We got into Nha Trang and they were loading the dependents of the military onto boats to take them out. We shot this graphic story of a baby being carried to the shore by a woman who said the mother was on board one of these boats. She had been given the baby to hold for a while and couldn't find the mother but knew she was on the boat. So they put this baby in a pail and sent it up to the boat like he was on a boatswain's line, this milk pail sort of thing. They got the baby up—and we shot the whole thing—and everybody cheered as the baby landed on the boat.

Two minutes later, it was determined that the mother was on the shore. She had never gotten on the boat. And they had to put the baby back in the bucket and send it back down. This is at a time when people are running around in jeeps and maneuvering madly. It was a very tense time.

We left the shore and decided to drive back into the heart of Nha Trang. The streets were pretty well deserted. We headed toward the hotel where we'd been staying and, as we came around the street, we saw a tank coming toward us. I knew goddamn good and well that this had to be the enemy heading in our direction.

We commandeered one of the cars in the compound and drove as fast as we could toward the airport. We went to the main terminal and it turned out to be the wrong place to go, so we got rides on the backs of motorcycles with a bunch of Vietnamese, and a whole group of ARVN [Army of the Republic of Vietnam] soldiers were there, extremely angry because they felt the United States had betrayed them. And they started shooting. One of the guys I was with, who was Vietnamese, realized they were shooting at me. He yelled at the motorcycle driver to turn around and get me out of there, which he did. I didn't get hit.

We all went to the Air America terminal, which was where the flights were leaving, and there was one plane left, with about a thousand refugees trying to get on that airplane. I finally got on the plane, a DC-4. There must have been 200 people on a plane built to hold 50 or 60. There were babies. Of the 200 people probably 50 percent were kids who just got thrown on the plane by their parents, who didn't get on the plane themselves.

The pilot just wheeled the thing off the tarmac and onto the taxiway. They were firing at us as we took off. We landed in Saigon about 40 minutes later. I arrived in Saigon carrying a kid under each arm as we got off the airplane, and we handed the kids to some Red Cross people who were there to meet us.

In Saigon, we walked into the office, and people were happy to see that we were alive because everybody thought we'd been killed. Word had already spread all over Saigon that Nha Trang had fallen and that anybody left there had probably been done away with. They seemed to be relatively happy that we'd gotten out of there. I think somebody even bought me a drink that night.

---

## WORKING THROUGH INTERPRETERS

In Southeast Asia, no one was required to understand Vietnamese, Khmer, Laotian, so you had interpreters and you had to rely on them. The reporters with the best interpreters, of course, did the best job.

But you lose the nuances. I don't like it. I don't like being dependent on somebody, standing there like a dummy while two people talk. But since everybody is in the same boat, you're not in a position where your colleagues know something you don't.

However, since then, having spent some time in El Salvador, and much more recently in Mexico, the situation is entirely different. I don't speak Spanish. It is required that you speak Spanish, if you're going to cover those countries. First, the people who live there expect you to speak Spanish and second, the people you're competing against speak Spanish. If you don't speak the language, even if you have wonderful interpreters, as I've had, you still lose a little bit of an edge.

After the earthquake [in Mexico in 1985] I'm sure I could have come up with quotes that I would have wanted. I got some, but I was never too sure that they were the best ones. I would like to make that decision, rather than having an interpreter tell me, as they're pulling babies out of the rubble of the hospital, exactly what is being said.

## COVERING DIPLOMATIC STORIES

You can't be covering stories that are complicated—diplomatic stories or economic stories—without knowing the language. The first thing a reporter does in any country where he doesn't speak the language is head for the U.S. Embassy and get a briefing from whoever is in charge of the section you're dealing with. I've found that's not always the most accurate source. They're going to tell you things that represent the position of the U.S. government, not necessarily what's really going on.

The Philippines is a good case in point. When you used to go to a briefing in the U.S. Embassy in Manila [in early 1985], Marcos was wonderful—maybe he has some excesses, but we don't think it's bad. We need those bases. Now, of course, the tune has changed entirely because there's a new threat of communist insurgence in that country, and the one thing the American government dislikes more than instability or repression in a country is the threat of communism.

Suddenly the U.S. government is saying, "Oh, my God, the communists could take over that country in three to five years." So we can't support Marcos anymore. And these are the same policies Marcos had been following for years that we perceived as good policies. Now, suddenly, they're bad policies. So the point is, you're not going to get the story by going to the U.S. Embassy.

## AMERICAN REPORTERS IN FOREIGN COUNTRIES

A reporter has to be smart enough to know that what the officials in a country are telling him may or may not be the truth, may not be valid based on the history and culture of the country you're working with. You can't take things at face value just because they fit into an American context. If you don't know that, if you haven't had the education or the opportunity to get a good backgrounding in that country, you're going to accept it because you don't have any other frame of reference.

## RETURNS TO THE U.S.

In January of '76, I got a call from New York saying they were short of people to cover the campaign and they wondered if I would be willing to come back. I came back to cover the Reagan campaign from mid-January.

I'll never forget the first day I was with the campaign. After living in the Orient for two years, we were in Winchester, New Hampshire, doing a luncheon, and we got the salad, and I had picked up the salad bowl and had the fork up underneath my lips as you would if you were eating with chopsticks. The sound man sitting next to me said, "We don't do that in this country." I didn't even realize it.

I stayed with Reagan until about the end of March and then shifted over to Jimmy Carter. I stayed with Carter until two days after the election, often awakening in the morning and having to look at the phone book to know what town I was in. I was on the road 300 days out of 360 in 1976. My home that year was the Best Western Motel in Americus, Georgia, where most of my worldly possessions were.

---

## BEING ON THE CAMPAIGN BUS

You wake up at about 5 o'clock, because you have a 6 a.m. baggage call. You have to have your bags down to the lobby by 6 o'clock so they can take them out to the airplane. If you're smart, the night before, you take out what you're going to wear the next morning and go down to the press room in your underwear and put your bag down with everything that you don't need in it. That way, you can sleep until about 7 for an 8 o'clock departure.

Generally, toward the end of the campaign, you have one event in New York City at 8 o'clock in the morning—a rally at Grand Central Station, time for the candidate to be seen live on the morning news program at all three networks. Once the candidate leaves on the train, you're still there live on the platform, telling the audience that the candidate's train has just pulled out.

Then you get in a car with a surly courier and he takes you to a helicopter pad on the East River, and you get up in the helicopter and you try to get ahead of the train. You are met by a producer somewhere in New Jersey, who's in a rental car, and he says, "We've got four and a-half minutes to get into the station before the train gets there."

When you get to the station, you get on the train and go as far as maybe Trenton, where the airplane, which had been in New York the night before, has flown on ahead of you. The whole entourage gets off the train and onto many buses and you go to the statehouse for a rally with the governor, if he's in your [the presidential candidate's] party. If he's not, you go somewhere else and have a rally with someone else who's running against the governor.

Then you get on the airplane after the rally in Trenton, you fly to Dallas/Fort Worth Airport and hold a rally. By then, it's probably 1 o'clock in the afternoon Texas time, so if Texas is an important state to you, you may fly to Houston, have another rally midafternoon, and then another one in El Paso.

Then you get on the airplane again and fly from El Paso to San Francisco, so you can arrive to get coverage on the 11 o'clock news. The candidate goes off to bed, while the rest of us who have morning news programs to worry about write a story and hand the narration track to the producer, who then has to go cut it. If you don't have a producer or you don't trust your producer to do it properly, you head for your affiliate or your office in that city.

Remember you've lost three hours going across the country and you've got a 5 o'clock wakeup call. Then it's 3 or 4 in the morning by the time you get back to the hotel and have a couple of drinks to quiet you down, and get to your room and tuck yourself in, like good reporters are supposed to do. The next morning, you do the same thing.

When you're on the bus or on the plane every day, all you know is what's going on in your immediate circle. But you don't know how people are reacting to the candidate. All you know is that you got on another plane that flew to another city—maybe in the same state, maybe halfway across the country. It becomes kind of roadless, and there's a tendency toward pack journalism. People tend to compare notes, and when they do, the coverage has a certain sameness to it.

I have made friendships that have existed for 18 years, people that I'd never know before, but I see every four years now—political reporters from Washington, D.C. Every four years, unfortunately, they get very old. Much older than I am.

## IN EGYPT FOR CHRISTMAS

In '77, I was in Egypt for about 10 days, when [Menachem] Begin went to Egypt. I remember I spent Christmas of 1977 in a hotel in Egypt, which had clammy walls, running water everywhere. There were lots of Americans there, from NBC and all over the world, gathered in this hotel. We had one stocking that someone had found and hung it up, and a couple of bottles of cheap, Bulgarian wine. And we celebrated Christmas Eve in the lobby of this hotel—one stocking, two bottles of wine, singing Christmas carols.

## THE IMPORTANCE OF GENERAL KNOWLEDGE

I'm a firm believer that you have to have a good grounding in political science, history, and, as I said, I regret not having taken a foreign language. Beyond that, economics, a journalism degree—I have two of them.

A journalism degree does give you a little bit of technique of the trade, but perhaps more important, journalism professors can give you an idea of the ethics, the honor in the business, the dos and don'ts. I certainly wouldn't advise somebody who was serious about getting into journalism to take communications courses that spend a lot of time talking about how radio waves go from one point to another, or how to set up a pedestal dolly on a television camera.

There's somebody around who will do that, or you'll learn it if you go to a small station. There's not going to be anybody around who can talk to you about the Peloponnesian War and how that may have affected wars that are going on now. You've got to have a context of history.

You've got to know what came before. If you're talking about labor strikes, you need to know something about the history of the labor movement in this country. You will know about precedents. You won't say this is the first time in the history of the labor movement that they've overturned cars, because you know it happened in Detroit during the organization of the Autoworkers' Union—I'm just using that as an example. Things have gone on before, and you may not use them, but it prevents you from saying or writing foolish things. You don't have to make broad generalizations—"many years ago."

## WHAT MAKES A GOOD TELEVISION REPORTER

For television, it's knowing how to combine the spoken word with the pictures and sound that are available to you. You should get more than two minutes worth of information from a two-minute story because you're attacking two senses, rather than just one. It's a prized ability in television to be able to write well for tape or film, to use them to complement each other. It's grand when you can do that.

You've got to be able to talk. So, to that extent, voice is important, but only if your voice is weird. It's going to detract from your ability to make yourself understood. I knew a guy who sounded like a eunuch wailing in the wind, and he was a pretty good reporter, but his voice detracted so much from what he was trying to tell people that when I heard him, all I could think was, "Boy, he's got a weird voice. Nobody's going to be able to get any information."

You've got to be able to write, of course. I don't think anybody who's interested in expository writing is going to be particularly suited or happy with television, because you've got to learn to write in simple sentences.

Having a sense of humor is important, because you're going to be frustrated a lot of the time because you're not given as much time as you think you need to do a story, or your story isn't used. You're either on the front page on television or you're not in the game. You can't say, "Look where they put me. They put me on page 18." There is no page 18.

You can't get excited, either. You have to be fairly calm without being so calm that people think you're dead. Television has as demanding a deadline as any business in the world. When the clock hits that certain point, if you're not ready, the picture goes black, and a lot of people flip their dials, which causes your bosses to be very agitated because they lose money. When they lose money, they don't think kindly of you. And you hear about it.

## THE IMPORTANCE OF DEADLINES

I have not arrived at a party in years without finding the host and hostess still in their underwear. Because of my conditioning to deadlines, if they say 8 o'clock, I arrive at 8 o'clock.

I guess it would be nice to have the luxury of saying, "When I finish this story, we'll put it on." But I'm not sure you ever feel like you've finished something. There's always something else you could do, so you have to have some kind of artificial deadline that says, "Now's the time. You can't tinker with it anymore."

You've always got to get used to new deadlines. Working on the West Coast, deadlines are a great deal more inconvenient than on the East Coast. We have to have everything done by 3 o'clock our time, which is 6 o'clock New York time, for the program that goes on the air at 6:30. Unless it's a disaster or something like that, you really can't go out and start working on a story before 8 o'clock in the morning, because nobody's in their offices. But you learn to live with that.

I pride myself on being a fairly fast writer. I've had to rewrite three-minute stories in half an hour. I've flown into towns where, literally, we were shooting as the airplane landed, and getting off that airplane running, trying to do what we could in an hour and a half.

## BACK-TIMING TO DEADLINES

When you hit an emergency situation, you're thinking in time segments. You begin back-timing everything: How long is the flight to get there? How much driving time are you going to have at the other end? How much flying time? Then, in the middle is the amount of time to cover the story, because it doesn't matter if you cover it wonderfully well. If you don't get it back in time to get on the air, you haven't accomplished much.

One time when I was working in Sacramento, a plane had crashed near Danville. We covered the crash, and two days later it was determined that the plane had crashed because the pilot had been shot in the back of the head. So we raced to the airport, got this helicopter, headed to Danville, got there, did an interview with the officials who were investigating, and headed back to Sacramento.

Unfortunately, the pilot was new to the area. We were flying over the Sacramento/San Joaquin Delta, which is a maze of islands and waterways, and he foolishly allowed me to navigate. I thought we were headed due north, but it turned out we were headed out due east. We ran low on fuel to the point where the fuel warning light came on, which meant you had another minute to fly. So the pilot had to put it down right where we were—which was along Interstate 99 between Stockton and Sacramento.

I grabbed the film magazine and climbed the fence to get on the freeway. After about two or three minutes, this car came shuddering to a stop. It looked like it had gone through the bombing of Berlin. It was a gutted hulk. The guy driving it was an itinerant laborer from San Jose who was on his way to Lake Tahoe to gamble.

So I said to him, "If you get me to Sacramento by 5, that'll get me enough time to get this stuff on the air." He kept saying, "I try." I have no idea how fast we were going because the speedometer didn't work, but the car was all over the road. I don't think it had been aligned in about 12 years. We drove up in front of the station with about two minutes to spare. The last thing he said to me was, "When I get back to San Jose, no one is going to believe I picked up a man in a helicopter."

But I had to get there. Otherwise what we had done would have been worthless. If I'd strolled in at 6:30 or 7 o'clock and said, "Boy, we've got a great story for the 11 o'clock," and somebody else had it on at 6, we'd have been at a disadvantage.

## REPORTING LIVE

The advantage of being able to go live is that in a developing story, you can provide your viewers with whatever's happened up to the moment. That, to me, is the only advantage of it.

When setting up to go live actually interferes with covering the story that, to me, is unconscionable, but it happens more and more because they place this great importance on saying, "Joe Blow is live at the scene." Then Joe Blow comes on and he says, "Just nine hours ago, at the corner of Maple and Grant, two cars collided. No one was injured in the crash, but many of the neighbors heard it. Mrs. Jones here didn't actually hear it—she was on the telephone—but her son heard it, but he's in school right now, so we can't talk to him, but she's right here with us. Tell us what your son heard this morning when these two cars collided just nine hours ago."

First of all, you gain nothing by being live, and probably you could have done a hell of a lot better job of covering the story if you hadn't been live. If it was worth reporting on at all, you could have taken that material back to the station and honed it a bit and not had to spend your time standing on a street corner.

A lot of PR people have realized that if something happens at 2 o'clock in the afternoon, no one cares. If it happens live at 5, it's going to be covered because the reporter can say, "We take you now to the Acme Supermarket opening at the corner of 4th and Grand, where they have avocados on special sale tonight."

I think the public has become too sophisticated. First of all, they don't care about satellite transmissions—so what? And they don't really care if somebody's live unless something's happening.

## MISTAKES REPORTERS MAKE

There's probably more of a tendency now because the art of public relations has gotten so sophisticated not to question what you're being told, to just look at it and say, "Well, they're telling me that. It must be the truth."

When you have the pressures to go live or to do five stories in a day, you don't have time to devote to one story. The person who is most accessible to you is the one who's going to get the most air time. So people who are schooled in the art of public relations are going to make themselves accessible.

It may take a little more time to find out what's really going on because the people you need to talk to aren't standing there with a press packet. A press packet is probably the worst thing that was ever invented because a reporter tends to think, "Well, I've got the press packet now. What else do I need? This should tell me everything I need to know." The reporter takes a few feet [of tape] of the people sitting around in the audience at the meeting and goes back to start the next story or go to lunch.

Also, prejudging is a problem. When you are limited in the amount of time to cover something, you may have a scenario fixed in your mind. Then you arrive at the scene of the story and things aren't what you thought they would be, but because the reporter has already fixed in his mind how he's going to write that story, he tends to go with his predisposition, rather than change it in the middle of the story. I've seen people do that.

## A SPECIAL INTERVIEWING HINT

The best thing is to try to be prepared ahead of time, to try to anticipate answers. You say, "I know you pleaded not guilty to the charge, but your ex-wife says that you weren't home that night and you offered no alibi for where you were. How can you justify your plea of not guilty when you don't have an alibi?" If you let the subject know that you know a little more than the average person, they feel that perhaps they can't snow you.

If somebody answers a question and you know that isn't the answer they really would give, you just sit there and watch them. Nature abhors a vacuum. People who are doing an interview hate dead air. If you just sit there and look at them, they feel compelled to keep talking, and usually you get a much better answer after that first answer—just by not saying anything, or by saying, "Please elaborate on that," or by just looking at them like, "Certainly you have more to say on that," and just wait and see what they say.

You're trying to get an answer that's under 20 seconds. Sometimes you have to ask the question 15 different ways. I don't consider it dishonest or unethical. If you ask a question and you get a rambling answer that you can't possibly use on television, then you think of another way to ask it, so you can get an answer that is useful to you. You don't say to the person, "I want a shorter answer." You re-ask it in a little different manner. They may say, "I already answered that," and you say, "Well, could you elaborate a little bit on it?"

The main thing is to ask people questions so that your knowledge of the situation is enhanced. Interviews aren't done strictly to get a talking head to put on the air. They're done so you know what the story is. I've seen reporters sit down with somebody and say, "Tell me about it," and give someone 15 seconds and say, "That's all I needed," and they walk out because they have just gotten the sound bite they needed for their piece. You need the sound bite, but you also need to know as much as that person can give you that is germane to the story.

## THE EFFECT OF RATINGS

The competition for space and time on the "Today" program, the "CBS Morning News" or "Good Morning America" is split between soft features, things that don't have any bearing on news, and news coverage. In the last few years, if you take a look at the mix, news stories have suffered. They're far fewer. If it's not Hollywood or if it doesn't have a little glitz and glamour to it, it's going to be tough to get on the air. To that extent, ratings do affect network correspondents, because they figure their ability to compete for ratings is enhanced by providing more of what we call "infotainment" segments.

Look at the nightly news programs—all three networks. There's a great deal more trivialization and not the intensity than at any time in the 20 years that I've worked for the network. Whenever you've got 21 minutes to fill, which is what you have with a half-hour news program, if you have more features, that means there's less time for hard news or investigative reporting or good, substantial, analysis pieces.

They're now saying that the network should provide more background stories because people already have seen the basic outline by watching CNN or some other news agency or their local station that has covered the hurricane that day. But sometimes the best thing you can provide is a little more context of what's going on.

That's what an experienced reporter has that somebody who hasn't spent that much time in the field does not have—the judgment to determine in a short period of time, two or three minutes, what's important and what isn't important. That's what they pay us for. Anybody can get the pictures, but if you don't have the judgment to determine what's important, the guy from XYZ station who has three minutes on the air may present a picture that is either faulty, inaccurate or biased because he didn't have the experience to know.

It takes a certain amount of training to gather the facts. If you're given only two minutes of air time, that's where the judgment comes in, having to condense what took place in half an hour down to two minutes—what you choose to tell the people.

The affiliates now are able to go out and cover major stories because it's the look-Ma-I'm-dancing syndrome. "Our anchor guy from KRAP is here at the scene of the summit in Geneva." The guy doesn't have the slightest idea what's going on there, but he can say, "Gee, I walked around the street here in Geneva and these people have signs in German and French." They don't bring you a lot of information, but they're there.

If they would just cover their own communities and spend that money on their own communities, their citizens would be a lot better off than them going to the summit or to the scene of a hurricane and adding one more voice to the babble. It doesn't do anything to improve the human condition.

That is the old Afghanistan theory, which came about before Afghanistan, that the further away something is, the more you can rail about the awfulness of it. If it's closer to home, then you begin wondering.

## HOW THE PUBLIC VIEWS THE PRESS

People see more of what goes on—the byplay between politicians and reporters, the reporting process. Because they see more of the process, they have formed opinions they didn't hold before. You've seen news conferences with people shouting at the president. People say, "Is that the way our government should be conducted?" Certainly excesses are committed by members of the media in their zeal to get a competitive advantage. When people see things like that, it gives them a bad impression.

Also, when they see interviews done with people who are under great stress, they have compassion for the people who are being interviewed. God knows, those of us who have had to go out and do those interviews have compassion, too, but sometimes it's the only way to find out. The public has a right to know about things.

We're more and more being castigated for intruding on people's private lives in order to protect the public's right to know. The public may have some valid points. But again, I think it's the old behead-the-messenger syndrome—they're hearing something they don't want to hear and they're blaming the people who are bringing the message.

## NEW TECHNOLOGIES IN TELEVISION

I would foresee a time in television when viewers will be getting television programs strictly by broadcast satellite, because as they get those little dishes down to $250, they will sprout like television antennas did back in the '50s and '60s. When people who produce entertainment programs realize they can reach 50, 60, 70 percent of the households in the United States without going through a television network, they are going to form their own network just for the programming.

So they're going to say, "You want to watch 'Dallas'? 'Dallas' will be on Westar II, Transformer 34 at 8 o'clock on Wednesday night." And they'll beam it up from wherever they are, and they'll sell the advertising, and they'll cut out CBS because they don't need that middleman.

So we'll wind up with the networks being able to offer only one service—news and information programming, because that would be something that packagers would not want to touch, and perhaps more 24-hours-a-day news services.

## SUITCASE SATELLITES

I think news will change. We [NBC] are now going out and distributing suitcase satellites, receivers and transmitters that you can carry in five suitcases. There are now, I think, 50 of them. NBC put these suitcase satellites out for our affiliates. These satellites are portable earth stations—both receivers and transmitters.

Let's say our affiliate in Denver is covering a trial in Seattle. They must now go into KING [the NBC affiliate in Seattle] to use their satellite uplink. If KING has a suitcase satellite, they can move the story right from downtown—from the courthouse. It's a lot more compact, and we're going to get to the point where we'll go out on a story carrying these things.

Rather than doing the entire story at 6:30 in the evening, the viewer may have a menu board that says, "If you want to see an interview with the mayor of London as part of the story that we're doing, it will be on at 11, followed by an interview with an opposing member of Parliament at 11:45"—that sort of thing. Where you normally put it together as a three-minute story at the end of the day, you may just be feeding elements to the satellite and people can choose what they want to watch.

Then go one step beyond that into some kind of combination of satellite and computer programming. You sit at home with your home computer and television screen and go to the menu board of whatever news organization you're interested in, whatever service you can dial up that your computer will receive. This might be a combination of *The New York Times*/CBS service or other combinations. That menu board will show you what you get on any given story on any given day. You can put together your own news program.

It doesn't affect me much because somebody still has to do the story. It does affect a lot of people who produce programs. Probably, there will be a program for the lazy man who wants to watch a ready-made program all together with an anchor. But you won't have to. You can decide what stories are important to you and make your newscast from those stories, just by programming your computer.

You may want to know more about the war in Afghanistan. There's been a development today—the Russians were attacked and television cameras were there. You see that and you say, "Gee, that's interesting. But I wonder how *The New York Times* reported it." You dial that up. You follow the picture story immediately with the story as it was reported by the newspaper.

## HOW I DEFINE MY JOB

My job is to try to cover things that are important to the American people. Sometimes I have to make subjective decisions about what is important and what isn't. I try to do that and be as fair as I can.

You try to be objective, but objectivity, I think, is unattainable because whatever you do, there are subjective decisions made. Once I've done the story, my obligation is to put it on the air in a manner that people can understand, that will keep their interest, and that will have bearing on their lives. I hope it's done in a way that lets them make up their own minds, that it provides them with enough information to be relatively informed. In the time we have, you can't really tell people as much as they need to know about any issue.

People ask me, "Are you ever recognized on the streets?" Very rarely does it happen, but there have been several occasions when I have been rewarded for what I have done. I never felt that I was a household word or that people were going to recognize me. I never cared about that. But I always get a good feeling when somebody knows what I have done—not necessarily that they know I've done it, but that they remember the story. My job is to inform people and to try to get them to remember what I say.

# NHA TRANG BABY 4-1-75

JOHN CHANCELLOR: For almost a month now, the South Vietnamese army has been in retreat and along with it, hundreds of thousands of refugees ... bewildered, frightened or despairing.

We've shown you some of those refugees at Da Nang, at Hue, at Nha Trang and Saigon. Tonight from Nha Trang, Don Oliver brings us another vignette of a Vietnamese refugee in the midst of a terrifying confusion.

DON OLIVER: The families of South Vietnamese sailors, lined up on the beach at Nha Trang—waiting for a landing craft to take them to safety as communist troops approached the city. This landing craft is filled. [PAUSE FOR NAT SOT]

The doors were opened one more time, but a soldier inside with a gun refused to allow any more refugees on board. Just as the ship was leaving, a woman rushed up with a two-week-old baby. The baby's mother, she said, was on board. The child had been left behind.

A bucket was lowered, [PAUSE FOR NAT SOT] the baby made it safely on board the ship. [PAUSE FOR NAT SOT] But then, just as the ship was headed out, the mother appeared on shore. There had been a mix-up. She'd never been on the boat at all. With reluctance, the transfer was made again. [PAUSE FOR NAT SOT] The Vietnamese woman had her baby back, but the family had an uncertain future as the communist troops closed in on the city. Don Oliver, NBC News, Nha Trang.

---

*Don Oliver talks about this story on pp. 196–197. The story was written on a piece of scratch paper and shipped with the film. Courtesy of NBC News.*

CBS

*I think it's possible for a dog or cat to watch television. I've seen them do it. . . . But I don't think I've ever seen an animal listen to the radio.*

# CHARLES OSGOOD

Charles Osgood writes limericks for radio, but he's never entered a limerick contest. Working in his shirtsleeves, with his familiar bow tie intact, Osgood says his constant companion is not a volume of Byron or Shelley, but *Bartlett's Familiar Quotations*.

Sure enough, there on the book shelf in his office at CBS News in New York is a copy of *Bartlett's*. Several tape cassettes and *Bartlett's* have given in to gravity and are leaning haphazardly against each other next to an unopened bottle of champagne. Pictures of Osgood's children are on the wall, and the only item on the wooden hat rack is a well-used terrycloth tennis hat.

Since 1972, Osgood has been bringing quick humor to more than seven million people on the morning "Newsbreak" and on "The Osgood File" on CBS radio every weekday. He doesn't write verse every morning. Sometimes he just tells a story. He knows that when he chooses to write poetry, he is making his job more difficult because he has the same amount of time to write every morning—an hour and 24 minutes.

One morning, Osgood's listeners were treated to his story about former President Gerald Ford's cat, Shan:

A low-key cat in the White House sat,
A Siamese named Shan,
And from where she sat in this habitat,
She could see how the country ran.
Now, it's hard to see how she stays low-key
Observing the things she can,
But we'll all be sad if this cat goes mad,
For the fit will hit the Shan.

Charles Osgood graduated from Fordham University, where he took several philosophy courses, but graduated with a degree in economics. He joined the Army and worked as a radio announcer for the U.S. Army

Band, his first job in broadcasting. He worked in local radio and television in Washington, D.C., and then in 1972 he was hired by CBS.

His radio columns have been collected in two books, *Nothing Could Be Finer Than a Crisis That Is Minor in the Morning* and *There's Nothing That I Wouldn't Do If You Would Be My POSSLQ*. Besides his radio duties, Osgood, 53, also writes stories for CBS television and anchors the CBS television Sunday News. This means that he puts in a six-day work week that begins at 5 a.m. Monday morning, when he gets up to start the week on the radio, and ends at midnight on Sunday, when he finishes the late television news show. He is off on Saturday. It's what Osgood calls "a fairly active schedule."

At a celebration of radio at the Museum of Broadcasting in New York, Osgood presented a poem that described how he feels about radio. To conclude the poem, he talked about his listeners:

> I have been riding with them
> For such a long, long time
> They're willing to put up with me
> When I resort to rhyme.
> And that may be the ultimate
> And quintessential test—
> That proves beyond the slightest doubt
> That radio is best.
>
> A friend will always stick to you
> 'Though your poems may not scan
> I'll see you on the radio,
> I can, you see, I can! ❖

*from Charles Osgood*

- How to interview for radio
- Why radio is a visual medium
- How to write for radio

# Beginnings

I was interested in radio when I was a kid, "The Shadow," "Jack Armstrong." They tried to do a film version of "The Shadow." In my mind, he really was able to make himself invisible. The radio version was always better than the visual.

At Fordham University, I majored in economics. I began to work as an announcer for the U.S. Army Band in Washington, D.C. We recorded recruitment shows. I didn't play an instrument.

After the Army, I went to work for a classical radio station in Washington, D.C. Then I became general manager of a pay TV station in Hartford [Connecticut]. The company went out of business and I found myself as the foremost expert on pay TV in the U.S. without anywhere to work. It's like picking a language that no one else in the U.S. speaks.

I went to work for ABC radio. They wanted people who would be different. They had a desk assistant at WABC who had never been on the air—Ted Koppel. He was 23 years old. Ted and I worked at ABC radio together, but I don't know whatever became of him. He stayed at WABC and I left. I went to work at 5 in the morning for four years at WCBS. Then I moved over to CBS. I had been doing news broadcasting for about three years.

I would not recommend that anybody follow my particular path. I did not do any news broadcasting until I was 30. But I don't think that anything I did was wasted.

## HOW I WORK

I've been working with Phil Chinn [his producer] for the last 10 years. Phil goes over the wires and picks out those things that he thinks are the best prospects for me, and then after I do the 7 o'clock news, he and I usually go downstairs in the cafeteria with a pile of prospects. He has these things printed out—the ones that he thinks are good. We just go over them, and I pick one, sometimes two. One is for Newsbreak, one is for The Osgood File.

We also talk about what's going to be happening on the morning news, whether there's going to be some interesting people who might be in to be interviewed or that I could do a separate interview with, or whether we could take sound off an existing piece that television has done and rework it for radio.

## STORIES I LIKE

I'm not looking necessarily for the most important stories, although I don't eliminate the important stories either, but ones that I can give some kind of treatment to which is not conventional. Once you have found your own voice as a writer, you must be able to recognize the stories that will give you the opportunity to write what you want to write.

If you're doing 10 original pieces a week, which is what I do—between the Osgood Files and the Newsbreaks—in no time at all that means that you've done hundreds of pieces, and you don't even remember them all, let alone be informed by them all, instructed by them all. So sometimes I'm sure you repeat yourself. I hope that I don't. I certainly don't do it on purpose—use the same phrases, the same sentences.

I don't really read poetry much at all. I don't like to read poetry that much. Every so often I'll come across what I think is a good line and try to remember it, but I'm certainly not the kind of person who brings his slim volume of Byron or somebody onto the plane to read on my way to do a story. I never entered a limerick contest. I'd be afraid that I wouldn't win.

## SYSTEMATIC DISORGANIZATION

Yes, as you can see. It's sort of a random, put it on your desk and maybe it will go away, system. Actually, what happens is that there will be ideas and I mean to use them and I find them again when it's too late—when the date has passed. I'm not very well organized.

But I find that to turn out as much stuff as I have to turn out—an end piece for the Sunday night television news every week and pieces for Rather with some regularity, I try to be working on something for him at all times—and then filling in for this one and that one, it really is very busy.

I've got to do Sunday night news at 11 o'clock for television. There's a repeat of that at 11:15, and I stay until the end of that feed, which means that I'm always here until 11:30 because the whole Sunday night schedule is pushed back, as it is during football season almost every week. That will keep me here until close to midnight. I still have to get up at 5 a.m. to do radio next morning. I work six days a week. So it's a fairly active schedule. I don't want to *not* do any of the things that I'm doing, and I can't do them all unless I work that kind of schedule.

## HOW TO APPROACH A SUBJECT

I have no interest in profound subjects. Sometimes you remember something or look something up. As far as quotes are concerned, I rely heavily on *Bartlett's*. Most of what's wrong professionally and especially with novice writers is that they are trying to be taken seriously, they are trying to prove something about themselves and how serious and how learned and how wise and profound they are. As a result, you are tying big boulders around your feet.

I think a much more productive thing for a young writer is to really try to take an almost childlike look at whatever it is that you're looking at that day and let the ideas be as simple as you possibly can make them. If there's something that puzzles you, just in the fact that you are puzzled there may be an idea. You may be able to go to work on that.

If something doesn't seem to make sense, then maybe that's what you should be writing about—not with the idea that you have discovered this gap in human knowledge, but just because there seems to be a little conflict there. Then you talk about those things in as simple a way as you can, the way you do at lunch with a friend, not trying to posture or be any smarter or more insightful than anybody else, because we're not.

## TRY TO MAKE SENSE

Making sense is the hardest thing. It's a very worthy goal. It's one that we don't seem to worry about too much. So much of what you read on the wires and so much of what you hear on the air just doesn't make sense. Why in the world were those words put down?

It's allowing information to somehow come into you from whatever source and then putting that information out without ever letting it pass through your brain. All your brain has to do with it is say, "Does this make sense?" Keep asking that about everything that you're dealing with. If it doesn't make sense, why? That's where you can make your contribution.

## REMEMBER YOUR IGNORANCE

Ignorance is a tool. Use your ignorance. If you're an interviewer who knows all the answers—there's nothing more boring to me than listening to a science reporter ask questions of a scientist about science because the reporter is trying to prove how much he knows about the subject.

If you listen to a specialist reporter talking to a specialist and you get the idea that the business reporter is trying to prove to Tim Pickens that he knows as much about acquisitions as Pickens does, you tune out and see if there isn't something else on to listen to. If the reporter really doesn't understand and says, "I don't get it. Tell me again," that's a good way to do an interview.

## HOW TO INTERVIEW FOR RADIO

I'm assuming that my curiosity is not going to be vastly different from somebody else's curiosity. I don't have a great deal of specialized knowledge about anything, and that puts me in the same boat with almost everybody. I'm talking to a general audience. So forgive me sometimes if I ask a question that the audience already knows the answer to, but if I don't know the answer, then I figure there are other people out there who don't know either.

I do most of my interviews on the phone. If you're trying to make an impression on an interviewee, if you are playing some kind of game with them to show what kind of a hotshot you are, you are going to put them off and you're not going to get anything out of them. You have to put yourself in their position. You're delaying them from whatever it is that they're doing.

## THE BEST QUESTION IN THE WORLD

I find it sometimes very frustrating, you talk to a local station that has interviewed somebody and they've got the tape. And you say, "Great. That's a wonderful story. Let's have the tape." And they haven't let the person tell the story. What this newsperson says is, "We know this. We know how you rescued the dog from the tree. Tell us, what is it in your background that motivated you to do what you did?"

This person will start talking about their childhood or something and it has nothing to do with the story. The best question in the world when you're talking to somebody who is an eyewitness or a participant in some event is, "Tell me about it." Even if you know about it, get them to tell you about it.

But a reporter who is trying to prove that he or she already knows everything has a very hard time doing an interview because they do not want to be told something they already know.

A much better thing is to say, "I'm Rip Van Winkle. They just woke me up. I've been in a deep coma for the last 10 weeks. Tell me about this. I don't know about it." Then you get somebody to give you the background. They can actually tell the story better than you can, if you give them half a chance.

---

## WHEN SOMEBODY DOESN'T WANT TO TALK

I find that even people who say generally that they don't want to talk about something will talk about it if you're on their side, trying to help them tell what they have to tell.

Occasionally you get somebody who is either afraid—they feel that they're on the spot—or somebody in the corporate or the military world. You'll talk to Major So-and-So, and he'll say, "Well, I think the colonel would really be the one who would want to be interviewed." And you say, "Yes, but you tell me that the colonel is not available. Can we talk to you?" "Well, no, you call Colonel So-and-So. He'll be back Tuesday." That's never any good for us. We need it now.

Sometimes there's a fear that somebody has stepped forward some-how to be on radio or television when really it should be the vice president or the colonel who should be doing this interview. In cases like that, where there are hierarchies and somebody really feels that they might get in trouble for talking—that's where you run into problems.

---

## FORGET YOURSELF

When you're doing an interview, you want a sound bite that you can use—at least one, maybe two, three or four. You know when you have it, but you also know when you don't have it. Sometimes you have to go back over the ground that you've already covered to get them to say something, if you get someone who's just giving you yes and no answers, who is being very guarded about what they do.

There are good interviews and there are terrible interviews. I think my batting average is pretty high. Part of that is that I don't think about myself at all when I'm doing these interviews, and I hem and haw and don't always ask the question in the way that would be the most professional way to ask because I'm going to cut myself out anyway. I'll write script into the tape that I use, so I don't give a moment's thought to, "Am I sounding like the professional broadcaster or the professional journalist or the smart person?" I don't care about that. It's just of no consequence at all.

It just bothers the hell out of me to see interviewers, and there are plenty of them on television, where the purpose of the interview seems not so much to find out what the guest is all about, but the guest is kind of a foil for the interviewer.

Dick Cavett is the world's best example of that. No matter who it was, you could have Mortimer Adler or somebody sitting there, and the whole purpose of that thing was to let you know that Dick Cavett was a smart fellow—not to find out anything at all about Mortimer Adler. In fact Dick Cavett would tell things to Mortimer Adler about his experiences at Yale, how he first encountered the Great Books Program or something like that. That absolutely drives me crazy.

## BRING PEOPLE OUT—QUICKLY

You try to bring people out by asking a question that evokes a usable response. When we're talking about radio shows, you can't really spend an awful lot of time beating around the bush. So that's where the editing knife comes in handy. Sometimes a certain amount of beating around the bush is necessary just to establish a little rapport. But we don't have much time, even in preparation, to deal with that.

If I talk to someone on the phone at 7:30 in the morning until a quarter to eight, the thing's going to go on the air at 8:30. You can't take 15 extra minutes just for the amenities, so we get them over in a hurry.

Politicians are wonderful because they know that their time is scarce and they know that you're working on a deadline. You say, "Good morning, Senator. I'm glad you could be with us, and I'd like to talk about so-and-so." They say, "OK, let's go." Boom! You get right into it. You don't have to ask them what kind of a day it is in Cincinnati.

## THE WRONG QUESTIONS

I'm just absolutely amazed at novice writers or broadcast people who try to get an eyewitness account of tornadoes or an earthquake. They'll say, "You're right there where they're having the forest fire?" And then they'll start asking a question that can only be answered in numbers.

There you are in the fire and they [the reporters] will say, "How many have been killed?" The person will say, "I don't know. The last I heard was 24." "OK, thank you. How many firefighters are there working on this fire?" "Oh, I'd say it must be thousands. Two or three thousand." And they write that number down. All the questions are not questions that you really want from the eyewitness.

Instead you say, "You were in the fire. It must be terrible. Tell me about that fire. Have you seen flames? Smoke? Where were you? Tell me about what you saw." Then they'll tell you about it. For some reason that seems hard to do for an awful lot of people.

You get some cop in a situation like that and they'll say, "Well, the national guard has sent in x number of people and we have x number of people out there on patrol." But what you're really looking for is for somebody to tell you how hot it is and what they saw—about the tree falling over or the house being blown away or the guy in the rowboat— something that is a human thing.

It's so obvious, and yet you listen to the tapes that come in. "There's a terrible blizzard out there. God, it sounds just awful." And somebody will say, "Yes, we had 34 inches of snow yesterday and we're expecting another 6 inches today." That's a cut. Then they'll say, "It must be very cold." And they'll say, "It's very cold—32 degrees below."

What you really wanted to find out is, "How do you have to dress for this? That sounds like an awful lot of snow. Is it up to the window? Up to the door? Can you open the door? How are you managing during all this? Did you step outside? What does it feel like? Is there wind in your face?" Sense impressions. Tell me about the hot and the cold and, if it hurts, tell me how it hurts.

Again, it is a question of wanting to be serious. "I'm here on Olympus and I'm keeping score here. Tell me the score." And so sure, they'll give you the score if that's what you ask for. Box score. It's like following a baseball game. People jump up and down at baseball games and they yell and scream, but you never saw anybody jump up and down and scream at a box score. They're just numbers. It doesn't have the same effect on you.

## WHAT I WANT FROM AN INTERVIEW

There's drama in there. Let's hear it. I don't think I'm any less of a newsman because I'm looking for that. There are stories. We still call them *stories*. The elements of a story—character and action and plot and all of those things—have to be there or it's not a good story.

We are telling true stories. Some people think they're being much more serious news people if they tell the facts and the facts are, "Here's who was in the charge. Here's how many people were arrested. So many counts of this, so many counts of that." Again, there's this obsession with counting things.

## WHY THE NEWS FASCINATES ME

What fascinates me in the news are stories that I find either amusing or sad, one that I have some kind of reaction to. The telephone book has a lot of useful information in it, but it doesn't make very interesting reading unless you happen to be looking up a telephone number.

There are good stories, fascinating stories, out of history. There's drama in everyday life and certainly drama in public life. Those things are interesting. If they're not interesting, it's not any fault of the story itself. It's just our lack of ability to grasp where the interest lies. What you're looking for is animation, enthusiasm, involvement of the person in the story.

## HOW I WRITE

I've found that the only way you can write as much stuff as I have to do is to develop the ability to concentrate on one thing at a time. What happens to me is that if I get too much stuff in my hands or too much stuff in my head at one time, everything gets in everything else's way. It's not just this messy desk. It's also that I can't grasp what's in my hand when I've got 83 things in my head.

So you have to be able to concentrate on one thing at a time and really wipe everything else out. If I do two things during the day, by the time I have done the second one, I have almost completely forgotten the first one.

I'll do Newsbreak, which comes on the air at 8:30—it's fed to the network at 8:30 and it's played within five minutes by the local station. I then do a newscast and then I work on The Osgood File. So I will have done another piece. Then I walk down the hall and I meet someone who's just heard my piece on the radio. And they'll say, "Hey, that was a terrific piece this morning." And I will look at them with a blank look. I won't know what they're talking about. I can't remember what I did.

You really have to wipe the slate clean or you won't be able to concentrate on the next thing you have to do. That same phenomenon of developing the concentration to work on the thing that you're working on right then requires that you not grow too fond of the things you've done in the past, or even think about them very much.

I suppose that if you were a writer of books or truly a poet and you really took time—weeks, months, years—to hone a work of art to perfection, then I suppose you could treasure that finishing touch that you were able to put at the end of Chapter 3. But this is a very different kind of work. It's not art or anything approximating art, so I really don't think that those kinds of satisfactions go with this territory.

I'm a specialized kind of a writer. What I can do is take material and quickly convert it into a radio piece or a television piece. I write fast and I try to come up with phrases that will help to tell the story, not phrases that are memorable in their own right. Nobody's ever going to collect the pithy phrases of Osgood and put them in a book. Nor will they ever make *Bartlett's*. But if they help to tell the story, that's all that you're asking.

## HOW LONG IT TAKES TO WRITE A STORY

I always take one hour and 24 minutes to write a story. The reason I know that is because the newscast I do at 7 o'clock is over at 7:06. Newsbreak goes on the air at 8:30. It takes me every second available to do Newsbreak, so it takes me an hour and 24 minutes. Sometimes I'm running down the hall with an unfinished script.

Ordinarily, if there are holes I allow a little time to write any missing lines during a commercial. But an hour and 24 minutes includes some three-minute poems. So sometimes it's pretty demanding, and sometimes you can tell.

## PICTURES ON THE RADIO

I cultivated my taste in radio back when that's all there was. There was no television at that time. I like television a lot, too. I like working in television. I don't like watching television very much.

I think radio is a more visual medium. It sounds paradoxical, but the truth is that television is a very literal medium because you're looking at a picture and that picture is whatever it is. It's whatever size your screen is and it only can take a picture of something where you were able to get a camera in and take a picture and bring the picture back out.

Radio isn't dependent on that kind of stuff at all, and you really do make a picture with words. That picture really can be a much better picture—much more vivid and colorful and helpful picture—than the specific literal picture that you can do on TV. It's because you engage the human mind.

I think it's possible for a dog or cat to watch television. I've seen them do it. They see the moving patterns of light. I'm assuming that they're not really following the soap opera. But I don't think I've ever seen an animal listen to the radio.

I guess what I'm saying is that I think that the engagement of the human mind is more obvious with radio than it is with television. It's so simple. It's easy to take a tape recorder almost anywhere. Its simplicity is one great advantage, and also the fact that there's so much more to be done.

I'm able to turn out 22 radios shows a week—two hourly newscasts a day and two feature shows—20 shows—and then there are two others. I'll do one on Sunday night. It takes me very much longer to turn out a television piece.

The other thing is that radio tends to be a one-man, maybe a two-man operation. Somebody helps you find the story. But then when the time comes to write it, you sit down and write it. Nobody fusses with my copy that much.

In television you keep having to change words because it doesn't quite go with the picture. Or, here's a picture and we really ought to say something so that we can use this picture we have. And you find yourself with the tail wagging the dog about half the time.

I think I've gotten to be pretty good at it. But with radio, if I think something is a dynamite radio piece, I can take some personal satisfaction and personal credit for having done it. In television, you've got producers and editors and camerapeople and sound people. It's such a group effort that if it worked, maybe it was because of your wonderful treatment, but maybe it was because of somebody else's work. So it's less individualistic than radio.

## DISADVANTAGES OF WRITING FOR RADIO

If you work in CBS news, at one time radio was the big brother and television was the stepchild. But the little stepchild has grown up and is now a giant that sort of looms over us all.

The recognition, the big money, everything else, is in television. I am fortunate in that I get to keep a foot in both boats. Sometimes that's a little conflicting. You end up with the boats moving in different directions and you end up in the water. Most of the time I'm glad that I get to do both.

## WRITING FOR TELEVISION

There are challenges in television, too. There are ways of using that picture where you can make the viewer see the picture totally. Sometimes you don't need to say anything. It's just knowing when to shut up.

It's hard for someone who's writing in radio all his life to make the transition to television because you don't need to tell somebody what they're looking at. One of the best producers in the business used to say, "If you have a bunch of men jumping out of an airplane, you don't have to say, 'The men jumped out of the airplane.' But if you have something else that you can say, some other line that says, "Now the time comes to do what you've trained to do," or "No matter how often you do it, stepping out of an airplane at 5,000 feet makes your heart stop"—say something that will make you look at a picture of those men coming out of an airplane and make you think about how that must feel.

Don't just caption it by saying what it is—"Members of the 8th Infantry jumping out of an airplane." Try to make the viewer imagine himself in that same situation. There's nothing original about what I'm saying to you, but so much of what you see on television is pure caption writing.

## WHAT'S FUNNY?

I don't think very much stuff is funny and I don't see humor in a whole lot of things. I almost invariably hate funny stuff that other people write for me to read. The things that are on the wires every day under the heading of "Brights" are usually just awful. Or somebody will write a piece for a newscast and they'll say, "Well, they're having the annual Cow Chip Throwing Contest in Bulldog, Montana, this week."

I hate funny events. They just don't seem to be funny at all. Not only do I fail to see the humor in them, I can't communicate the humor in them. I never read them. If I get one of those things, I say, "Next time, spare me the Frog Jumping Contest."

On the wires this morning, it's a serious story, but nevertheless there's humor there. It's funny to me. There were a whole bunch of stories on the wires under the heading Law Enforcement. "Today's subject in the exciting field of law enforcement is spying something fishy."

There's a detective in Miami who watches a woman getting on a train to New York and she's carrying a bag of fruit. There's nothing unusual about that—lemons and oranges—but she's also carrying a 20-pound watermelon and struggling with this watermelon. And the detective finds that suspicious and, sure enough, there are 4 pounds of cocaine stuffed into the watermelon. I just think that the picture of someone getting on the train is funny, and the cop saying, "Why would somebody be taking a watermelon to New York? They have watermelons in New York."

Then there's another case of a guy in prison. U.S. marshals are bringing him refund checks from corporations. The reason the guy's in prison is because he's been submitting phony refund claims to corporations, claiming that their product was rotten, that he ate something and got sick and he wants his money back. So he gets a $20 check, $14 checks, whatever, and the U.S. marshals are actually delivering the checks to him in prison because he did it from his jail cell. He continued to do the thing that he had been doing that got him in jail in the first place. It's a real story, the thing really happened, but it's really sort of bizarre, and I think that's funny.

## DO YOU MAKE A DIFFERENCE?

I think everything makes a difference. I think everything that everybody does makes a difference. It seems to me that the world is in a constant state of flux. It's the operating principle for the natural world. You can never change just one thing. Any change always involves a lot of other changes. That's what makes the news business so interesting. If you are going to change the tax plan, that means that several other things have to change to accommodate the first change.

There's a line from an English poet, Francis Thompson, "You can't touch a flower without troubling a star." In a way, that is saying the same thing. What everybody does affects the lives of everybody they come in contact with. I come in contact with seven million people a day on the radio. I have no idea what difference that makes for them. In most cases, I'm sure it makes no difference whatsoever, but I think sometimes it does.

It's likely that if you talk to several million people first thing in the morning when their alarm clocks go off or when they're driving to work or shaving, your vision of reality, such as you express it, is going to make some difference to them. They're either going to agree with you or disagree with you and they're going to love it or they're going to hate it.

But it has an effect on them, just as the other people you deal with in the morning—the bridge tolltaker, the doorman at the apartment building or whatever. It's not that it's going to change your whole day if somebody is rude or pleasant, but it has some effect on the way you're going to have your own day. I like to think that there may be some cases out there where, having heard my version of what is in the news that day, I make a difference to some people.

And I try never to be mean. It's easy in this business to be mean, or at the very least callous, anyway. Very often you are reporting calamitous events—cyclones and tidal waves and earthquakes and many disasters of one kind or another—and again, it's just that you can get yourself up on this pedestal that says, "I do this and I'm just telling about it, and it makes no never mind to me whether 5,000 people are wiped away."

I don't mean that you have to be sobbing about the deaths in Bangladesh, but the audience has to know that you understand what you're talking about, not that you know all about tsunamis [tidal waves], but that you can imagine what it's like for somebody to be confronting a 32-foot wall of water, and to have a proper sense of the tragedy in the sad stories you tell.

I think that's important and I think it makes a difference if people think that what they're hearing is an account of the world we're living in by somebody who they perceive to have some sense of decency. I don't care whether they think I'm smart, but I want them to think that I'm decent.

The stuff I do, I don't do for the ages. It disappears literally with the speed of light.

# Newsbreak: The Fascinating Field of Law Enforcement

CHARLES OSGOOD: Newsbreak, news and comment. I'm Charles Osgood, CBS News.

Today, some stories from the fascinating field of law enforcement. Our subject: how to spot something fishy. Stand by.

(ANNOUNCEMENTS)

OSGOOD: U.S. marshals delivered a check to Lawrence Peyton, a prisoner at the federal penitentiary in Sandstone, Minnesota. It had been addressed to Peyton, care of Post Office Box 280, which is the address for the Clay County jail in Moorhead, Minnesota, where the prisoner was held before being transferred to Sandstone. Another check came in and then another one and another one, and the U.S. marshals delivered those, too, until they began to smell a rat. Was this not the Lawrence Peyton who was in jail in the first place because he'd defrauded hundreds of companies by sending for refunds on food products, claiming they were spoiled or contaminated? He'd been convicted of that and ran off from a halfway house, fled to Canada and Europe and all the while kept writing to companies demanding refunds. So, recently, he turned himself in but, while in jail, would allegedly pen little notes in his cell to companies demanding refunds—nothing big, mind you. In a new mail-fraud indictment handed up yesterday, there's mention of five such refund checks, the biggest one being for $19 from the Swift meat company. That was one of the checks the U.S. marshals had delivered to Peyton at the penitentiary until some shrewd officer realized there was something fishy about all those refund checks being delivered to the prisoner who is the famous refund swindler.

If you want to make it in the law-enforcement field, you really have to keep a sharp eye out for the suspicious-looking characters. Take Detective John Facchiano in Miami. At the Miami train station, he spotted a woman getting on a train for New York the other day who was carrying some fruit. Some of it was citrus fruit, oranges and lemons—nothing suspicious about that—but the woman was also carrying a great big watermelon. Detective Facchiano thought to himself, "This is pretty fishy. Why should someone carry a watermelon to New York, when you can buy a watermelon up there for the same price, maybe cheaper." So he stopped the woman, 36-year-old Migueline Rodriguez, who was struggling with this 20-pound watermelon. Facchiano then noticed that the end of the watermelon had been taped up; and, sure enough, it turned out that part of the watermelon had been hollowed out, and what was in there was cocaine, 4.4 pounds of it.

Another woman, getting on the very same train, Estelle Sanchez of Miami, was stopped because another detective, Claudius Noriega, said that she was carrying very little luggage and was looking at him nervously. She was carrying 2.2 pounds of cocaine in a little package neatly wrapped in red, green and white paper and with a tag that read, "Especially for you."

And in Cincinnati, Hamilton County park ranger Glenn Smith thought he saw something fishy—a green, 10-foot dinosaur inside a van traveling to a park at 2 in the morning with a bunch of teen-agers. It turned out to be a plastic dinosaur, but, sure enough, Ranger Smith was right. There was something fishy. The kids had lifted the dinosaur as a prank. They've been booked on charges of receiving stolen property. I tell you, you gotta get up pretty early in the morning to fool today's lawman. Now this.

(ANNOUNCEMENT)

OSGOOD: . . . I'm Charles Osgood, CBS News.

# &IDEAS ISSUES

These questions, listed by topic, are designed to compare and contrast the ideas and the issues from the 12 interviewees with one another. Section VI, for example, will help compare Doug Kriegel's ideas about the qualities necessary for a good television reporter with any one or all of his colleagues who discuss the same topic.

Or, you can compare David Brinkley's interviewing hints with those of one or all of his colleagues listed in Section II. For quick reference, the page numbers for individual topics are listed after the interviewee's name.

I.   Working Conditions

1.  How does the work schedule of a television reporter differ from the traditional 9–5 job?

2.  How do daily news events affect how a broadcast journalist works?

3.  How much control does each of these broadcast journalists have over what they cover and when they cover it?

4.  What is the importance of deadlines to each of these reporters?

5.  How do the working conditions for general assignment reporters differ from working conditions for broadcast journalists in other assignments?

II. Interviewing Techniques

1. What role does interviewing play in the reporting process for each of these writers?

2. What are the benefits and the drawbacks of interviewing for broadcast?

3. How do these people differ in their interviewing approaches for private, as opposed to public, figures?

4. Why is it important for reporters to adapt to each individual interviewee?

5. List five approaches suggested by these reporters that will help you to improve your interviewing techniques.

III. Writing for Broadcast

1. List five (or more) specific suggestions from these writers to help improve your writing.

2. What role do pictures play in telling a story for television, according to these writers?

3. Examine the scripts for these writers. What do you notice about how these journalists (except David Brinkley, who wrote a commentary) use the pictures and the words together to tell their story?

4. Compare each script to the journalist's explanation of his or her story approach. Which of their writing goals do they achieve?

IV. Characteristics of Different Assignments

1. What are the differences among the specific subject beats (Science, Business, Local and Network General Assignment, the White House)?

2. How do these reporters' interests match their backgrounds or their beats?

3. Are there special problems that reporters should recognize with certain beats (international reporting, for example, or political reporting)?

V. Criticism of Journalists and Journalism

1. What are five (or more) criticisms of the journalistic profession raised by these reporters?

2. Is their criticism justified? Why? Why not?

3. How do members of the press affect the events they cover?

4. What is the press's social responsibility?

5. What is the press's professional responsibility?

VI. Characteristics of a Good Reporter

1. On which characteristics of a good reporter do these journalists agree?

2. To you, which five characteristics seem most important?

3. Which characteristics of a good reporter, as described by these journalists, do you have? Which should you work to improve?

VII. The Quality of Local Television News

1. How do the standards of reporting in local news differ from the standards of reporting in network news, according to these journalists?

2. What pressures does the local television journalist face?

3. What are the mistakes that local reporters sometimes make, according to these reporters? Why?

VIII. The Role of Consultants in Television News

1. How important are consultants in the day-to-day operation of the newsroom, according to these reporters?

2. Does the work of the consultants interfere with covering the news? Why? Why not?

3. How do these reporters say television reporters are responding to having consultants in the newsroom?

4. Why are television consultants increasingly important in local television news?

5. What effect are the consultants having on the people who are anchoring and reporting the news?

IX. How the Public Views the Press

1. How does the public's view of a journalist's job compare with the reality, according to these reporters?

2. What accounts for the glamorous image of people who work in television?

3. Is some of the public criticism of the press warranted?

X. Role in Personal Life

1. What role does their profession play in each of these journalists' lives?

2. What choices have these journalists made about their personal lives?

3. Are the personal lives of any of these journalists enhanced by their professional responsibilities?

XI. Ethics

Spencer, 10                    Harris, 106–108

Kriegel, 33                    Sanders, 129

Woodruff, 53–55                Whitaker, 163–164

Dow, 74–75, 77–78              Wornick, 179–181

Donaldson, 99

1. Would you have made the same choice these journalists made when faced with specific ethical situations they describe? Why? Why not?

2. Is it possible to create a list of ethical principles that would cover the ethical dilemmas described by these reporters? Why? Why not?

XII. Discussion of Script

Spencer ("The Learning Disability Called Dyslexia"), 16–18

Kriegel ("Is Your Money Safe?"), 35–37

Woodruff ("What Price Defense?"), 57–63

Dow ("Juarez Radiation Accident"), 80–83

Donaldson ("ABC World News Tonight—The U.S. and Nicaragua"), 100–101

Harris ("Quality of Mercy"), 117–119

Sanders ("Casinos in Atlantic City"), 132–134

Brinkley ("Commentary on the Russians and the Press from 'This Week With David Brinkley' "), 151

Whitaker ("The Jesse Helms–Jim Hunt Campaign"), 168–169

Wornick ("Follow-up to the Revere Police Investigation"), 185–187

Oliver ("Nha Trang Baby 4–1–75"), 209

Osgood ("Newsbreak: The Fascinating Field of Law Enforcement"), 225–226

1. How do the elements of each story match the reporter's description of his or her approach to the story or the subject?

2. How do the reporter's biases or point of view about the story influence what is written?

3. Which elements of good television writing do you see in each script sample?

4. Does a writer working on a quick deadline necessarily have to write differently from a writer with no imminent deadline? Why? Why not?

5. Compare the script samples of each of these journalists with what they say about writing and reporting. Which of their writing and reporting goals do they achieve?